Stagflation and the Bastard Keynesians

Stagflation and the Bastard Keynesians

John H. Hotson,
Professor of Economics
University of Waterloo

with Hamid Habibagahi,
Ministry of Finance, Iran

and George Lermer,
Economic Council of Canada

University of Waterloo Press

ISBN 0-88898-008-6

1st Printing

University of Waterloo Press
University of Waterloo
Waterloo, Ontario, Canada
N2L 3G1

Printed in Canada

Cover Drawing by *David B. Hotson*

Contents

Preface

1 The Parable of the Cliff Diver

Economic theorists are a little like the cliff divers of Acapulco or the aquatic urchins on surfboards who cluster beside cruise ships.

Confident in our powers of inductive summary of complex reality, and holding tight to our life line of theory bequeathed us by the great deductive divers of the past, we plunge deep into the swirling, churning mass of historical and statistical data, of flotsam and jetsam, that life throws up to us. We disappear into the whirlpool of complexly interrelated phenomena. Deep into secret grottos far beyond the ken of the onlooking layman we twist our labyrinthian way, down to the bottom, the root causes, the essential principles of economic life. Then we return to break surface where, after catching our breath, we triumphantly explain to our admiring audience what we have seen. The wonders of the deep being too marvelous for their limited apprehension we have to simplify and present only a "model" old or new, but 99 per cent of the time old, of the wonders we beheld.

Why do we do it? Partly for the thrill of the plunge, of intellectual *joie de vivre,* but largely because the tourists pitch coins into the whirlpool; research grants, royalties, and salaries, and like the Acapulco beach boys we dive for these coins.

Occasionally, however, an onlooker expresses disappointment with our performance, maintaining that even from his limited vantage point he can see that our description is faulty. There is a dark cave over to the left he wants explored and a shoal on the right where strange shadows dart menacingly. This beach jockeying, this dry diving, is most unwelcome and is usually ignored even though it is often well founded.

For our high divers, though deep, are narrow in their approach. They take off from the same familiar rock, do their customary swan or half gainer as a crowd pleaser, and hit the water at an angle and in a spot which experience has shown to be safe, if unenlightening. And actually, if the audience were able to follow the typical diver beneath the waters they would be surprised to find his eyes are tightly shut, or if open are intent only on the flash of the illusive coin. Why? Why not? The diver has seen the grotto before. At least he has heard it described by others – the light *is* bad down here, and the salt hurts his eyes.

Consequently, once a given description, or model, of the pool becomes current among the divers it persists, despite catcalls from the shore, until perhaps some diver hits the water "wrong" and explores things from a new perspective, or sees things never before beheld; a new grotto inhabited by creatures defying hitherto accepted principles. He returns to the surface and splutters out his discovery. Most often his immediate reward is merely to be told he's all wet, but if he persists he can eventually get others to retrace his plunge, confirm his insights and the "model" is changed, or even scrapped.

All analogies limp, and this analogy is not only limp but soggy. The history of economic thought does abound, however, with examples of partial insights which for too long were taken as the whole reality and which, becoming dogma, stood in the way of further progress. Thus Smith's one-sided "labor theory of value" delayed the attainment of an adequate model of relative prices, and the general equilibrium model of the market led economists to deny the possibility of deep and lasting depression, even though the watchers on the cliffs could see the trench was there and demanded an explanation of this important phenomenon. Finally Keynes plunged into the deep waters and emerged to explain them. However, it is generally contended that he spluttered more than a little in his explanation, the famous *General Theory,* so it became customary to substitute his Expositors', Hicks, Hansen, Lerner and Samuelson's explanation of his explanation for his own. Their savings – investment, and multiplier models hung on a 45° line, or IS = LM diagrams have been taken as preserving the kernel of truth in Keynes, while the husk, *The General Theory,* was thrown away and today is generally neglected.

Indeed, Samuelson placed himself between Keynes and a whole generation of "Keynesians" explaining that the book was a disjointed collection of "random notes" and advising the "young and innocent" to ignore Book 1 of *The General Theory,* "especially the difficult Chapter 3," where Keynes first sketched his Aggregate Supply and Demand analysis, and Book 5 entitled *Money – Wages and Prices.* In place of this analysis Samuelson raised the "Keynesian Cross" or 45° diagram and in this sign conquered, much like an earlier Paul changing the new doctrine even as he spread it. The 45° "Classical Keynesian" or "Bastard Keynesian" (in Joan Robinson's tart phrase) model throws all emphasis on aggregate demand and its components and appears to indicate that all aggregate economic ills can be cured by manipulating demand by suitable fiscal and monetary maneuvers. To their everlasting credit the 45° theorists, or Paulist Fathers, did convince dubious governments and electorates that deep depression was both an avoidable and curable disease, and that the right medicines were easy money and deficits.

To their shame, however, they stripped macro theory of the theories of the price level, aggregate supply, money, uncertainty and of income distribution contained in *The General Theory.* The result was that economists and policy makers who followed their advice were unable to cope with world inflation. Belatedly, experience has forced us to rediscover some of the basics of Keynes' Aggregate Supply analysis, but so little is he read that propositions clearly stated in *The General Theory* are hailed as independent discoveries, as the "Phillips curve" and the income policies so long ago urged by Keynes are treated like illegitimate children in their father's house. Because these policies are considered illegitimate their use has been hesitant, tentative, and fitful, when it is with these weapons that the main battle for high levels of employment and a stable price level must be fought.

Fortunately, while the American Keynesians sank into a dark age, their energies sapped in fending off the pagan hordes subscribing to the *Reader's Digest,* and later, Friedmanian, barbarisms; the lights were never extinguished in the east. At Cambridge and other English centres post Keynesians, most notably Joan Robinson, Sir Roy Harrod, Michal Kalecki and Nicholas Kaldor, continued to build on firm foundations. In the west, Sidney Weintraub has played a Martin Luther, or "back to the Good Book" role, and more recently Robert W. Clower, Axel Leijonhufvud and Paul Davidson have done much to rescue Keynes from "Keynesianism."

Finally, the continuing failure of "bastard Keynesian" policies to control inflation have brought forth a host of insights on the theory of macroeconomic policy, to which this book makes a modest contribution. A second crisis in economics is upon us which can lead to a second Keynesian Revolution through discarding the "bastard Keynesian" heresies and thinking anew.[1] To this end this effort is dedicated. I was once a bastard Keynesian myself and I write this book in atonement for sin.

In Joan Robinson's lively terms, we have been until recently living alternately in "bastard" and "limping" Golden Ages.[2] In a "bastard" Golden Age, even though the actual, warranted, and potential growth rates are approximately equal, real incomes are not growing rapidly enough to satisfy all the claims organized groups demand and the result is inflation. The "bastard Keynesian" response is to convert the situation into a "limping" Golden Age, where $G_a = G_w < G_p$, so that unemployment increases. Lately we have even "achieved" a "limping bastard" age of growing inflation *and* unemployment, a far from golden situation!

I am intellectually indebted to Sidney Weintraub, Joan Robinson, J.K. Galbraith, Robert W. Clower and Sir Roy Harrod for much that appears here, although none of them may approve of the use I have made of their insights. I am also indebted to Robert R. Kerton for valuable suggestions which much improved my presentation. I am indebted to the Canada Council for financial support of the quantification of several chapters and to the University of Waterloo for financial aid to publication, to my research assistants, Margaret Darling, Christopher N. Georgas and Uwe Lilje for their skill and dedication, to our able departmental Secetaries Donna O'Brecht and Sandra Hertzberger, to George Roth for his professional assistance in design and production, to my father, Dr. Clarence P. Hotson and to my daughter, Eleanor, for help with the proofreading and to my sons Howard and David for computational and graphic aid. I am indebted to my wife Elisabeth, for her patience during the seemingly endless process of my writing a book. I am indebted to *The Canadian Journal of Economics* and *Economic and Business Bulletin* for permission to reprint previously published materials as Chapters 3 and 6, to my co-authors, Professors Hamid Habibagahi and George Lermer for their invaluable contributions, and to authors and publishers too numerous to mention here for permission to quote others' work. I hereby wholly absolve my mentors and collaborators from blame for any remaining shortcomings, inaccuracies and wrongheadedness of this book, taking same upon my own head.

---

[1] See Alfred S. Eichner and J. A. Kregel, "An Essay on Post-Keynesian Theory: A New Paradigm in Economics," *Journal of Economic Literature,* 13, December 1975, pp. 1293-314.

[2] Joan Robinson, *Essays in the Theory of Economic Growth,* London, Macmillan, 1962. For the most recent statement of Lady Robinson's views on growth and Bastard Keynesians see her "The Age of Growth," *Challenge,* May/June 1976, pp. 4-9.

In reviewing what I have written below about bastard Keynesianism in general, and the macroeconomics of Paul A. Samuelson and Milton Friedman in particular, I feel an almost over-mastering urge to apologize to both of these eminent scholars and gentlemen. What right do I have to savage such distinguished economists, suggesting that their Keynesian intellectual "father" did not know their neoclassical "mother" very well? My only defense is the same as Keynes' for his attack on the economics of Arthur Pigou – the matters involved are of the utmost urgency and the above two gentlemen are the two most formidable developers and expositors of the "Keynesianism" which has failed and in failing has done much damage. Only very great men can do great harm for, as Keynes put it, " ... the ideas of economists and political philosophers, both when they are right and when they are wrong, are more powerful than is commonly understood. Indeed the world is ruled by little else."

I dedicate this book to my students, whose mental anguish at being told the textbooks are wrong, confirms again Samuelson's judgment that "once an idea gets into these [textbooks, but also students,] however bad it may be, it is practically immortal."

1

Towards a More General Theory of Inflation

Introduction – From "Fine Tuning" to "Stagflation"

Economic theory and policy making are in a bad way, so much so that Joan Robinson speaks of a "second crisis" in economics.[1] How have the mighty fallen! Less than a decade ago the leading economists of the "Keynesian" school were, at last, achieving the "measure of respect" accorded "scientists whose theoretical results are confirmed by observation when they are applied to the facts."[2] As the U.S. tax cuts of 1964 and of Canada in 1965 worked their predicted magic in expanding output and employment with only a minor inflationary joint product, the prestige of the economist soared right up there with that of the astronaut.

The last few years have been bad for the prestige of many of the heroes of the mid 1960's and not the least of those to have "lost face" have been the "Keynesian" economists. When inflation became a serious problem in the later 1960's, policy went into reverse. After many "decision lags," taxes and interest rates were raised and the growth of the money supply was slowed. The result was an "administered recession" in which unemployment rose, but inflation continued unchecked. Indeed, inflation became more severe after the "anti" inflationary doses had been administered than it had been before, and the ugly words "stagflation" and "slumpflump" were coined to describe our dilemma. The latest experience has been the most disturbing of all with a tripling of basic food prices and a quintuppling of oil prices setting off the most severe inflation the world has seen since the Korean War (at least) coupled with the worst unemployment since the 1930's.

What went wrong? Did we over-sell the public and raise their expectations regarding "fine tuning" beyond what we could possibly deliver? Or were valid theories discredited merely by poor execution? Or were the theories upon which restrictive monetary and fiscal policies were based hopelessly deficient? It is my contention that the blame for our troubles lies not with excessive public expectations, nor merely with the faulty execution of Nixon, Ford, Trudeau, Wilson, and their henchmen. Rather our inability to stop inflation flows directly from our bad theory of the price level. Until this is corrected we will continue to mis-describe and therefore mis-prescribe for the malady. As I hope to show, the medicines with which we have dosed the economy are part of the cause, rather than the cure, of inflation.

---

[1] Joan Robinson, "The Second Crisis of Economic Theory", *American Economic Review, Papers and Proceedings,* May 1972, 62, pp. 1-10.

[2] J.M. Keynes, *The General Theory of Employment, Interest, and Money,* Harcourt, New York 1936, p. 33, (*G.T.* henceforth).

In building up an adequate theory of the price level there is no better starting place than Keynes' *General Theory*. Although this book is the very "magna carta" of modern economics, it is a remarkable fact that "Keynesian" economics has very little to do with Keynes' own views and the price level theory developed in *The General Theory* is practically unknown.

Keynes lumped together all economists of the English school as "classical"[3] and attacked them for the following theoretical errors: (1) They accepted "Say's Law" that "supply creates its own demand", that "equilibrium" and "full employment" are synonymous. (2) They downplayed the importance of money in a monetary economy, thinking of it as a mere convenience to exchange and determining only the price level *i.e.* they held the quantity of money theory of prices. (3) They held the rate of interest on money moved to equate saving and investment at full employment thus validating Say's Law. (4) They held that labour was to blame for any unemployment through an "irrational" insistence upon a real wage too high for "equilibrium." (5) They dichotomized economic theory between "value" or "micro" theory of relative prices, and "monetary" or "macro" economics, involving the theory of the price level.

Keynes argued that Say's Law was false because saving and investment, being functions of different variables, cannot be coordinated through the interest rate, however flexible. Saving is a largely passive "propensity" not to consume out of present and past realized income, while investment is an active decision to acquire new capital based on the expectation that to do so will be profitable. It is of the essence of the human condition that the future is unknowable, irreducibly uncertain.

How business investors collectively view the future has powerful effects upon how much output they wish to offer now, and therefore how much labour they wish to employ. As long as there are sufficient profitable investment outlets thrown up by expansion into new lands, profitable colonial wars, rising population and invention – as was the case during much of the 19th Century – investment will be sufficient to make Say's Law appear valid to the uncritical. If, however, for any reason investment opportunities "dry up" – or investors collectively merely believe that they have – the economy will *not* coast into the full employment for consumption and replacement world of the classical "stationary state." Instead, it will fall into a "cyclical" and perhaps secular depression of mass unemployment.

In the real world, money is not a mere convenience, a "veil" behind which Say's Law works its equilibrating wonders to perform.

---

[3] Keynes was unaware of, or unimpressed with, the work of "unBritish" or even "unCambridge" economists whether Swedish, German, Polish or American who collectively had all the essentials of his *General Theory* long before he did. (In this regard see J.R. Davis, *The New Economics and the Old Economists* (Iowa State Press, Ames, 1971) and George Garvey, "Keynes and the Economic Activists of Pre-Hitler Germany," *Journal of Political Economy*, April 1975, pp. 391-405.) Indeed, the Ohio horse breeder Coxey, founder of Coxey's army, had the policy prescriptions in the 1890's.

Keynes' usage of the term "classical" – while right for his polemical purposes, conflicts with another well established usage, in which the economists from Adam Smith through Karl Marx – who had in common some variant of the labour theory of value, are termed "classical" economists, while the "marginalists" from Jevons through Pigou are termed "neoclassical" economists. As Joan Robinson has pointed out, Keynes' own analysis has much in common with the real world analysis of Smith, Ricardo and especially Marx, and his real target is the unreal world of the "neoclassicist."

"The importance of money essentially flows from its being a link between the present and the future."[4] The monetary – or better, the financial – sector has powerful effects for good or ill upon the "real" economy. The institutions of money, contract, and debt; so central to the workings of an actual "monetary market" or "capitalistic" economy, make it impossible for Say's Law to be valid because: (a) the existence of cash and near cash liquid assets (such as time deposits and short-term debts of other "strong" institutions) provide a leak of savings into "idle hoards" rather than into new investment. In times of crisis, savers will much prefer the "safe" liquid assets and the rate of interest investors must pay to tempt them into departing from liquidity will rise, just when by the classical theory it should fall.[5] (b) The great overhang of existing debts makes impossible overcoming depression "disequilibrium" via a general deflation of wages and prices. The "Pigou effect", as it was later to be termed, has nothing to hold to as most money is "inside" or "endogenous", being based on credit extended to business and would disappear together with defaulting firms should such deflation gain momentum.[6] Thus, runaway deflation would be as destructive to the continuation of "market" economies as runaway inflation. It is, therefore, fortunate, rather than the reverse, that wage contracts make impossible such galloping deflation – or galloping inflation, unless this safeguard is removed, perhaps by the "indexing" now advocated by some misguided monetarists.

For the price level, to Keynes, was not determined by the quantity of money, but by the level of money wages and the laws of returns.[7] This being the case, it is truer to say that the level of wages determines the amount of money in existence, than the reverse. Over the long run, this is precisely what Keynes does say.[8]

To cure the worst faults of the capitalist system, while avoiding the still worse faults of totalitarian planning of either the "left" or the "right", Keynes in various places prescribed the following medicine. (a) A short *and* long-range commitment to full investment via low interest rates. This entails an active monetary policy – a "green cheese" factory to satisfy the demand for liquidity.[9] The ultimate goal is capital "saturation", and the "euthanasia of the rentier",[10] by making it impossible to live off the fact that capital is scarce. (b) A "somewhat comprehensive socialization"[11] of investment by which the state takes on many entrepreneurial functions; mobilizes the desired level

---

[4] Keynes, *G.T.* p. 293

[5] See J.M. Keynes, "The General Theory of Employment," *Quarterly Journal of Economics*, February 1937, pp. 209-23 for a discussion of the crucial importance of money and uncertainty in real-world economics.

[6] These and other neglected monetary aspects of Keynes' thought are highlighted in Paul Davidson's important *Money and the Real World*, Macmillan, London 1972.

[7] *G.T.* p. 294

[8] *G.T.* p. 309, 340n

[9] *G.T.* p. 235

[10] *G.T.* p. 376

[11] *G.T.* p. 378

of savings via taxation and bond sales, and invests in public works. (c) An incomes policy looking toward a non-inflationary and increasingly more just and equal distribution of society's output.[12]

It is perhaps the fate of all profound insights to be debased and vulgarized as they are popularized sufficiently to become policy. This was especially the fate of Keynes, whose epoch-making *General Theory* quickly attained the status of a classic – a book that everybody thinks they know about and that nobody reads. So far has the process of vulgarization gone that Joan Robinson. a close colleague of Keynes' in writing the *G.T.* dismisses the entire American "Keynesian" school – from the simplest version offered the college freshman in Nobel Laureate Paul Samuelson's textbook through the most "sophisticated" mathematical or econometric versions – as "Bastard Keynesianism."

I have adopted this spleen-did term in my title as descriptive of the current bankrupt American school, rather then founder Samuelson's persuasive term "neo-classical synthesis"[13] or long-time critic Weintraub's gentlemanly "classical-Keynesianism",[14] or Robert W. Clower's term "Keynesian Counter Revolution"[15] in order – at the danger of "too keen" controversy – to contribute to its demise and replacement by better theories and policies.

What are the hall-marks – the bar sinister – of Bastard Keynesianism, which distinguish it from Keynes' legitimate "brain child"? The distinguishing characteristics include: (1) At the level of "pure" theory a willingness to concede that Say's Law, or Walras' Law, is "really" correct, or would be if it were not for "frictions", such as sticky wages and interest rates from "irrationalities", such as "money illusion" and "administered prices". This is to make the General Theory merely a "special case" of the classical theory – thereby neatly changing the doughnut for the hole. (2) At the level of policy, bastard Keynesianism has been perverted to a technique for *causing* unemployment by "deflating" "excessive" aggregate demand. Whether the argument for so doing is that of the "Phillips Curve" or the "natural rate" of unemployment, it is a bitter irony, and bastardization of Keynes, that we have exchanged the classical business cycle for a "policy cycle" of administered semi-boom and

---

[12] We shall explore this last aspect of Keynes' prescription at some length, particularly in the last chapter. Here I wish merely to document that an anti-inflationary and anti-deflationary incomes policy is advocated, *G.T.* 270-1, and a reduction in the degree of inequality, pp. 373-4.

[13] Samuelson defines his "neoclassical synthesis" as follows: "by means of appropriately reinforcing monetary and fiscal policies, our mixed enterprise system can avoid the excesses of boom and slump and can look forward to healthy progressive growth. This fundamental being understood, the paradoxes that robbed the older classical principles dealing with small-scale "microeconomics" of much of their relevance and validity will now lose their sting. In short, mastery of the modern analysis of income determination genuinely validates the basic classical pricing principles . . ." *Economics: An Introductory Analysis*, 6th Ed. McGraw Hill, New York & elsewhere 1955.

[14] Sidney Weintraub, "Classical 45⁰ Keynesianism: A Plea for its Abandonment," *Classical Keynesianism, Monetary Theory, and the Price Level*, Chilton, Philadelphia 1961.

[15] Robert W. Clower, "The Keynesian Counter-Revolution: A Theoretical Appraisal," *The Theory of Interest Rates*, F.H. Hahn and F. Brechling (eds.) Macmillan, 1965 pp. 103-25.

semi-depression.[16] Furthermore, particularly in the U.S., "Keynesian" policy has been perverted into "military Keynesianism" – the maintenance of high levels of income and employment by high armaments spending, CIA subversion and "brushfire" wars. This development was perhaps inevitable given U.S. foreign policy imperatives. However, the bastard Keynesian model – with its sole regard for the short-run effect upon demand, its neglect of the short and long-run supply effect of various government programmes, and its lack of concern with what the output is for – was particularly vulnerable to this corruption. (3) An ignoring, forgetting or jettisoning of Keynes' more disturbing and "radical" ideas – such as that of true uncertainty, his concern with the top-heavy income distribution in a capitalistic society as the root cause of social injustice, inadequate demand and mal-distribution of resources – his call for "euthanasia of the rentier" via low interest rates, and for partial socialization of investment. (4) Ignoring Keynes' entire analysis of aggregate supply and his wage-cost theory of the price level in order to preach either an "excess demand" theory of the price level (early Samuelsonians), "Phillips curve" tradeoff (later Samuelsonians) or a refurbished quantity theory (Friedmanians). These analyses restore the classical "dichotomy" between the "real" and "monetary" aspects of the economy, and between "micro" and "macro" analysis which it was one of the chief purposes of the *G.T.* to bridge.[17]

It is on this last aspect of Keynes and "bad", "45°", or "bastard" Keynesianism that I wish especially to focus. For Keynes rejected the classical dichotomy with stinging words regarding the "opposite side of the moon" and "waking and dreaming lives",[18] and set forth a theory of the price level which was in "close contact with the theory of value."[19]

Why did economists adopt, in large part, Keynes' theory of Aggregate Demand, Income and Employment, but neglect and even forget his theory of Aggregate Supply, Distribution, Money and the Price Level, and his focus upon uncertain expectations?

---

[16] In his prescient 1943 article, "Political Aspects of Full Employment," *Political Quarterly*, 14, 1943 pp. 322-31, M. Kalecki foresaw just such a perversion as governments responded to rentier and business pressure to *prevent* continuous full employment.

[17] Since Milton Friedman's "monetarists" combine all these shortcomings of Bastard Keynesianism with peculiarly simplistic analysis and policy views, I do not regard them as constituting a separate "school", but as merely the "right wing" of illegitimate Keynesianism. Friedman once said, "in one sense we are all Keynesians now; in another, no one is a Keynesian any longer." (Milton Friedman, *Dollars and Deficits*, Prentice Hall, Englewood Cliffs, 1968, p. 15.) I would hold that he might better have stated, "we are all Bastard Keynesians now, and thus none of us are Keynesians any longer." For Friedman's own reassertion of Say's Law (without actually using the term) see his "A Theoretical Framework for Monetary Analysis," *Journal of Political Economy*, March-April 1970, pp. 193-238, esp. pp. 206-7. Indeed, Friedman's entire monetarist chain of causation amounts to the assertion of Say's Law for money – the supply of money is the demand for money (though perhaps with a lag). Friedman's views will be examined further in Chapters Two and Eight.

[18] *G.T.* p. 292

[19] *G.T.* p. 293

A full exploration of answers to this question would entail an entire book, rather than the few pages I wish to devote to it.[20] The following points seem most relevant.

Bastard Keynesianism, whether of the 45⁰ diagram or of the more "sophisticated" IS ⩵ LM approach, has been useful in popularizing the basic lesson that major "deflationary gaps", such as the Great Depression, will not occur if proper demand creating policy moves are made. Once the profession was converted to this new aggregate demand analysis, a great problem of salesmanship was involved. Keynes' cure of depression necessitated a revolution of public and official opinion regarding public policy. Specifically, the public had to be educated to the proposition that in a depressed economy, easy money and deficit finance were conservative, prudent, responsible and wise public policies, rather than the work of the great red devil. It was no mean task to save the "capitalist" world from its long established "conventional wisdom", which called for further "belt tightening" when the belt was far too tight already.[21]

How much harder it would have been if his disciples conceded that the expansionary medicine would be somewhat inflationary (as Keynes did).[22] Since conservatives were bound to hammer endlessly[23] on the theme that deficit finance would cause run-away inflation, a flat denial – "this isn't going to hurt a bit" – was a better bedside manner to adopt than a completely truthful approach.

---

[20] For some exploration of these matters of Keynesian exegesis, see Sidney Weintraub, "Keynes and the Monetarists," *Canadian Journal of Economics*, 4, February, 1971, pp. 37-49; Warren S. Gramm, "Natural Selection in Economic Thought, Ideology, Power, and the Keynesian Counterevolution," *Journal of Economic Issues*, 7, March 1973, pp. 1-27; Ron Stanfield, "Kuhnian Scientific Revolutions and the Keynesian Revolution," *Journal of Economic Issues*, 8, March 1974, pp. 97-110. Richard X, Chase, "Keynes and U.S. Keynesianism: A Lack of Historical Perspective and Decline of the New Economics," *Journal of Economic Issues*, 9, September 1975, pp. 441-70. A look to the future is provided by Alfred S. Eichner and J.A. Kregel, "An Essay on Post-Keynesian Theory: A New Paradigm in Economics," *Journal of Economic Literature*, XIII, December 1975, pp. 1293-314.

[21] Thus in the 1932 elections in the U.S., Roosevelt castigated the Hoover administration for reckless deficit finance and the Democratic Party platform called explicitly for a "federal budget annually balanced on the basis of accurate executive estimates within revenues". Further, the Democratic Platform pledged to balance the budget by an "immediate and drastic reduction of government expenditures" by at least 25 per cent. In February 1933, when the depression was at its very worst, Mr. Hoover had the following advice for the President-elect:
"It would steady the country greatly if there could be prompt assurance that there will be no tampering or inflation of the currency; that the budget will be unquestionably balanced even if further taxation is necessary; that the Government credit will be maintained by refusal to exhaust it by the issue of securities." (All direct quotes as in J.K. Galbraith, *The Great Crash,* Houghton: Boston, 1961 pp. 188, 190.)

[22] "The increase in effective demand will, generally speaking , spend itself partly in increasing the quantity of employment and partly in raising the level of prices. Thus instead of constant prices in conditions of unemployment, and of prices rising in proportion to the quantity of money in conditions of full employment, we have in fact a condition of prices rising gradually as employment increases." *G.T.* p. 296.

[23] It would be an interesting exercise (not carried out here) to count and evaluate the changing arguments of the articles denouncing government spending (except for armaments) in general, and deficit finance in particular in *The Reader's Digest* from the 1930's through the 1960's. All those who have taught the "Principles of Economics" course, particularly those old enough to have taught it prior to about 1964, know what an antagonist *The Reader's Digest* is in the "struggle for young minds" and how hard it is to destroy its peasant wisdom equation "the national debt = the national sin", in the week or two one can spend on this subject.

Secondly, the profession was able to convince itself quite early that the law of diminishing returns, so central to Keynes' macro analysis and neoclassical micro analysis, was of no practical importance at the macro level.[24] Finally, Keynes' analysis, whether short-run or long-run, pointed directly to labour and, by implication, the labour union as the chief "culprit" in secular inflation,[25] a conclusion many of his disciples wished to avoid in order to maintain their "liberal" *bona fides*.

As the originator of the 45⁰ analysis was later to write, it is only a "caricature"[26] of Keynes' own system. However, the fact that this caricature was taken to be the essence of the system by a generation of Keynesians has importantly affected the real world.

In this world, which reads on the run it is difficult to convey more than a "compound fracture" of an idea, as Woodrow Wilson once put it. The older generation of Keynesians cannot be fairly criticized, in my opinion, for stripping down Keynes' system as much as possible and discarding everything that was not relevant for controlling the post-war depression they thought was imminent. All's fair in fighting off *The Reader's Digest.* However, much confusion and unnecessary delay in launching an adequate policy of inflation "containment" might have been avoided if our teachers had more clearly distinguished between their roles as expositors and as reshapers of *The General Theory,* and if they had not forgotten what Keynes' theory of inflation had been. And clearly, the Aggregate Demand chapters were the "exciting" and "relevant" chapters of the *G.T.* for the world of the 1930s'.

But more is involved than mere necessary simplification, inattention, forgetfulness, and the "white lies" of salesmanship. While Hicks, Hansen, Samuelson, Patinkin *et al.* were quick to make pieces of Keynes' analysis their's, at a deeper level his vision was wholly alien and repugnant to them. The mutation from "the economics of Keynes" to "Keynesian counter-revolution" is the result of their attempt to behave as "normal scientists" and stuff Keynes back into the "neo-classical" paradigm.

It is central to Keynes' argument that there is no "Say's Law" to guarantee either the "short" or the "long-run" equilibrium of the economy be at full employment, because investment decisions depend upon the state of long-run profit expectations relative to the rate of interest. But what do these expectations depend upon? As Shackle puts it, to find Keynes' answer

"stated, with full uncompromising explicitness, we have to look in a part of the canon which few economists seem able to endure the sight of – or else they have never heard of it. . . . It appeared in the Quarterly

---

[24] For a review of this controversy and the evidence see, Ronald G. Bodkin, "Real Wages and Cyclical Variations in Employment: A Reexamination of the Evidence," *Canadian Journal of Economics,* 2, August 1969, pp. 353-72. More on this presently.

[25] *G.T.* 307, 309 and 340n.

[26] "It is a caricature of Keynes to say that wages and prices stay constant until we move the system to full employment; after that point, there is an inflationary gap and we must turn to his *How to Pay For The War,* (1939) to describe the resulting demand-pull inflationary process. Yet this caricature is a useful classroom expository model." P.A. Samuelson, "A Brief Survey of Post-Keynesian Developments," in Robert Lekachman, ed., *Keynes General Theory: Reports of Three Decades,* New York, St. Martin's Press, 1964 p. 338.

Journal of Economics *for February 1937, and it declares unequivo-*
cally that expectations do not rest on anything solid, determinable,
demonstratable. 'We simply do not know'."[27]

Keynes of *The General Theory* envisions the economy as an underdetermined system. The human condition is not one in which "complete information" of the past or present, still less of the future, can
ever be obtained. Instead, lack of knowledge totally dominates human
affairs. There are not as many "equations" as there are
"unknowns".[28] Long-run expectation is a "wild card"; exogenously
given and subject to violent shifts as new information and rumor is
dealt us by history's unfolding, to feed our hopes and fears. The level
of money wages, also depends largely on expectations and, therefore,
does not depend in any "solid, determinable, demonstratable" way
on short-run market phenomena, or a simple lag structure from the
past, thus frustrating all attempts to find an invariant "Phillips curve".
The rate of interest does *not* tend to a "natural" rate which will equate
saving and investment at "full employment".

This view is wholly alien to economic scholars "trained to treat
economics as a geometry in the old sense, a complete and self-
sufficient axiom-system for generating as many propositions as
required."[29]

Shackle thus sees "classical Keynesian", "monetarist", "Walrasian general equilibrium analysis", and *all determined* models that
we can create, as alien to Keynes' own vision of our situation.

"All are concerned with a model of economic society, an economic
world, where knowledge of circumstance is (miraculously, impossi-
bly, unexplainedly) sufficient. Keynes in many places exploited a
superlative mastery of language to repudiate such a model, such an
invented world, as totally alien to our real predicament. We are not
omniscient, assured masters of known circumstance via reason, but
the prisoners of time."[30]

---

[27] G.L.S. Shackle, "Keynes and Today's Establishment in Economic Theory. A
View", *Jour. Econ. Lit.,* 11, June 1973, pp. 516-19. Quotation is from p. 516.

[28] Thus Shackle would hold that Samuelson's central misunderstanding of
Keynes is contained in Samuelson's claim that the *G.T.* provides us with "a well
reasoned body of thought containing . . . as many equations as unknowns."
(Paul A. Samuelson, "Lord Keynes and the General Theory," *Econometrica,*
July 1946, pp. 315-31) p. 318.

In view of the central role Paul Samuelson has played in American
Keynesian theory, education and policy, it is worthwhile to quote further
regarding his "conversion" from classicism to Keynesianism.

"I must confess that my own first reaction to the *General Theory* was not at
all like that of Keats on first looking into Chapman's Homer. No silent watcher,
I, upon a peak in Darien. My rebellion against its pretensions would have been
complete, except for an uneasy realization that I did not at all understand what
it was about. And I think I am giving away no secrets when I solemnly aver –
upon the basis of vivid personal recollection – that no one else in Cambridge,
Massachusetts, really knew what it was about for some twelve to eighteen
months after its publication. Indeed, until the appearance of the mathematical
models of Meade, Lange, Hicks, and Harrod, there is reason to believe that
Keynes himself did not truly understand his own analysis." p. 316.

Shackle would contend that Samuelson and his ilk never did understand
Keynes, but only the counter-revolution started by Hicks in his 1937 IS = LM
model. (J.R. Hicks, "Mr. Keynes and the Classics: A Suggested Interpretation,"
Econometrica, April 1937, widely reprinted.) Shackle sums up thirty-six years
of Keynesian exegesis and criticism in the words "He did escape," from the
made-up world of classicism, "his critics did not." Shackle p. 518.

[29] Shackle, p. 517

[30] Shackle, p. 519

But Keynes' is not a council of despair. The very fact that the economic system is underdetermined is what gives economic policies; monetary, fiscal, incomes, foreign trade, and international agreements, scope to move us toward desired outcomes that the "market system" is incapable of achieving by the interplay of blind forces and individual decisions.

These policy interventions will only work as planned if we have a clear knowledge of the system interrelationships it is the task of economic model building to illuminate – however imperfectly. An analogy with the conscious and unconscious levels of the brain seems appropriate – only if the automatic mechanisms, the scarcely conscious habits and reflexes, *and* the conscious learning, evaluating, decision making centres are all working well may the organism hope to survive.

In kicking their "Say's Law" props out from under them, Keynes invited his fellow economists to join him in facing and mastering the real world with its "horrid void of indeterminacy and irrationality."[31] Instead, most economists sought to regain their "mental equilibrium" by a retreat into determinate systems. Say's law is dead? – long live Say's law! Not that anyone, except Schumpeter,[32] cared to reassert Say's law boldly – that way lies rejection as a "classical" fuddydud.

What to do? It was Samuelson who found the answer – substitute "Walras' Law" for "Say's Law" and go on as if nothing (essential) has happened. Thus Samuelson's "neoclassical synthesis" was born as a "dash of Keynes in the Walras soup." R_x whenever Walras' Law – that in equilibrium the sum of excess demands and supplies is zero – seems not to be yielding full employment (*i.e.* whenever the assumed law is not a law) add a dash of Keynesian monetary and fiscal policy until the "law" is "validated."

We have it from Scripture that a man cannot serve two masters – "He is bound to hate one and love the other, or support one and despise the other".[33] And, certainly, the attempt to have it both ways – to hold with Walras that the economy is self-regulating, and can "settle down" *only* at full employment; *and* to hold with Keynes that it can "settle down" anywhere, is schizophrenia.

Despite Samuelson's many panegyrics on Keynes and his great success in putting across his "caricature" of Keynes' system, it is clear that the "master" he supports is Walras. A few more quotations will indicate his relative evaluation of Keynes and Walras. In the next quotation he comes, like Marc Anthony, to bury Keynes not to praise him, at the time of his death in 1946.

---

[31] Shackle, p. 517

[32] Schumpeter objected to Keynes' rejection of Say's Law as follows:

"Since . . . the only reason he had for objecting was that people do not spend their whole income on consumption and do not necessarily invest the rest – thus barring, according to Keynes, the way to 'full employment', it would have been more natural not to object to this proposition [that the competition between firms always tends to lead to an expansion of output to the point of full utilization of resources or maximum output] either, just as we do not object to the law of gravitation on the ground that the earth does not fall into the sun, but to say simply that the operation of Say's Law, though it states a tendency correctly, is impeded by certain facts which Keynes believes important enough to be inserted into a theoretical model of his own . . . (continuing in a footnote). This would have made Keynesian theory a special case of a more general theory." Joseph A. Schumpeter, History of Economic Analysis, *New York, Oxford University Press, 1954 p. 624.*

[33] Matthew 6:24. However, Samuelson maintains, "On Monday, Wednesday and Friday, I can be a Say's Law man and a Keynesian on Tuesday, Thursday and Saturday." Remarks at Conference on Keynes, Cambridge and *The General Theory*, University of Western Ontario, October 10, 1975.

"The General Theory *is a badly written book, poorly organized; . . . It is not well suited for classroom use. It is arrogant, bad tempered, polemical . . . It abounds in mares' nests or confusions . . . In it the Keynesian system stands out indistinctly, as if the author were hardly aware of its existence or cognizant of its properties . . . When finally mastered, its analysis is found to be obvious and at the same time new. In short it is a work of genius."* [34]

The following quotation is from Samuelson's Presidential Address to the American Economic Association in 1961.

"When I began graduate study at Harvard in 1935, Schumpeter rather shocked me by saying in a lecture that of the four greatest economists in the world, three were French . . . And who were the Frenchmen? Of course, one was Leon Walras, whom Schumpeter had no hesitation in calling the greatest economist of all time, by virtue of his first formulation of general equilibrium. Today there can be little doubt that most of the literary and mathematical economic theory appearing in our professional journals is more an offspring of Walras than of anyone else . . . The comparison that Lagrange made of Newton is worth repeating in this connection: Assuredly Newton was the greatest man of science, but also the luckiest. For there is but one system of the world and Newton was the one who found it. Similarly, there is but one grand concept of general equilibrium and it was Walras who had the insight (and luck) to find it." [35]

Schumpeter's remaining three greatest economists were Cournot Quesnay, and Marshall. Samuelson makes clear that he agrees with the first two choices, but rates Adam Smith somewhat more highly than Marshall. And Keynes? Well, in this address entitled, "Economists and the History of Ideas," the motto – "For there are, in the present times, two opinions: not, as in former ages the true and the false; but the outside and the inside," is from Keynes and one is given to understand that, like Walras, he is more important than his father. Other than that, Keynes is mentioned merely as one who was wrong in thinking that "Ricardo's mind was the greatest that ever addressed itself to economics,"[36] and wrong in thinking that "practical men . . . are usually the slaves of some defunct economist." (because "the Prince often gets to hear what he wants to hear"). Keynes was also, we are told, "known for one famous quotation, the casual remark: 'In the long run we are all dead',"[37] and presumably even Samuelson is prepared to concede he was right about that! He also quotes Keynes approvingly for having once dismissed Marx as "turbid" nonsense.

I remember, as a rather bastardized graduate student – I see now – reading Samuelson's Presidential Address and wondering whether a

[34] Samuelson, "Lord Keynes and The General Theory", pp. 318-9.

[35] "Economists and the History of Ideas," *Am. Econ. Rev.* 52, March 1962, pp. 1-18. Quote from pp. 3 & 4.

[36] Ibid p. 9. Samuelson doesn't here push his own nominee, but the "message" of the whole is that he is Walras.

[37] Ibid p. 17

man who could dismiss Karl Marx as "from the viewpoint of pure economic theory . . . a minor post Ricardian."[38] was always right.

Now, after the experience of watching the collapse of bastard Keynesianism, I reread this speech as an abstract of all that is wrong with establishment economics of the first "Keynesian" generation in its decline. It is all there – the "normal science" pride in the manipulation of mathematical abstractions[39] while ignoring the anomalies with which the neoclassical paradigm cannot cope and ignoring indeed, the central contradiction of that paridigm – the putting down as an "outside opinion" the view that epoch-making economists such as Smith, Marx and Keynes were the great economists, on the showing that Smith was a mere "synthesizer" (Schumpeter's term again), Marx "wrong" in "his façade of economics" but of some importance for some of his other ideas, while Keynes is at the highest level of "pure theory" a "theoretical charlatan who hid his trivial manipulations in fogs of words on irrelevant topics."[40]

If, as I would maintain, "bastard" Keynesianism has collapsed, what, or who, has brought about its downfall? Certainly there have been increasing, and increasingly important anomolies, or non-correspondence between fact and theory. But as Samuelson wrote long ago;

"Theorists can always resist facts; for facts are hard to establish and are always changing anyway . . . Inevitably, at the earliest opportunity, the mind slips back into the old grooves of thought, since analysis is utterly impossible without a frame of reference, a way of thinking about things, or, in short, a theory."[41]

As long as establishment Keynesians were content with their "neoclassical synthesis" it was vain for empiricists to push anomolous facts at them and for Weintraub, and following him Davidson and myself, to point out to them that their "Keynesianism" was neither Keynes nor in accord with plain facts. They knew better than Keynes – better than to read that "incomprehensible" book again, and facts were irrelevant! It remained for Joan Robinson and R.W. Clower independently to refute the Bastard Keynesian theory *before* the recent stagflation convinced even its practitioners that it was hopelessly inadequate. I would date the collapse of Bastard Keynesian theory from about 1966. In that year Cambridge, Mass. conceded defeat to Cambridge, England in the "reswitching"

[38] Ibid p. 12. But despair not, spirit of Marx, for lately, finding that like Keynes you can be mathematized, Samuelson has rehabilitated you, and declares *(Economics 10th edition)* "It is a scandal that, until recently, even majors in economics were taught nothing of Karl Marx except that he was an unsound fellow." You may yet be canonized in Cambridge, Mass.

[39] "My own scholarship has covered . . . questions like welfare economics and factor-price equalization; turnpike theorems and osculating envelopes; non-substitutability relations in Minkowski-Ricardo-Leontief-Metzler matrices of Mosak-Hicks type; or balanced-budget multipliers under conditions of balanced uncertainty in locally impacted topological spaces and molar equivalences." "Economists and the History of Ideas," p. 1.

[40] The words are Leijonhufvud's as expressing not his own opinion but that of "high-brow" theorists such as Samuelson after the Hicks-Patinkin exchange of 1957-59. Axel Leijonhufvud, *Keynes and the Classics*, Institute of Economic Affairs, London, 1969, p. 19.

[41] Samuelson, "Lord Keynes" p. 318.

debate,[42] and Clower's "The Keynesian Counter-Revolution" began to sink into the professional consciousness.[43]

The "reswitching" debate demonstrated that the "neoclassical capital and profit" theory – the aggregate production function with "well behaved" marginal productivities – was untenable as an explanation of income distribution and growth. This realization undermined economists' confidence in the neoclassical paradigm and, I believe, made them more receptive of the points raised by Clower. Clower's contribution consisted of re-interpreting the *General Theory* as a refutation of Walras' Law as well as Say's Law. Clower demonstrates that once we drop the assumption that Walras' "auctioneer" (who costlessly and instantly transmits the information necessary to coordinate all markets) exists, Walras' Law goes out and what he might have termed "Keynes' Law" or "Clower's Law" takes its place. Walras' Law asserts that in equilibrium the sum of excess demands in all markets is zero, *i.e.* if there is an excess supply of labour (involuntary unemployment) in the labour market, there is an excess demand for goods in the product market and the "auctioneer" will go to work finding and transmitting the new vector of wages and prices at which both markets will clear. However, since no such miraculous auctioneer exists, unemployed workers' "notional demand" for goods (how much they would buy at current prices if they could sell all the labour they wish to) is not "effective demand", as they are income constrained to offer to buy less than their "notional" demand. It is "effective" demand that the market system responds to, and Walras' Law must therefore "be replaced by the more general condition *the sum of all market excess demands, valued at prevailing market prices, is at most equal to zero.*"[44] Thus, "full employment" is just a special case and the "classical theory" is just a special case of Keynes' *General Theory.* Since this is merely common sense, as Clower shows, and it's all there in Keynes, at least tacitly as the basis of the Keynesian "consumption function," as Clower shows, what's all the fuss about? Is the trip necessary? Yes, it is necessary; theorists are immune to "common sense". Given that "neoclassical Keynesians" are enamoured with Walras, it is necessary to show that his equilibrium law wholly depends on the very special assumption of perfect knowledge – that "miraculous, impossible, unexplained" denial of the human condition. Clower concludes:

---

[42] The debate demonstrated that a technique which minimized the cost of production with a high rate of profit, and which did not minimize costs for an intermediate range, might also minimize costs with a low rate of profit. Samuelson and Levhari set off the debate by denying that reswitching (first suggested by Joan Robinson, "The Production Function and the Theory of Capital," *Review of Economic Studies*, 21, no. 55 (1953-4), 81 - 106; and D.C. Champernowne, "Comment," *ibid.*, 112-35) can occur. P.A. Samuelson, "A New Theorem on Non-Substitution," in H. Hegeland ed., *Money, Growth, and Methodology and Other Essays in Honor of John Akerman* (Lund, 1961), and D. Levhari, "A Non-substitution Theorem and Switching of Techniques," *Quarterly Journal of Economics*, Feb. 1965, 98-105. The November 1966 issue of the *Quarterly Journal of Economics* is largely given over to a symposium on reswitching which concludes with Levhari and Samuelson's retraction, "The Non-Switching Theorem is False," 518-9, and Samuelson's "A Summing Up," 568-83, which shows that re-switching is plausible, and possibly important. See also G.C. Harcourt, "Some Cambridge Controversies in the Theory of Capital," *Journal of Economic Literature*, VII, June 1969, 369-405; Joan Robinson "Capital Theory Up to Date," *Canadian Journal of Economics*, III, May 1970, 309-17.

[43] Clower's paper was presented to a Conference on the Theory of Interest and Money at the Abby of Royanmont, France in 1962, but not published until 1965.

[44] Clower, p. 120

"I shall be the last one to suggest that abstract theory is useless; that simply is not so. At the same time, I am convinced that much of what now passes for useful theory is not only worthless economics (and mathematics), but also a positive hinderance to fruitful theoretical and empirical research. Most importantly, however, I am impressed by the worth of Keynesian economics as a guide to practical action, which is in such sharp contrast to the situation of general price theory. As physicists should and would have rejected Einstein's theory of relativity, had it not included Newtonian mechanics as a special case, so we would do well to think twice before accepting as 'useful' or 'general' doctrines which are incapable of accommodating Keynesian economics." [45]

In addition to Clower's central point regarding non-transmission of "notional" signals, and Shackle's point regarding the impossibility of transcending the human condition, it has also been adequately demonstrated that Walras' equations describe essentially a barter world, and all attempts to add a "numerare" money are artificial.[46] All goods and services are equally exchangeable – everything is liquid so nothing is money. Again, this is not the real world, and such abstractions are not helpful, as Keynes said so clearly and as Davidson has so helpfully elaborated.[47] Finally, as Joan Robinson has shown repeatedly, Walras' model cannot be made into a useful starting point for studying the real world because it is a model of pure exchange of already existing stocks and the real world is a world of production in historical time.

"Anyone who tries to introduce a flow of production with Walras immediately falls into contradictions. Either the whole of future time is collapsed into today or else every individual has correct foresight about what all others will do; while they have correct foresight about what he will do, so that the argument runs into the problem of free will and predestination. This could not be of any use to Keynes. The very essence of his problem was uncertainty." [48]

What these attacks, taken together, do is to prove, even to the Bastard Keynesians, that the "neoclassical synthesis" is hopelessly foolish and self-contradictory. If they want to progress in understanding, and dealing with, the real world, they must go back to the good book, *General Theory* and this time understand it, as they struggle to develop a workable paradigm – to quote Scripture again, "the stone which the builders rejected has become the head of the corner."[49] What a pity that almost 40 years have been wasted!

To turn again to the Walras – Newton analogy used by Samuelson; as Clower mentioned, Newton's "world" is only a "special case" of Einstein's "world". However, Newton's world does happen to be the world we "live in" – that is, relativity makes no practical difference

---

[45] Clower p. 124-5. See also Axel Leijonhufvud "Keynes and the Classics" for further elucidation of Clower's central point. See further, H.I. Grossman, "Was Keynes a Keynesian? A Review Article", *Jour. Econ. Lit.*, 10, March 1972, pp. 26-30 for the view that Clower is too generous in attributing his own ideas to Keynes.

[46] "... the Walrasian economy ... is essentially one of barter," F. Hahn, "Some Adjustment Problems", *Econometrica* 38, 1970, p. 5.

[47] Davidson, *Money and the Real World*, Chapter 6.

[48] Joan Robinson, "The Second Crisis of Economic Theory".

[49] Psalm 118:22-3; also Matt. 21:42.

to an astronaut who wants to predict the motions of the planets in order to get to Mars. By exact analogy, Walras' theory of general equilibrium at full employment is only a special case of Keynes' *general* theory. However, Walras' "world" is *not* the world we "live in". It matters very much to practical affairs that "notional" demand is not "effective" demand, and that information is *never* sufficient – so that neither Say's nor Walras' "laws" are valid.

Furthermore, what would we think of a physicist who first gained fame and fortune explaining what Einstein "really meant", then led a retreat to Newton because he found relativity scientifically and politically disturbing and because he found uncertainty impossible to treat mathematically?

Commenting upon this strange mental aberration, Martin Shubik writes the following:

"General equlibrium economics is undoubtedly a splendid intellectual achievement. But it is not by any means on the level of Newtonian mechanics. In a world with large complicated corporations, selling thousands of goods and services (and often selling whole systems), the way we stick to our simple models (which at best cover one simple limiting case) is ludicrous. I am reminded of the story of the drunk who had lost his keys at night and spent his time searching for them under a streetlamp fifty yards from where he had lost them because that was the only place where he could see anything."[50]

Let us leave this drunken search and turn to the task of freeing Keynes' "lost" theory of the price level from the "Keynesian" incubus.

---

[50] Martin Shubik, "A Curmudgeon's Guide to Microeconomics," *Journal of Economic Literature*, June 1970, p. 415.

Keynes' Theory of the Price Level vs the "Keynesian Theory"

The difficulty economists have in distilling Keynes' Price Level theory comes not from any inherent difficulty in this theory. Keynes merely applied micro price theory to the economy as a whole, with important *caveats* concerning wages. Rather, the source of the difficulty is two-fold. First, economists thought they already had an adequate price-level theory in the Quantity Theory of Money, and are in the habit, particularly if they are sufficiently mathematically trained to grasp Walras' equations, of treating money wages as "just another price" which adjusts to clear markets.

Secondly, the Keynes theory has been neglected because of inconsistencies in his exposition. In Chapter 4 he proposed to have nothing to do with so "vague and non-quantitative" concepts as "the price level" and "real output", and instead promised "to make use of only two fundamental units of quantity, namely quantities of money value and quantities of employment".[51]

Keynes argued that:

"The first of these is strictly homogeneous, and the second can be made so. For, in so far as different grades and kinds of labour and salaried assistance enjoy a more or less fixed relative remuneration, the quantity of employment can be sufficiently defined for our purpose by taking an hour's employment of ordinary labour as our unit and weighting an hour's employment of special labour in proportion to its remuneration; i.e. an hour of special labour remunerated at double ordinary rates will count as two units. We shall call the unit in which the quantity of employment is measured the labour-unit; and the money-wage of a labour-unit we shall call the wage-unit.[1] Thus, if E is the wages (and salaries) bill, W the wage-unit, and N the quantity of employment, $E = N.W$.

[1] *If X stands for any quantity measured in terms of money, it will often be convenient to write X_w for the same quantity measured in terms of the wage-unit."*[52]

---

[51] *G.T.*, p. 41.

[52] Ibid.

This decision of Keynes was a source of impatience and annoyance to his disciples. As Hansen points out, Keynes' wage-unit is just as ambiguous as the price index,[53] so that Keynes' sarcasm concerning the ambiguity of the "real output" and "price-level" concepts[54] applies in equal measure to his "money value of output" and "wage-unit" concepts also.

Furthermore, Keynes later abandoned his self-imposed restriction of having nothing to do with such a vague concept as "the price level" and, as we have seen, wrote Book V on the subject! In their impatience and annoyance, his disciples ignored his theory of the price level with its base in the cost function, threw out the hallowed Law of Diminishing Returns and converted the "Keynesian" model from one running in terms of employment, money values and wage units, into one in terms of real output and real expenditure. Thus, within a few years of the writing of the *G.T.* Keynes' Aggregate Supply Function was wholly stripped of price level implications and reduced to a truistic 45⁰ line, while all emphasis was placed on the intersecting Aggregate Demand for Real Output Function (D), wholly reversing Keynes' statement that,

"The Aggregate supply function, . . ., which depends in the main on the physical conditions of supply, involves few considerations which are not already familiar . . . it is the part played by the aggregate demand function which has been overlooked."[55]

Recovery of Keynes' theory of the price level and inflation merely entails disregarding his qualms in Chapter 4 and applying what he says about the price level in Book V.

---

[53] Hansen, *A Guide to Keynes, New York, McGraw,* 1953, pp. 43-4.
    There are, however, some advantages to Keynes' deflation by wage-units:
    1) When money variables are expressed in constant wage-units the variable is tied directly to the level of employment. If the wage share is constant (and as we shall see in Chapter Two it is indeed close to constant) then

$\dfrac{Yw}{w}$ is proportional to the level of employment since if

$\dfrac{Yw}{k} = wN$ then

$\dfrac{Yw}{w} = kN.$

Income in wage-units will vary only with employment if shares are constant. The letters

$k = \dfrac{PY}{wN},\ w = \dfrac{W}{N},\ \text{and}\ Yw = \dfrac{Y}{w}$

all terms being expressed as index numbers.
    2) $\triangle w$ will tend to be uniform in the capital goods and consumer goods industries if labour is mobile between them, while the price level and $\triangle P$ may vary widely between capital and consumer goods industries over the cycle, necessitating separate price deflators. See Axel Leijonhufvud, *Keynesian Economics and the Economics of Keynes*, New York, Oxford, 1968 for emphasis on relative price distortion problems.

[54] "To say that net output today is greater, but the price-level lower, than ten years ago or one year ago, is a proposition of a similar character to the statement that Queen Victoria was a better queen but not a happier woman than Queen Elizabeth – a proposition not without meaning and not without interest, but unsuitable as material for the differential calculus. Our precision will be mock precision if we try to use such partly vague and non-quantitative concepts as a basis of a quantitative analysis". *G.T.* p. 40.

[55] *G.T.,* p. 89.

Here, again, Samuelson has placed himself between the "unintelligible" *General Theory* and a whole generation of students and set up a bowdlerized 45⁰ Keynesian canon.

"Like Joyce's Finnegan's Wake, *the* General Theory *is much in need of a companion volume providing a 'skeleton key' and guide to its contents: warning the young and innocent away from Book I (especially the difficult Chapter 3) and on to books III, IV, and VI. Certainly in its present state, the book does not get itself read from one year to another even by the sympathetic teacher and scholar."*[56]

Yet it is precisely in Chapter 3 that Keynes first sketches his model of Aggregate Supply, Aggregate Demand and the Price Level which he developed further in Book V entitled "Money – Wages and Prices". Keynes might have saved himself the trouble of writing these chapters for all the use his "Neoclassical Synthetic" disciples have made of them.

For a generation the "young and innocent" have been led down just the garden path Samuelson prescribed for them. They receive their all-important first impressions from Samuelson's text, or a host of imitative books. Those who major in economics are introduced to the "fine points" of Keynes, i.e. Hicks, more algebra, Phillips curves and Harrod's growth model in "intermediate" and "advanced" macroeconomics courses. The few who persist until graduate school are finally assigned to read Keynes themselves. The students find him difficult, as they were told to; there aren't any pictures, or rather there is one but it is new and indeterminate. Where is the good old 45⁰ line and IS = LM? Here Samuelson's great teacher Alvin H. Hansen comes to his rescue with the "guide" that Samuelson had called for and the fledgling economist relaxes, resolved to learn *The General Theory* here with all the dear familiar aids. Despite Hansen's prefactory statement that the aim of his *Guide to Keynes* is:

"to assist, and induce, the student to read The General Theory . . . *It is not a substitute for Keynes,"*[57]

it seems clear that most graduate students, and their teachers have got their Keynesianism from *A Guide* rather than *The General Theory* itself.

But what is the harm? Is not Hansen a reliable guide to Keynes; one who has extracted the essence, put it more felicitously, but faithfully to the original and illustrated Keynes with 18 diagrams? No, *A Guide to Keynes* is both more and less than the "tutorial guide" it purports to be. Hansen undertook not only to improve upon Keynes' exposition, but upon his theoretical system, and, perhaps through modesty, he is not always candid regarding where Keynes stops and Hansen begins. In some of these corrections Hansen is undoubtedly right – Keynes did gloriously botch his interest rate theory[58] – but in others he was quite wrong, in this writer's opinion, with serious consequences to the understanding of Keynes, to the development of economic theory and to the design of effective policy.

[56] Samuelson, "Lord Keynes", p. 319.

[57] Alviᶇ H. Hansen, *A Guide* v.

[58] See *The General Theory*, Chapter 14 and Hansen's discussion in *A Guide*, Chapter 7.

In his foreword, Seymour E. Harris gives his evaluation of what Hansen has done:

"He has not only weeded and raked the rich field of The General Theory *but has fertilized the soil and replanted to achieve the landscape envisaged by Keynes . . . Hansen's* Guide *also reflects many of his own contributions to the system about which he modestly remains silent."*[59]

No analogy is perfect, and the fertilizer metaphor is perhaps unfortunate, but in these terms it is here contended that Hansen discarded as weeds one of Keynes' finest flowergardens – his theory of the price level – and replanted this area with far inferior stock. Only when this patch is cleared away and planted as Keynes directed will we achieve the "landscape" he envisioned – and be on our way to understanding and controlling inflation.

Keynes accepted, and Hansen rejected as valid for macro theory, the law of variable proportions and all its implications for the marginal cost and aggregate supply functions. Hansen is forthright regarding his disagreement with Keynes[60] – that replanting is in process – except at one crucial point. After stating clearly how central diminishing returns are to Keynes, as to classical theorists,[61] and illustrating Keynes' argument with a diagram, Hansen presents in his Figure 2, as Keynes' Aggregate Supply analysis, a diagram which is wholly inconsistant with diminishing returns and thus with Keynes.[62] This diagram is here reproduced.

---

[59] *A Guide,* xi.

[60] *A Guide,* p. 21 including footnotes, pp. 186, 192n, 194.

[61] "On this point Keynes was emphatic. He accepted the marginal productivity theory of wages. If industry is operating under decreasing returns (rising marginal cost), real wage rates must decline (in the short run) as employment is increased." *A Guide,* p. 21.

[62] Hansen's discussion at this point contains one of the most puzzling "clarifications" in the literature in the form of Table 1 and its explanation.
"The schedule of sales-proceeds required to cover the cost (i.e., the payments to all factors including normal profits) of producing the output associated with the employment of varying quantities of labor, Keynes called Z. Table 1 is an illustrative table showing the numerical values of Z for different quantities of O (output) and N (employment). Z is the Aggregate Supply price of output from employing N workers. Thus $Z = \emptyset N$."

Footnote continued on p. 29.

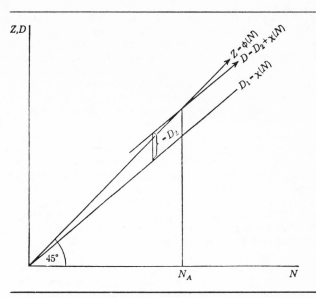

Figure 1.1 Aggregate Demand and Aggregate Supply.

Note

Realized employment (N_A) is determined by the intersection of the Aggregate Demand function, $D_2 - X(N)$, and the Aggregate Supply function, $Ø(N)$.

Hansen's Interpretation of Keynes' Aggregate Demand and Aggregate Supply Model. Source: Alvin H. Hansen, A Guide to Keynes, p. 31. (Copyright 1953 by McGraw-Hill Book Company and used with their permission.)

Continued from p. 28.
Table 1

Z	O	N
Aggregate supply price of output in constant-value dollars, billions	Output base year $= 100$	Number of workers employed, millions
300	100	60
270	90	54
240	80	50
200	67	40

Source: Hansen, *A Guide*. Used with permission of McGraw-Hill Book Company.

Table 1 presents Z as a complicated function involving first increasing returns (as employment expands from 50 to 54 million) and then decreasing returns (as N grows from 54 to 60 million). Most likely, however, Hansen intended constant returns throughout with the index of output growing at $1^2/_3$ for each increment of employment and $VMP_n = \$5,000$. Thus if we change 80 in the O column to 83.3 and the \$240 in the Z column to \$250 all relations are linear as in Figure 1.1. Hansen's misinterpretation remains since Keynes' model specifies diminishing returns.

It is our old friend the 45⁰ line with the difference only that the horizontal axis is labelled N, for Employment, rather than Y, for Real Income as in Samuelson. A few pages later the 45⁰ format is complete, Hansen noting the transition from N to Y with the following footnote,

"Here we jump ahead a little and assume that since employment N and output, or real income Y, are likely to fluctuate together in the short run, the functional relation $D_1 = X(N)$ can equally well be stated as $C = C(Y)$."[63]

Hansen's little jump is a momentous one, however, for it was right here that Keynes' theory of the Price Level was lost. An Aggregate Supply curve which is a function of the level of employment is meaningful and operational. It is not bound rigidly at 45⁰, indeed it cannot be linear once we posit diminishing returns as Keynes did, but is free to reflect the cost and price level implications of wage and output changes. It is fully consistent with our Theory of the Firm and when it is properly developed fulfills Keynes' aim of bringing, "the theory of prices as a whole back to close contact with the theory of value."[64] An Aggregate Supply curve which merely represents the truism that Real Output (Q or Z/P, thus Z deflated by a Price Index) is identical to Real Income (Y) can merely indicate the level of Real Income at which the equilibrium with Aggregate Real Demand (D/P) is attained.

As an old saying has it, first impressions are important, and though in later discussions[65] Hansen shows fully why Figure 1.1 cannot represent Keynes' $Z = \emptyset(N)$ it is already far too late to get a student raised on Samuelson and Hicks to "buck" his teachers and understand what Keynes' theory of supply and the price level actually was, much less consider the possibility that Keynes was nearer right than Hansen. This is doubly so since by the old Chinese equation one picture is equal to one thousand words and Hansen nowhere supplies a visual corrective to Figure 1.1.

It seems safe to say the 99 out of 100 students have taken the representation in Figure 1.1 as all there is to Keynes' $Z = \emptyset(N)$ despite Keynes' continual emphasis on the law of returns. Nor were lazy graduate students the only ones who have confused "45⁰ Keynesianism" with Keynes' own views. Even Abba Lerner, a famed expositor of Keynes who became dissatisfied with all attempts to rescue the 45⁰ analysis and who developed a more adequate "sellers' inflation" model in its place, once confused "45⁰ Keynesianism" with what Keynes actually wrote. Thus Lerner then wrote:

"Keynes, like the 'classical' economists, assumed that . . . prices would not rise unless there was excess demand," and *"Keynes assumed that the point of full employment is also necessarily the point of price-level equilibrium, so that only buyers' inflation is possible."*[66]

---

[63] *Ibid.*, p. 34.

[64] *G.T.* p. 293.

[65] *Guide* – Chapter 11. "The Keynesian Theory of Money and Prices" esp. pp. 186-7, 191-3.

[66] A.P. Lerner, "On Generalizing the General Theory", *American Economic Review*, March 1960, pp. 135, 140.

In both these statements Lerner was simply incorrect, as he later recognized. They are included here merely to indicate the pervasiveness of the misinterpretation of Keynes' price-level views. In his "uncanonical" Chapter 21, "The Theory of Prices," Keynes made perfectly explicit why the price level could rise before full employment is reached. His analysis may be summed up in two sentences: The price level may rise because the cost level may rise. Among the forces pushing up costs as employment advances the most important is the increasing wage level.

Keynes' analysis of the price level was not in terms of a $C+I$ line crossing a 45-degree line. Samuelson contributed this diagram and popularized it in his very successful introductory textbook;[67] the Hicksian $IS=LM$ "suggested interpretation" being reserved for the sophomores. The world view of "Bastard Keynesianism" is set forth in Figure 1.2. Keynes briefly considered the kind of world described by these models only to show that it is "not the real world." He wrote:

"let us . . . assume (1) that all unemployed resources are homogeneous and interchangeable . . . and (2) that the factors of production entering into marginal cost are content with the same money-wage so long as there is a surplus of them unemployed . . . It follows that an increase in the quantity of money will have no effect whatever on prices, so long as there is any unemployment, and that employment will increase in exact proportion to any increase in effective demand brought about by the increase in the quantity of money; whilst as soon as full employment is reached, it will thence forward be the wage-unit and prices which will increase in exact proportion to the increase in effective demand. Thus if there is perfectly elastic supply so long as there is unemployment, and perfectly inelastic supply so soon as full employment is reached, and if effective demand changes in the same proportion as the quantity of money, the Quantity Theory of Money can be enunciated as follows: 'So long as there is unemployment, employment *will change in the same proportion as the quantity of money; and when there is full employment,* prices *will change in the same proportion as the quantity of money'."*[68]

---

[67] The 45° apparatus first makes its appearance in the literature in Paul A. Samuelson, "A Synthesis of the Principle of Acceleration and the Multiplier," *Journal of Political Economy*, 47 December 1939. Samuelson's *Economics: An Introductory Analysis* New York, McGraw 1948 is now in its tenth U.S. edition and fourth Canadian edition.

[68] *G.T.*, pp. 295-6.

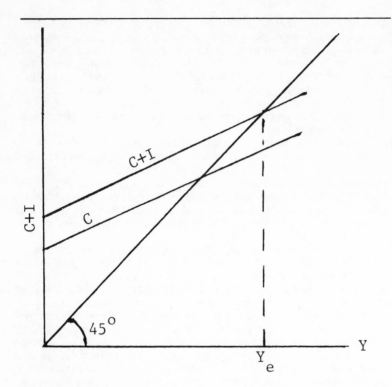

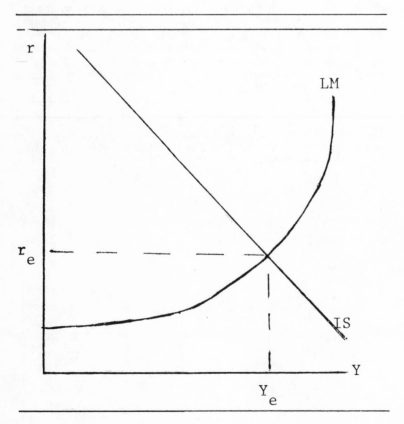

Figure 1.2 Bastard Keynesianism:
Above 45° Diagram of Aggregate Equilibrium where C + I = Y. Below IS = LM Diagram of Equilibrium Real Income (Ye) and Rate of Interest (re) simultaneously determined by the joint equilibrium of Investment and Saving (IS) and the Demand for and Supply of Money (LM).

The "Bastard Keynesian" models which a generation of students have been taught are based squarely on these simplifying assumptions, which Keynes dismissed in the next paragraph! He continued:

"Having, however, satisfied tradition by introducing a sufficient number of simplifying assumptions to enable us to enunciate a Quantity Theory of Money, let us now consider the possible complications which will in fact influence events:

(1) Effective demand will not change in exact proportion to the quantity of money.

(2) Since resources are not homogeneous, there will be diminishing, and not constant, returns as employment gradually increases.

(3) Since resources are not interchangeable, some commodities will reach a condition of inelastic supply whilst there are still unemployed resources available for the production of other commodities.

(4) The wage-unit will tend to rise, before full employment has been reached.

(5) The remunerations of the factors entering into marginal cost will not all change in the same proportion."[69]

Keynes summarized his "contraquantity" or "micro based" theory of the price level as follows:

"In a single industry its particular price-level depends partly on the rate of remuneration of the factors of production which enter into its marginal cost, and partly on the scale of output. There is no reason to modify this conclusion when we pass to industry as a whole. The general price-level depends partly on the rate of remuneration of the factors of production which enter into marginal cost and partly on the scale or out-put as a whole, i.e. (taking equipment and technique as given) on the volume of employment."[70]

Despite all this, despite the price experience of the 1930's through the 1950s, bad analysis has so driven out good that not until the advent of the "Phillips Curve" would any Keynesians acknowledge the reality of rising prices with unemployment!

When the inadequacies of 45^0 Keynesianism as an explanation of inflation became more and more evident economists retreated from it in confusion, introducing as partial explanations trade-off curves and ratchet effects, instead of making use of Keynes' actual system. We could not make use of it because we had not learned it ourselves! Let us therefore retrace our steps, reestablish what Keynes' model actually was and then modify it only where further experience or the exigencies of a particular problem require "replanting", being careful to distinguish between Keynes' and others' contributions.

---

[69] *Ibid.*

[70] *Ibid.*, p. 294.

Keynes' Model of Income, Employment and the Price Level

Let us start our search in Chapter 3 of *The General Theory* – surely it is not as arcane as Samuelson maintained. Keynes' analysis runs in terms of an Aggregate Supply Function (Z) and an Aggregate Demand Function (D):

"Let Z be the aggregate supply price of the output from employing N men, the relationship between Z and N being written Z = Ø(N), which can be called the Aggregate Supply Function. *Similarly, let D be the proceeds which entrepreneurs expect to receive from the employment of N men, the relationship between D and N being written D = f(N), which can be called the* Aggregate Demand Function.*

Now if for a given value of N the expected proceeds are greater than the aggregate supply price, i.e. if D is greater than Z, there will be an incentive to entrepreneurs to increase employment beyond N and, if necessary, to raise costs by competing with one another for the factors of production, up to the value of N for which Z has become equal to D. Thus the volume of employment is given by the point of intersection between the aggregate demand function and the aggregate supply function; for it is at this point that the entrepreneurs' expectations of profits will be maximised. The value of D at the point of the aggregate demand function, where it is intersected by the aggregate supply function, will be called the effective demand. *Since this is the substance of the General Theory of Employment, which it will be our object to expound, the succeeding chapters will be largely occupied with examining the various factors upon which these two functions depend."*[71]

The Aggregate Supply and Demand functions are to be derived on the assumption that "the money wage and other factor costs are constant per unit of labour employed".[72]

Figure 1.3 incorporates Keynes' argument.

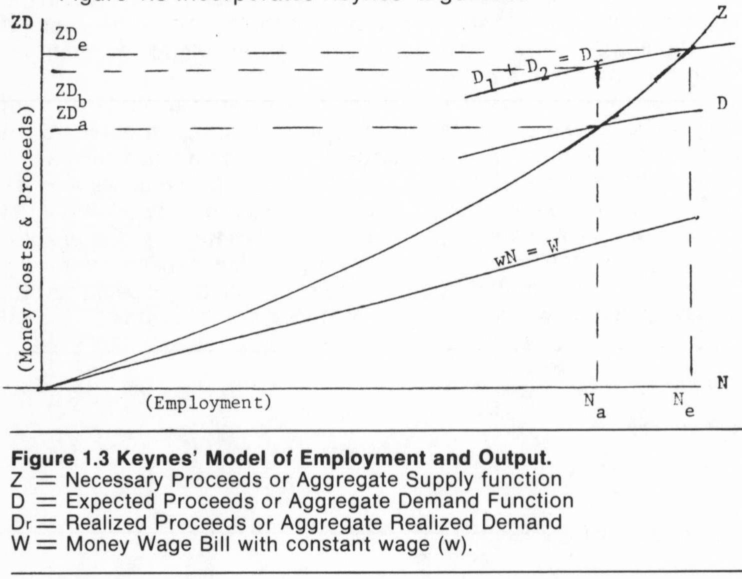

Figure 1.3 Keynes' Model of Employment and Output.
Z = Necessary Proceeds or Aggregate Supply function
D = Expected Proceeds or Aggregate Demand Function
D_r = Realized Proceeds or Aggregate Realized Demand
W = Money Wage Bill with constant wage (w).

[71] *G.T.*, p. 25.

[72] *Ibid.*, p. 27.

The Aggregate Supply Function (Z) is drawn on the assumption of a) constant money wage rate (w), b) diminishing returns, c) profit maximizing behaviour under pure competition. As is well understood, c) entails that supply price is set equal to marginal cost. Assuming that labour is the only variable factor we have $P = MC = (w/m)$ where m is the (declining) marginal product of labour. Multiplying both sides by Q, or real output, we have:

$$PQ = (w/m)Q = Z$$

which expresses the necessary proceeds, or Z, required to support a level of real output Q. However, it is the relation between Z and N, or employment, upon which Keynes focused. Since $Q = aN$, where 'a' represents the average product of labour, we may rewrite our equation as Keynes' Aggregate Supply function, $Z = \emptyset(N) = w(a/m)N$.

The ratio (a/m) is the inverse of the elasticity of output with respect to employment, and if this elasticity is assumed constant, Z is a straight line from the origin, à la Hansen. Keynes' assumption of diminishing returns, or $a > m$, involves a decreasing elasticity of output as employment advances.

The Expected Proceeds Function, $D = f(N)$ states the proceeds sum which businesses *expect* to receive from the sale of the output resulting from the employment of varying amounts of labour. Expected Proceeds may be taken as the product of the price expected by firms, P, times the real output Q they plan to produce. On the assumption that expected price diminishes at higher output levels the expected proceeds function, D, increases at a decreasing rate. In Figure 1.3, Expected Proceeds, D, are equal to Necessary Proceeds, Z, at Na. This is the employment level and corresponding output and proceeds level (ZDa) which firms will choose, as this employment level maximizes their expected profits.

Suppose, however, that at Na the realized proceeds (D_r) sum from Consumption (D_1) and Investment (D_2) exceed ZDa? A short period disequilibrium is the result since at employment level Na, consumption plus investment expenditures sum to ZDb while only ZDa is being currently produced. Clearly, inventories will be run down, and, (to the extent that price is demand determined rather than supply determined) prices will rise leading to some upward revision of expected proceeds and an increase in employment and output toward Ne. If investment decisions are based on long-run expectations and are not revised because of the unexpected increase in business, the equilibrium at Ne will eventually be attained where $D_1 + D_2 = D = \emptyset(N)$[73] and the profit maximizing proceeds ZDe are being received.[74]

Keynes pictured the firm as basing its short-run output upon its short-term expectations and continually adjusting these expectations in the light of realized receipts, as in the following passages:

". . . the behaviour of each individual firm in deciding its daily output will be determined by its short-run expectations – expectations as to the cost of output on various possible scales and expectations as to the sales-proceeds of this output . . . The actually realized results of

---

[73] *G.T.*, p. 29.

[74] For a clear statement of Keynes' short-run model of Employment, Proceeds and Output see Paul Wells, "Keynes Dynamic Disequilibrium Theory of Employment". *Quarterly Review of Economics and Business*, January 1974, pp. 89-92.

the production and sale of output will only be relevant to employment insofar as they cause a modification of subsequent expectations.''[75]

''. . . the process of revision of short-term expectations is a gradual and continuous one carried on largely in the light of realized results; so that expected and realized results run into and overlap one another in their influence. For although output and employment are determined by the producer's short-term expectations and not by past results, the most recent results usually play a predominant part in determining what these expectations are.''[76]

Keynes' model was almost wholly neglected until it was resurrected by Sidney Weintraub in 1958, and through his students Paul Davidson, and Eugene Smolensky, incorporated in a textbook only in 1964.[77]

---

[75] *G.T.*, p. 47.

[76] *G.T.*, pp. 50-1.

[77] See Weintraub, *An Approach to the Theory of Income Distribution*, Chilton, Philadelphia, 1958; *Classical Keynesianism, Monetary Theory, and the Price Level*, Chilton, Philadelphia, 1961. Paul Davidson and Eugene Smolensky, *Aggregate Supply and Demand Analysis*, Harper, New York, 1964.

Weintraub's Model of the Price Level and Income Distribution

The model presented in Figure 1.3 is identical with that derived from Keynes by Weintraub, except that Weintraub adopted the by now more familiar $C + I$ notation instead of $D_1 + D_2$, focused on the equilibrium at N_e rather than short-run disequilibrium phenomena, and has no truck with deflation by the wage unit. To this model I have added a real output function, Q, subject to diminishing returns. Weintraub used this model as one of income distribution and the price level as well as one of income and employment. Thus, on the assumption of a governmentless economy, and that labour is the only variable factor of production, we have: $TC = V + F$ where variable cost $(V) = wN = W$, or the total wage bill, and $F =$ fixed cost, consisting of interest payments on long-term debt. Income distribution at an employment level is given by $Z = W + F + R$ where $R =$ gross profit residual after explicit costs are paid. Clearly a higher level of employment and output entails: a) a higher price level from diminishing returns, b) a fall in the real income of fixed income recipients, c) a fall in the wage share, d) a fall in the real income of employed workers, e) a rise in the profit share.

On the assumption of pure competition and profit maximization, supply price at a level of employment is given by $P = MC = \dfrac{\partial TC}{\partial Q} = \dfrac{w}{m}$. Figure 1.4 sums up the analysis.

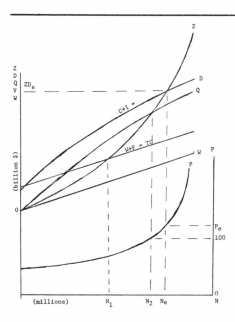

Figure 1.4. Extension of Keynes' Model

Z $=$ Aggregate Supply   D $=$ Aggregate Demand
Q $=$ Real Output   TC $=$ Total Contractual Cost
W $=$ Total Wage Bill   P $=$ Price Level with
N $=$ Employment   Constant Money Wage

Employment level N_1 represents a level of activity so low that firms as a whole would merely cover their wage and fixed costs leaving nothing for depreciation and net profits. Level N_2, where the real output function Q intersects the Aggregate Supply function (Z), represents the level of employment which would make this period's price level equal to that of the base period in which Q is denominated. Suppose that aggregate demand (D) is equal to Z at employment level N_e. This employment level entails some diminishing returns inflation, as $P_e >$ 100. Note that the price level curve

$$P = \frac{w}{m},$$

is implicit in the Z/Q ratio at each level of employment and, therefore, may be omitted without loss of information.

Weintraub tied the aggregate demand analysis closely to the supply side income analysis by focusing upon the varying pro-pensities to consume of wage, interest, and profit recipients. Thus $C = C_0 + C_w W + C_f F + C_r \lambda R$, where $C_0 =$ "autonomous" consumption; C_w, C_f, and C_r represent the marginal propensities to consume of the "factor" income groups and λ is equal to the pay-out ratio of firm profits. Higher levels of employment will entail lower aggregate mar-ginal propensity to consume because of the shift to profits.[78] Invest-ment is, of course, a function of past, present and expected future profits, income, and interest rates.

In this writer's opinion, Figure 1.4 is what Keynes "said", in Books I and V. The model needs to be made "complete" by bringing in the labour and money markets and elaborated by introducing the gov-ernment and foreign sectors. Also, as Leijonhufvud and Shackle have so well pointed out, no static equilibrium model can accurately cap-ture Keynes' analysis of persistent disequilibrium due to dynamic movement with "positive" deviation amplifying feedback.[79] However, the model does fulfill Keynes' desire to *integrate* price level theory with micro theory. Also it opens up several alternative specifications. Thus, it can be used as a Kaldor-Kalecki model by assuming that "capitalists (F + R) get what they spend while workers spend what they get"; consequently, that $C = W$ and $Z - W = F + R = S = I$. Where S is defined as aggregate savings.

Furthermore, when the government sector, together with the money market, are incorporated into both the demand and the *supply* side of this model, the hollowness and even perversity of much of "Bastard Keynesian" monetary and fiscal policies are exposed.

---

[78] ". . . the increase of employment will tend, owing to the effect of diminishing returns in the short period, to increase the proportion of aggregate income which accrues to entrepreneurs, whose individual marginal propensity to consume is probably less than the average for the community as a whole.", *G.T.*, p. 121.

[79] On "positive" feedback see, Axel Leijonhufvud, *Keynes and the Classics*, pp. 25-32.

Complete Keynesian Macro Model

Figure 1.5 brings together the $IS = LM$ diagram (graph e) and the Aggregate Supply (Z), Aggregate Demand (E)[80] and Employment (N) model (graph b). As the $IS = LM$ (or "Islamic") model is familiar to all students of macroeconomics, little time needs to be spent here on its derivation from equating the sum (S) of Saving (s), Taxes net of transfers (T) and Imports (m) (graph h) with the sum (I) of Investment (i), Government Expenditure (G) and Exports (X) (graph d) to derive the IS line. The LM line is derived from summing the Transactions Demand for Money (L_1, graph i) and the Speculative Demand for Money (L_2, graph f) and equating the resulting L functions to the Money Supply (M) to derive the LM function. The final equilibrium (graph e) determines Real Income (Y_e) and the Rate of Interest (r_e).

As we have seen, however, the great defect of the $IS = LM$ system is that it is drawn up on the basis of a constant price level. Thus L is the demand for *real* balances and M is the supply of real, rather than nominal, money. It is a mistake to draw price level inferences from such a model, such as that a reduction in M will raise r and depress Q and therefore reduce P. Whether such a move will lower, or raise, prices depends upon the degree of response of aggregate expenditure (E) and aggregate supply (Z) and the shape of these functions over the relevant range, thus on matters which are entirely neglected in the $IS = LM$ format. These matters are explored in graphs a, b, and c.

Graph 'a' examines labour market relationships. By the marginal productivity theory, the demand for labour (D_n) is equal to the (declining) marginal revenue product of labour, while the supply of labour (S_n) is an increasing function of the real wage (w/P). Competition is supposed to ensure a continuous equilibrium in which the wage is equal to that real wage just sufficient to induce a marginal worker to offer his labour for its "marginal product." Thus the equilibrium of the labour market was by assumption and definition a "full employment" equilibrium in that all those willing to work at the prevailing real wage were able to do so.

How then are we to account for the real world observation of the existence of a fringe of involuntarily unemployed workers? Keynes' explanation ran in terms of inadequate aggregate demand from a pessimistic view of the profitability of new investment, coupled with imperfectly flexible wages, prices (particularly capital goods prices) and interest rates, in turn the product of uncertainty and generally inelastic expectations. These forces were seen as sufficient to make invalid Say's "Law" that demand would always equal "full employment" supply.[81] Thus in graph 'a' the Demand for Labour (D_n) is not

---

[80] I use the letter E (for Expenditure) rather than the familiar D, (a) to indicate that E is not "constant dollar" or deflated demand, as in the 45° diagram, (b) so I can dub this model "ZEN" Keynesianism in contrast to "Islamic" Keynesianism and "Keynesian Cross" or 45° analysis.

[81] Leijonhufvud follows Clower in recasting Keynes' argument as a refutation of Walras' Law – that the sum of excess demands and supplies in all markets is zero – rather than of Say's Law. While Leijonhufvud's argument is highly illuminating, it is not Keynes' own argument but rather yet another idea of what he "should have said." Also following Clower, Barro and Grossman distinguish between "notional" demand and supply schedules at full employment and "effective" or income-constrained schedules given that other markets are not clearing. Their treatment has the advantage of not "requiring" that real wages move countercyclically when they are nevertheless observed to move procyclically. R.J. Barro ahd H.I. Grossman, "A General Disequilibrium Model of Income and Employment," *American Economic Review*, LXI, March 1971, pp. 82-93.

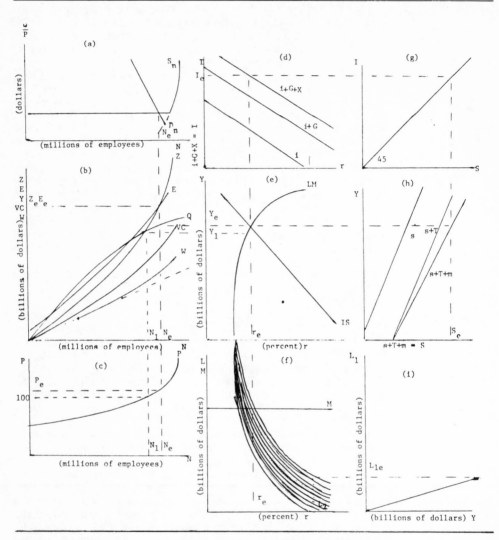

Figure 1.5 Complete Keynesian Model of Aggregate Supply (Z), Aggregate Demand (E), Employment (N), Price (P), Output (Y), and Interest Rate (r).

simply the marginal physical product of labour when combined with certain fixed and variable factors, the product being sold in markets which always clear at prices which equal marginal cost and which were foreseen when production was undertaken. Rather, D_n is a function of all those uncertainties regarding the saleability of the product underscored by Keynes. It is shifted to the left or right by the multiplier effects of a change in aggregate demand. Thus a fall in investment demand does not lead smoothly, much less instantaneously, to a rise in government and consumer demand. Rather, the unemployed investment goods workers must cut their consumption while searching for employment, hopefully at wages as good as, or at least not too inferior to their former pay. However, this causes a fall in demand for consumer goods and consequent induced unemployment of some of those who produce and distribute them: the "multiplier" in Keynes' terminology, "positive feedback" in Leijonhufvud's.

It is particularly when we attempt to draw a "Keynesian" supply of labour (S_n) function that the limitations of comparative statics in describing a dynamic economy become more evident. Some have seen the essence of the difficulty in a "money illusion" on the part of workers which makes the labour supply a function of the money wage rather than the real wage. Keynes' argument, however, was that there might not, in fact, be any way in which workers, by taking money wage cuts, could reduce the real wage (w/P) and bring about full employment, since prices would fall as fast or faster than wages so that aggregate demand would be little affected.[82] Here, the S_n function is

---

[82] Later, Pigou was able to show that if all wages and prices were "fully flexible" downward the classical medicine would eventually work as the increased purchasing power of the money stock shifted both the LM and IS functions to the "full employment" income and interest rate equilibria. This argument has been seen by some as making "classicism" the truly general theory and Keynes' theory merely a special one of rigidities. It is perhaps Leijonhufvud's greatest contribution to show that it is instead the classical theory which depends upon the special and unrealistic assumption of instantaneous adjustment to equilibrium, while it is Keynes who deals with the real world where the past cannot be changed, the future is unknowable and Walras' "auctioneer" does not exist.

drawn horizontal to a level of employment beyond its intersection with D_n to indicate that "involuntary unemployment" is present: there are workers willing to work at the prevailing real wage who cannot find employment.[83] The point where S_n begins to slope upward may be thought of as "low" full employment, while complete, or "high" full employment would be indicated by the point where S_n becomes vertical. The dotted line section of S_n indicates that some of the unemployed would be willing to take a lower real wage in order to achieve employment so that, in time, a classical equilibrium would be achieved if D_n would hold still (which it won't).

The ZEN model drawn in graph 'b' is a modification of that presented in Figure 1.4. The modifications consist of treating the money wage as "weakly" responsive to the current level of employment, à la "Phillips Curve"[84] rather than as an exogenous constant, and that other variable costs, notably interest and indirect taxes, are recognized as affecting price determination. These modifications in turn entail that the Aggregate Expenditure (E) may be of increasing upward slope to the right, rather than of decreasing or constant upward slope. A positive marginal propensity to save (the sum of the "leaks" from personal and business savings, marginal rate of taxation and propensity to import) would assure a stable equilibrium between Z and E at $Z_eE_eN_e$.

The Price level function (in graph c) is given by

$$P = MC = \frac{\partial VC}{m_v},$$

where $m_v =$ the marginal product of the variable factors. We may take VC as $wN + rB_s + tY + poY$, where r is the nominal rate of interest, B_s represents the amount of short-run borrowing for inventories, payrolls, etc., and t is the marginal rate of those taxes which affect business costs and thus selling prices. Those last would include indirect taxes i.e. excises and sales taxes, and perhaps, the corporate profits tax as well. The term poY allows for the impact of the price (p) of imported goods (o) on the variable costs of domestic firms: o may initially be thought of as a constant fraction of Y. More on these matters in Chapter Three. The Fixed Cost line is eliminated from graph 'b' as it plays no part in price making and the graph is quite complicated enough without it.

Approximately one-half of business debt is short-term. Moreover, as will be documented in Chapter Two, the Debt to Income (B/Z) ratio is one of the more nearly constant of the "great ratios" of economics, changing but little in all U.S. experience save the Great Depression. For simplicity, we may take B_s to be a linear function of the wage bill (wN) since the degree of factor substitutability between capital and

---

[83] For some purposes it would be better to draw the S_n function as downward sloping to the right. Thus multiple, stable and unstable, equilibria between S_n and D_n are possible. It would carry us beyond our present purposes to explore these matters further here.

[84] That the "trade-off" may exist between unemployment and price-level change is evident in the following, "That the wage-level may tend to rise before full employment has been reached, requires little comment or explanation. Since each group of workers will gain, cet. par., by a rise in its own wages, there is naturally a pressure in this direction, which entrepreneurs will be more ready to meet when they are doing better business. For this reason, a proportion of any increase in effective demand is likely to be absorbed in satisfying the upward tendency of the wage-unit". (G.T., p. 301) Indeed, the "Phillips Curve" may also be traced back to Marx. It would be difficult to find a more succinct statement of the relationship than Marx', "The general movements of wages are exclusively regulated by the expansion and contraction of the industrial reserve army, and these again correspond to the periodical changes of the industrial cycle". Karl Marx, Das Kapital, Vol. 1, Ch. 25.

labour is small in the short-run.[85] The nominal rate of interest is a function of all the forces determining the IS = LM equilibrium *plus* the price level and expectations concerning its future level. Thus the rate of interest determined in the IS = LM graph 'e' should be thought of as the real rate of interest, and the nominal rate of interest will diverge from this if expectations of a higher future price level outweigh expectations of an unchanging or falling price level.

The equilibrium price level (P_e) is determined by the Z_eE_e equilibrium, the link between the ZEN diagram and that of IS = LM being given by the corresponding equililbrium real output (Q_e). As Figure 1.5 is drawn, some inflation is indicated in that P_e is greater than the base period price level, $P = 100$, in which "real output" is denominated, even though there are some unemployed resources. According to the conventional wisdom of "bastard Keynesianism" this "semi-inflation" can be eliminated only by repressing aggregate expenditures and causing some further unemployment. Thus, if a lowered Expenditure function (E') could be made to intersect Z at N_1, where Z intersects Q, the initial price level will attain with real income reduced from Y_e to Y_1. In terms of the IS = LM functions it doesn't matter fundamentally to the attainment of the new equilibrium whether it is achieved by the various "fiscal policy" tools which shift IS (cut G, raise taxes to depress C and I, or, more rarely discussed, encourage imports and discourage exports to boost aggregate supply) or by cutting the money supply and thus shifting LM. Generally, a coordinated policy of fiscal and monetary restraint is advocated, but advocates of "money alone" and "tax hikes alone" are not lacking. What is missing from this debate between "monetarists" and "fiscalists" is any realization that the desired N_1,Y_1, $P = 100$ constellation may be unattainable by any combination of interest and tax hikes they might engineer.

If it is possible it curb demand by cutting "wholly wasteful" government expenditures, events may well follow the scenario envisioned by IS = LM theorists. However, tax and interest hikes cause an upward shift in the Variable Cost, and therefore, in the Aggregate Supply function. Thus at every level of employment and real output, the Price Level function will be higher than the P function of graph 'c'. The new equilibrium price level will be lower only if the rise in the marginal product of the fewer factors now employed, together with the lower wages induced by moving to a lower point on the "Phillips curve", outweighs the cost increases through the higher taxes and interest rates. Economists should demonstrate that this will be the case rather than merely assuming the net effect of contractionary policies will be deflationary. Recent events suggest strongly that the opposite has been the case; that our contractionary policies have been inflationary, while some, at least, of our expansionary policies have been deflationary.

These matters are explored at greater length in subsequent chapters, particularly Chapter Three, where the questions are posed in a Canadian setting. Here, suffice it merely to say that the diminishing returns phenomenon appears to be strong only when the economy is very close to its full employment potential. At other times, the marginal product of factors may be constant or even increasing. It has been widely documented that firms do not achieve short-run cost minimization in recessions. Instead, for several quarters after a fall in de-

---

[85] For the development of a two variable factor macro model with some discussion of the resultant ambiguitites regarding the effects of policy moves see, Arthur Benavie, "Prices and Wages in the Complete Keynesian Model", *Southern Economic Journal*, 38, April 1972, pp. 468-77.

mand they have many redundant employees with a consequent fall, rather than rise, in marginal and average products. Therefore, a rise in demand will be accompanied by rising, rather than falling productivity until very full employment has been achieved.[86] Furthermore, there is considerable evidence that increasing direct and indirect taxes lead to a rise in wage demands "to pay the higher taxes."[87] Thus the increased level of taxation in recent decades, as the public sector expands more rapidly that the private sector, becomes a factor shifting upward the supposedly invariant "Phillips Curve." This possibility is explored more fully in Chapters Four and Five.

Finally, the real economy is not one of pure competition in which all prices are the result of the play of anonymous forces. Rather, in much of the economy, Galbraith estimates about half,[88] prices are "planned" or "administered" by firms with considerable market power. This has several important implications regarding the response of the economy to "anti" inflationary policy moves. Firstly, it may account for the finding that the corporate profits tax is fully shifted, or even more than fully shifted, in the short run, making this tax a dubious anti-inflationary device indeed.[89] Secondly, there may be "long and variable" lags between a change in aggregate demand and decisions to change prices. Moreover, prices may be maintained or even increased in the face of declining demand.[90] Thirdly, prices may be quickly and fully responsive to cost increases, but only slowly and partially responsive to cost decreases, imparting a "ratchet" effect to the overall price movement. Chapter Seven explores some of the complexities of Galbraith's vision of a planning-market dichotomy entails for the policy makers in a Harrod's Dichotomy world.

---

[86] See, T.A. Wilson & O. Eckstein, "Short-Run Productivity Behavior in U.S. Manufacturing", *Review of Economics and Statistics*, 46, Feb. 1964, pp. 41-59, for demonstration of this and explanation in terms of the "short-run maladjustment curve." As A.M. Okun puts it, "The record clearly shows that man-hour productivity is depressed by low levels of utilization, and that periods of movement toward full employment yield considerably above average productivity gains." Arthur M. Okun, "Potential GNP: Its Measure and Significance, "*Proceedings of the Business and Economic Statistics Section of the American Statistical Association*, 1962. Reprinted in *Readings in Money, National Income, and Stabilization Policy Revised Ed.*, W.L. Smith & R.L. Teigen, eds., Homewood 1970 pp. 313-22. R.G. Bodkin concludes that "Classical diminishing returns is probably confined in its operation to a range very close to the full utilization of the labour (and capital) factors of production," R.G. Bodkin, "Real Wages and Cyclical Variations in Employment: A Reexamination of the Evidence, *Canadian Journal of Economics*, 2, August 1969, pp. 353-74.

[87] Robert J. Gordon, "Inflation in Recession and Recovery", *Brookings Papers on Economic Activity*, 1970, no. 1 pp. 105-58. Gordon finds that the short-run Phillips curve is very nearly flat so that the partial forward shifting of payroll and personal income tax outweighs the wage-reducing unemployment effect. He holds, however, that as the restrictive fiscal policy is continued the Phillips curve becomes steep enough to reverse the initially "perverse" impacts. See also C.J. Bruce, "The Wage – Tax spiral: Canada 1953-70", *Economic Journal*, 85, June 1975, pp. 372-6.

[88] John Kenneth Galbraith, "Economics as a System of Belief", *American Economic Review, Papers and Proceedings*, 60, May 1970, pp. 469-78.

[89] See discussion in Ch. Three, pp 91-5. For indications that the corporate tax is shifted forward in the form of higher prices to consumers rather than backward in lower factor payments see William R. Moffat, "Taxes in the Price Equation: Textiles and Rubber", *Review of Economics and Statistics*, 52, Aug. 1970, pp. 253-61.

[90] For recent evidence regarding the prevalence of "administered" pricing by one of the originators of the concept see Gardiner C. Means, "The Administered-Price Thesis Confirmed, "*American Economic Review*, 62, June 1972, pp. 292-306. Means finds a "new dimension" in the adminstered price
Footnote continued on p. 45

Harrod's Dichotomy

Sir Roy Harrod has recently suggested that "anti" inflationary monetary and fiscal moves may in some circumstances cause inflation
rather than cure it, thus that a "dichotomy" may exist. He writes:[91]

*"The 'dichotomy' is as follows. If aggregate demand is running ahead
of supply potential, this will tend to pull prices up. In these circumstances deflationary policies, designed to reduce aggregate demand,
will have the effect of reducing, or, in the absence of wage push
troubles eliminating, any price increase . . . But, if initially aggregate
demand is not above supply potential, it is no longer clear that deflationary policies, so called, will have the effect of reducing or
eliminating any price inflation that is occuring. It may even be the
other way round." (p. 624)*

Harrod offers two reasons why demand restriction may raise the price
level. First, if imperfectly competitive firms face downward sloping to
the right marginal cost curves, a reduced demand may cause them to
raise their prices.[92] Secondly, the interest and tax hikes used to "fight
inflation" raise costs as we have seen above. Figure 1.6 is a visual aid
to Harrod's argument.

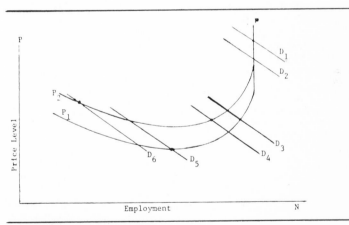

Figure 1.6 Harrod's Dichotomy

Continued from p. 44
thesis in that "industrial prices in recent years have disclosed many cases in
which price behavior has been the *reverse* of that to be expected from classical
theory, the price rising with recession and falling with recovery." (p. 297) Such
a result is fully consistent with "Harrod's Dichotomy" to which we turn in the
following section. See also John M. Blair, "Market Power and Inflation; A Short
Run Target Return Model," *Journal of Economic Issues*, 8, June 1974, pp.
453-78 for a theoretical rationalization of such firm behavior. See also Willard
F. Mueller, "Anti Trust in a Planned Economy," *Journal of Economic Issues*, 9,
June 1975, pp. 159-79.

[91] Sir Roy Harrod, "Reassessment of Keynes' Views on Money," *Journal of
Political Economy*, 78, July-August 1970, pp. 617-25.

[92] This case was analyzed long ago by Joan Robinson, *The Economics of Imperfect Competition* London, Macmillan, 1933, pp. 60-75.

Suppose that the Price Level curve (P_1) relating the employment and price possibilities for a given year, has shifted upward from some previous period (P_0) for whatever reason (too rapid a money supply increase, wage push, pollution abatement, food or fuel crisis, resource exhaustion). The rise in the price level, potential or realized, induces the authorities to raise taxes and interest rates in an attempt to lower aggregate demand (D).

However, these moves raise the Price Level function still further to P_2. Again, the price and employment level impact of these moves depend upon the degree of shift of the D and P functions and their shapes. Suppose the initial equilibrium is given by the intersection of D_1 with P_1 where supply is completely inelastic, and demand repression reduces demand to D_2. The policy move will reduce the equilibrium price with no reduction in employment. Suppose instead, that demand is more affected by the policy move than is supply price, so that demand is reduced from D_1 to D_4 as price shifts upward from P_1 to P_2. Clearly, price is much reduced even as employment falls. Suppose instead, that the intersection of D_3 and P_1 describes the initial situation and that restrictive policy succeeds in reducing demand only to D_4. Clearly employment, and real output, has been reduced but inflation has not been. Finally, let us suppose that the intersection of P_1 and D_5 describes the initial situation and the intersection of P_2 and D_6 the post-policy equilibrium. Here we have the "perverse" side of Harrod's dichotomy as employment falls and prices climb. Chapters Six and Seven explore the comparative statics and some dynamics of "Harrod's Dichotomy" argument.

Note that the horizontal scale in Figure 1.6 need not start at zero employment, as in Figure 1.5. Rather, Wilson and Eckstein's "short-run maladjustment" argument would entail that stern demand repression might encounter downward sloping Price Level curves within a few percentage points of "full" employment. Thus the American and Canadian economies may well have been moved from "P_1, D_5" to "P_2, D_6" by the demand repression policies of 1969-70. At any rate, as unemployment climbed (from 3.5% in 1969 to 4.9% in 1970 in the U.S., from 4.7% to 5.9% in Canada) the rate of price level increase did likewise (rising 4.8% in 1969 and 5.4% in 1970 in the U.S.; 4.5% to 4.7% in Canada over the same period) and the economics profession lost considerable repute. Much worse has been the most recent experience. As the level of unemployment climbed (from 4.9% in 1973 to 5.6% in 1974 in the U.S., and from 5.6% to 5.8% in Canada) the rate of change of prices also increased (rising 5.2% in 1973 and 10.2% in 1974 in the U.S., and 7.6% and 13.1% in Canada).

Inflation and the Rise of the Government Sector

Harrod's dichotomy discussion is set in a short-run context of demand suppression policy in which the government taxes more but does not spend more. However, the more usual reason for raising taxes is to spend more, either for new or expanded programmes, or to grant a pay boost to the civil servants. Might a secular rise in taxes per unit of output account for part of the secular rise in the price level in most developed countries in recent decades? Economists have much neglected this possibility even though, by the balanced budget multiplier theorem, a larger government sector is clearly expansionary, and thus, given diminishing returns, inflationary. Furthermore, if citizens have a more perfect perception of loss from higher taxes than they have of their gain through new or expanded government services, they may demand higher money incomes to compensate them for an imagined fall in their real incomes. Thus taxes may trigger a wage or profits push to restore net income. Similarly, redistributional schemes, such as unemployment compensation, negative income taxes, and old age pensions may result in some inflation if those who pay the extra taxes are able to demand higher pre-tax incomes, as well as from a tendency of such programmes to shift income from savers to spenders.

It would seem that economists have neglected the importance of "government push" inflation for several reasons. The first is the "quantity theory of the price level" tradition. As long as the "too much money chasing too few goods" explanation is accepted as the beginning and the *end* of inflation analysis, the government's culpability is limited to its role in forcing the creation of money to finance its deficits, and its permissive role in allowing too much private credit expansion. However, even a modicum of further analysis would indicate that a larger government sector would raise money "velocity" since the government seldom saves, while taxpayers and businesses do. The quantity theory played a key role in Ricardo's loss of the "scent" of "tax push inflation", and thus tended to relegate the concept to the realm of unimportant and unlikely matters best forgotten. Ricardo, like Smith, argued that taxes tended to shift forward in higher prices. He held that, by and large, this would merely change relative prices, i.e., the price of the taxed items would rise and those of non-taxed goods would fall. He also held that a general rise in the level of taxation in a country can raise the general price level, but saw that this would quickly lead to a fall in exports and a rise in imports. This in turn would lead to a gold drain and a consequent fall in prices in the high tax country to about the initial level.[93]

Ricardo seems never to have asked himself, however, what would happen if in most, or all, trading countries the public sector was expanding more rapidly than the private sector? Nor did he attempt to analyze the behaviour of a world economy where gold does not call the tune, and in which the money supply can easily be expanded, but can never be allowed to contract. Nor is this surprising. It is surprising, however, that so few later economists concerned themselves with such questions. M. Kalecki's analysis indicates that taxes shift forward and that consequently a growing government sector will raise the price level, but he does not develop the insight at any

---

[93] David Ricardo, *The Principles of Political Economy and Taxation* London, Dent, 1960, [1817] pp. 197-208. See also p. 98 passim.

length.[94] Colin Clark suggested that if taxation became greater than
25% of net national income the price level would rise cummulatively
due to a general reluctance to finance such a large public sector.[95] His
suggested limit was dismissed by the profession with considerable
snickering, although some conceded that there existed some limit to
taxation as an anti-inflationary force.[96]

More recently, William Krehm has offered a comprehensive
model of a "non-inflationary" price rise from an increasing "social
lien", defined as "the total accretion of all taxes upon price."[97] He also
developed the concept of the "aggregate shift function determining
the proportion of total taxation shifting into aggregate price," and of
"social revalorization" the non or extra market pulling and hauling by
which groups increasingly attempt to raise their share of the
economic pie, as they more and more come to see through the
"marginal productivity" explanation of income distribution to the
actual game of smash and grab that resulted in the existing shares.
More on this in Chapter Four.

Perhaps economists have been reluctant to look squarely at the
government sector inflation puzzle for "political" reasons. Most of us
consider ourselves to be "liberals" and, at least until the Vietnam War,
this predisposed us to favour increased government activity. Why do
the *Reader's Digest's* work for it by demonstrating the inflationary
"joint product" of pollution abatement or the war on poverty? So
perhaps, again, we were involved with "salesmanship" rather than
objective science. There is this difference, however. The "wage push"
inflation thesis was debated at great length, even during the heyday of
"demand pull" as *the* cause of inflation, but I search my memory of my
graduate education in vain for the slightest suggestion of a theory of
"interest and tax push" inflation. If some inner circle of "Paulist
Fathers" were keeping these concepts from falling into the "wrong"
hands, they also kept the secret from their Ph.D. candidates. I suspect,

[94] Michal Kalecki, "A Theory of Commodity, Income and Capital Taxation," *Economic Journal*, Sept. 1937, pp. 444-50; reprinted in M. Kalecki, *Selected Essays on the Dynamics of the Capitalist Economy* (Cambridge, University Press, 1971).

[95] Colin Clark, "Public Finance and Changes in the Value of Money," *Economic Journal*, 55, Dec. 1945, pp. 376-89.

[96] See Joseph A. Pechman & Thomas Mayer, "Mr. Colin Clark on the Limits of Taxation, "*Review of Economics and Statistics*, 34, August 1952, pp. 232-42; Dan Throop Smith, "Note on Inflationary Consequences of High Taxation", *ibid.,* pp. 243-7; Richard Goode, "On Economic Limit on Taxes: Some Recent Discussions", *National Tax Journal*, 5, no. 3, 1952, pp. 227-33 for a review of this controversy. See also Benjamin Higgins, "A Note on Taxation and Inflation", *Canadian Journal of Economics and Political Sciences*, 19, Aug. 1953, pp. 392-402; J.N. Wolfe "Professor Higgins on the Limits of Taxation", *Canadian Journal of Economics and Political Science*, 20, May 1954, pp. 236-7. Virtually the only economist to take Clark's concepts seriously and use them as a point of departure for his own work appears to be Amotz Morag. See his, *On Taxes and Inflation* (Random, New York 1965). See also James Tobin and Challis A. Hall, "Income Taxation, Output and Prices," *Economic Internazionale*, Aug. 1955, pp. 522-42; Nov. 1955, pp. 742-61; and Feb. 1966, pp. 1-8. Reprinted in James Tobin, *Essays in Economics*, Vol. 1., North Holland, London 1971.

[97] William Krehm, "La Stabilité des Prix et le Sectreur Public" *Revue Economique*, 21, May 1970, pp. 425-66. For a full statement of Krehm's views see his, *Price in a Mixed Economy*, Thornwood, Toronto, 1975.

instead, that, bemused by the 45⁰ line, they never thought such disturbing thoughts at all. Now that the spell is broken by the rude rush of
events, we must face the matter squarely, even if the *Reader's Digest*
will misuse the argument. For there *are* more important problems
than inflation, and we shall not make it easier to solve them by keeping
millions of men idle. The subsequent chapters explore several aspects of the "government inflation" problem.

Summary

The contention of this chapter has been that economists have seriously misunderstood the causes of, and cures for, the inflation of
recent decades. Neither "excess demand" nor any simple "quantity
theory" explains the inflationary creep. The proper starting place for a
"General Theory of the Price Level" is Keynes' "contraquantity" or
"micro based" Theory of the Price Level expounded in much neglected chapters of his *magnum opus*. But we should not stop with
Keynes' formulation and his almost solely "wage-push" explanation
of continued inflation. Rather, we should recognize the impacts of
interest and taxes on the aggregate supply, as well as the aggregate
demand, function. Further, we should incorporate into our short-run
analysis the realization that, whenever there is slack, production will
expand subject to increasing returns. Finally, we need to consider
carefully the interrelations between the rise of the government sector
and our creeping inflation.

2

Income Distribution, Money, Debt, and the Price Level

Introduction: Three Simple Theories of the Price Level.

It is often said that "economists must have a simple theory or they have no theory". It is the purpose of this chapter to explore three simple theories of the price level in the light of the Canadian and United States data. The first theory views inflation as an "income push", or less inclusively, a "wage push", thus that inflation is caused by "too much income for too little output". A very considerable literature exists concerning this theory with various elaborations such as "dilemma models" and "trade-off" curves. As we have seen, and will document further, "wage push" was Keynes' own theory of "creeping inflation", or in his terms, "semi-inflation". Keynes reserved the concept of true inflation, or inflation proper for situations such as World War 1, or hyperinflation in defeated countries, and held to "excess demand" and monetary overexpansion explanations of these phenomena. We shall say little of this aspect of his thought here both because it is overfamiliar and because it is irrelevant to present concerns. Not since World War II, when prices were heavily controlled, has North America known "excess demand" from an "inflationary gap", and yet in every post-war year save 1949 when prices fell slightly, the GNP deflator has crept, crawled or trotted upward. There is one other exception: in 1953, when employment was at a "peacetime" high (unemployment only 3.0% in Canada, 2.9% in the United States) and growth was at about the long-run "target" rates (5.3% in Canada, 4.5% in United States) the price level neither rose nor fell in Canada while the increase in the United States GNP deflator of 0.9% was the smallest of any year since 1940. 1953 fits but poorly into either "inflationary gap" or "Phillips curve" explanations.

The second simple theory of inflation is the Quantity Theory explanation which holds that the basic cause of all inflation is the money supply increasing faster than real output, i.e. "too many dollars chasing too few goods". This was the "Good Old Theory" from the time the gold of the New World flooded into Europe and in recent years has enjoyed a mighty revival and refurbishment under the leadership of Milton Friedman[1] and other "modern Monetarists". These

---

[1] Among Milton Friedman's voluminous writings in this area should be mentioned, "The Quantity Theory of Money – A Restatement", in Milton Friedman ed, *Studies in the Quantity Theory of Money* (Chicago 1956) reprinted in his, *The Optimum Quantity of Money and Other Essays* (Chicago 1969) and his mammoth empirical study with Anna J. Schwartz, *A Monetary History of the United States* 1867-1960 (Princeton 1963). For recent statements of Friedman's views see his, "A Theoretical Framework for Monetary Analysis", *Journal of Political Economy* April 1970; and "Have Monetary and Fiscal Policy Failed?", *American Economic Review* May 1972. For recent assessments of

Continued on P. 52

theorists go considerably beyond the Equation of Exchange and the classical assumption that, the output level being at full employment, and "velocity" being a constant, the price level was uniquely determined by the quantity of money in a country. Instead they argue that money is the most important, almost the sole, determinant of money (or current dollar) GNP, and that velocity, while not a constant, is a stable function of a few other variables. Friedman maintains that short-run fluctuations in velocity are largely the result of rapid changes in the rate of growth of money caused by inappropriate central bank policies. Because of human errors of foresight and policy execution, and the lags between execution and impact, he urges a policy of "steady as she grows" with the money stock growing at about the same rate as full employment real GNP can grow, thus about 5% in Canada and 4% in the United States.[2]

A recurring difficulty with the quantity theory is the problem of defining precisely the "money" magnitude, which supposedly controls all else. At one time, money and the precious metals were coextensive. Then paper currencies and bank deposits were developed and the question arose whether these were "money" or merely "money substitutes". After a long "recognition lag" involving considerable controversy, it became accepted that paper currency and deposits subject to check were indeed money, both because they were commonly used to fulfil all the functions of money, and because it was so clear that the level of prices could hardly be accounted for by the volume of gold and silver alone. But what about personal savings accounts and other time deposits? Are not they also so highly liquid that transactors consider them to be part of their "cash balances" once it becomes customary to pay them immediately upon presentation of the savings account book? At present the Canadian definition of money includes such time deposits while the United States definition excludes them. Friedman and other monetarists generally favour the broader definition "M_2" including time deposits rather than the narrower "M_1" concept. But this is not the end of the difficulty. If time deposits are to be included within the charmed circle of "money" rather than considered as poor relation "near moneys", what about deposits in the "near bank" financial intermediaries, short-term public debt issues, Canadian Tire certificates, credit cards and so on? "Moneyness" or "liquidity" is a matter of degree rather than of kind and unkind critics have pictured the monetarist as reduced to saying, "I don't know what money is, but whatever it is it ought to grow at 5%".

Continued from P. 51
monetarism see Harry G. Johnson, "The Keynesian Revolution and the Monetarist Counter-Revolution", American Economic Review May 1971 and Nicholas Kaldor, "The New Monetarism", Lloyds Bank Review, July 1970. See also Friedman's "Comment" and Kaldor's "Reply" in the October 1970 issue of Lloyds Bank Review. The September 1972 issue of the Journal of Political Economy is largely given over to a symposium on "Friedman's Theoretical Framework" featuring assessments by K. Brunner and A.M. Meltzer, James Tobin, Paul Davidson, Don Patinkin, and Friedman's reply. Further regarding these matters, see, P. Davidson and S. Weintraub, "Money as Cause and Effect", Economic Journal, 83, December 1973.

[2] Or, at least, he urged this policy until a few years ago. In a recent article he has urged instead that money supply growth be brought down to little more than the rate of growth in population, so that with increasing output and constant money incomes the price level could slowly fall. See, Milton Friedman, The Optimum Quantity of Money and Other Essays, pp. 45-8. Thus, if zero population growth continues in the United States, the Bureau of Printing and Engraving would have little more to do than replace bills as they wear out.

As he has done with many subjects, Kenneth Boulding has summed up the basic difficulty of monetarism in doggerel verse.[3]

"We must have a good definition of Money,
For if we do not, then what have we got,
But a Quantity Theory of no-one-knows what,
And this would be almost too true to be funny,
Now, Banks secrete something, as bees secrete honey;
(It sticks to their fingers some, even when hot!)
But what things are liquid and what things are not,
Rests on whether the climate of business is sunny.
For both Stores of Value and Means of Exchange
Include among Assets a very wide range,
So your definition's no better than mine.
Still, with credit-card-clever computers, it's clear
That money as such will one day disappear;
Then, what isn't there we won't have to define".

This difficulty with monetarism is cited by Robert Eisner in a recent article.[4] Friedman is fond of comparing attempts to restrain alleged "cost push" inflation with price and wage controls to pushing in one part of a balloon. The balloon will merely bulge elsewhere.[5] In the following, Eisner turns the balloon analogy against Friedman.[6]

"What we define as money, essentially those obligations of commercial banks called demand deposits, are after all but one very small part of a wide spectrum of assets (liabilities) which can be used for the various functions which we associate with money. The obligation of any large and well-known company could serve almost as well as the obligation of a bank. If we were forced to, we could use obligations of smaller companies, known only in smaller areas. To try to constrict the economy by operating on the very narrow part of the spectrum currently defined as money is, to apply a metaphor recently used by Friedman in objecting to price controls, like attempting to constrict the volume of a large balloon by pressing in some particular spot; the balloon will bulge elsewhere. It is a long, long path from the curtailment, even the total elimination, of bank money to barter."

It is possible to consider this insight as a third theory of inflation and to hypothesize that inflation is the result of "too much debt (credit) creation for too little output". This theory has been little considered by economists who have instead focused either on a particular kind of credit labelled "money", or looked for inflation's roots directly in a struggle over income distribution. So little has debt creation been considered as a source of inflation that no Canadian statistics gathering agency has developed a comprehensive series on the growth of all debts public and private. To assess the penetrative power of a simple "excess debt creation" theory of inflation we must therefore have reference to United States data.

---

[3] Kenneth Boulding, 1969, as quoted by Arthur B. Laffer, *Journal of Political Economy,* March/April 1970 p. 239. Here reprinted with the permission of Professor Boulding.

[4] Robert Eisner, "What Went Wrong?" *Journal of Political Economy* May/June 1971.

[5] Milton Friedman, "What Price Guideposts?" in George P. Schultz and Robert Aliber, eds *Guidelines: Informal Controls and the Market Place* (Chicago 1966) Reprinted in M. Friedman, *Dollars and Deficits* (Englewood Cliffs, 1968).

[6] Eisner, p. 635.

Theory and Truisms

The simple "quality theory" of the relationship of money and prices is often expressed in the form of the "Equation of Exchange" (EOE) developed by Irving Fisher;[7] $MV \equiv PT$, where M represents the stock of money, and V is the rate of turn-over. The triple bar states that M times V is identically equal to P times T, where P is the price level and T is the volume of money transactions. If, in the short-run, the volume of transactions is fixed by the amount of production, employment, and exchange people are engaged in, and V is fixed by payments habits and contracts requiring payments at fixed intervals, it must follow by mathematical necessity that M and P are directly proportional to each other. This, in itself, is not a "quantity of money theory of the price level," as distinguished from a "price-level theory of the quantity of money". However, the essence of monetarism is the belief in "left to right" causality, the belief that by and large an increase in the money supply causes a rise in the price level rather than the reverse.[8]

Since the rise of national income accounting, it is customary to express the equation of exchange as $MV \equiv PQ$, where Q represents real, or constant purchasing power dollar, income and output, and PQ is the current dollar value of output, thus Gross National Product, GNP. Since the concept Q excludes many transactions such as dealing in existing assets and intermediate products which are included in T, the "income velocity" of the second equation is considerably smaller than the "transactions velocity" of the first.

The remaining theories of inflation we wish to consider can likewise be expressed as truisms. Thus we may write: $MV \equiv PQ \equiv GNP \equiv C + I + G + (X - m) \equiv kW \equiv hB \equiv DPY + DBY + DGY + DFY \equiv jS$. Our new terms express that GNP is identical to the sum of Consumption (C), Investment (I), Government Expenditures (G), and Exports (X), less Imports (m). GNP is also identical to some multiple (k) of the Wage Bill (W). It is also identical to some decimal multiple of Total Net Debt (B), and the sum of Disposable Personal Income (DPY), Disposable Business Income (DBY), Disposable Government Income (DGY), and Disposable Foreign Income (DFY). We shall postpone the consideration of the implications of these disposable income relations until Chapter Five. Finally, GNP is identical to some very large multiple (j) of my salary (S). Each of these identities may be expressed as a price level equation by dividing through by Q, thus with rearrangement we have: $P \equiv V(M/Q) \equiv GNP/Q \equiv (C + I + G + (X - m)/Q \equiv k(W/Q) \equiv h(B/Q) \equiv j(S/Q)$. It will be recognized that each of the expressions to the right of an identity sign is merely an alternative definition of the price level. However, each expression may also be considered to be a causality statement. Thus the first, or equation of exchange, states that the price level is caused by the ratio of money to real goods (times velocity) and will change as this ratio changes (unless velocity varies). Skipping over the second term we come to its expansion in the third

---

[7] Irving Fisher,*The Purchasing Power of Money* (New York 1911).

[8] For a clear statement of the "modern" quantity theorist's *credo,* complete with left-side to right-side causality (MV to PQ) and the contention that independent changes in P and Q are necessarily offsetting and cannot be transmitted to the left side, see George Horwich, *Money, Capital, and Prices* (Homewood, Irwin, 1964) pp. 447-8. I was going to quote Horwich directly but the copyright holder required that I pay $20, or about 14c a word, for the privilege. After a careful calculation of the marginal value product of Horwich's statement and the relevant opportunity costs, I decided to hold onto my twenty. Thus

$$P \cdot Q = M \cdot V$$
$$\$20 \quad 0 \quad \$20 \quad 0$$

or "excess demand" expression, that the price level will rise whenever the sum of expenditures on Consumption, Investment, Government and the foreign balance exceed the real output of the economy. Next we have the 'Wage Cost Mark-up" equation explaining the price level as the ratio of the wage bill to real output, (times k, or "mark-up"). Next we have the "excess debt" explanation and finally we "explain" the price level as the ratio between my salary and real output times j. Now, all these statements are equally true, but they are not equally plausible as "right to left" causality statements. It appears particularly implausible that my salary is in some "butterfly that stamped" way the cause of Canada's inflation over, say, my adult life. Suppose that it could be demonstrated that the multiplier j is a true constant so that my salary has risen at exactly the same rate over time as has GNP. We would still reject any causality inference, other than a reverse causality inference that the rise of money GNP causes most of us to get raises from time to time, and that among the millions receiving raises there must be quite a few who for quite a period just happen to receive raises yielding them a constant share of money GNP. However, suppose that it could be demonstrated that V, or k, were invariant over a considerable period, so that the price level varied exactly as did the ratio of money to goods, or wages to goods. Such a finding would be taken as strengthening greatly the quantity theory, or wage-cost theory, of the price level, even though the causality might be reversed, or run both ways, or all magnitudes focused upon might be "caused" by some forces excluded from our analysis (such as debt creation). Thus, acceptance of a theory is at least as much a matter of plausibility as it is of demonstration of the exact manner and degree to which a cause produces its effects. It strikes us as quite plausible that the quantity of money, or the general level of wages, has a lot to do with the general level of prices, but highly implausible that any one individual's wage determines anything beyond his own standard of living.

Of what use then are truisms, or tautologies, since true statements can be very implausible causality statements, and it is causes that the theorist is after? Can anything come from tautologies but tautologies? On the contrary, tautologies expressing necessarily true relationships are of the greatest importance to the economic theorist, bookkeeper, physicist, etc. Thus the tautologies Assets = Liabilities + Net Worth, and Income – Expense = Profit are the basis of all accounting, including national income accounting. Such accounts tell us what has happened, and thus form our point of departure as we seek to learn *why* things happened as they did, and to attempt to predict how they will happen in the future.

The essence of all attempts at prediction is the recognition of regularities; the recognition that X always goes with Y, or that X always follows Y after a certain interval of time. Some regularities are so well established that we take them completely for granted: Monday always follows Sunday, most crops are harvested in late summer, and payday is always the last Friday of the month. Other regularities are less well established, but are still often the basis of useful economic prediction; the price level tends to rise as the level of unemployment falls, or as the ratio of money to goods rises. The simplest and most satisfying relationship an investigator can discover is a constant. It was a great step forward for physics when it was recognized that the acceleration of a body falling in a vacuum is a constant, and another great step forward came in the recognition that the speed of light is a constant. Similarly, if it could be established that the income velocity of circulation of money, or the capital/output ratio, or the marginal propensity to consume, or the wage share, were constants, our ability to forecast and to "fine tune" the economy would be much enhanced.

In our need for simple theories, a "second best" result is to establish that the relationship we are concerned with is an invariant determinate of one or more other variables, for in order to predict or influence the path of the determinate we need to predict, or influence, the path of its determinants. These determinants, all too often, turn out to be themselves determined by still other economic variables and our theory becomes lost in the maze of interrelationships. Thus the "sophisticated" theories of modern monetarism are a step *backward* from the "naive" theories of Fisher, made necessary because V turned out not to be constant after all. It therefore became necessary for those convinced of the plausibility of the money to prices and outputs causality chain to spin and test far more elaborate theories of the manner in which a change in M influenced P and Q in the search for dependable relationships. At the same time, the monetarists experimented with alternative definitions of M in the hope that some, perhaps changing, money magnitude might yet turn out to be invariantly related to P and Q, or failing that to its own determinants. Thus Selden tried out some 40 velocity series[9] and Friedman fastened on M_2, as a better measure of liquidity than M_1. To my mind, the monetarists are in no way to be criticized for the energy, zeal and singleness of purpose with which they seek to illuminate the "channels" by which the money supply determines all other "money magnitudes", such as money GNP, the money wage, the average price level, or even "all plant and animal life".[10] However, I believe they may be fairly criticized for a general "oversell" of a relationship which they are unable to demonstrate to anyone who is not already convinced. The quantity of money is a good starting point for a theory of inflation, but an inadequate ending place.

Let a few quotations establish Friedman's propensity for sweeping claims. When pressed on the specifics of the evidence for a uniquely causal role of the money supply, Friedman has willingly, even eagerly, conceded that statistical correlation and leads and lags can never settle causality questions, that causality probably runs both ways in that increased economic activity sometimes induces the banking system to create more money, and that fiscal policy changes, labour and product market concentration, price expectations, and so on can modify the relationship between the rate of change of the money supply and the rate of change of output and prices. However, none of this is allowed to alter the premise that "inflation is always and everywhere a monetary phenomenon" nor the conclusion that "the only effective way to stop inflation is to restrain the rate of growth of the quantity of money". A brief statement of the monetarist credo is given by Friedman in his slashing attack on the U.S. "guidepost" attempt at direct control of inflation.

"Inflation is always and everywhere a monetary phenomenon, resulting from and accompanied by a rise in the quantity of money relative to output. This generalization is not an arithmetical proposition or a truism, and it does not require a rigid relation between the rates of rise in prices and in the quantity of money. The precise rate at which prices rise for a rate of rise in the quantity of money depends on such factors as past price behaviour, current change in the structure of labor and

---

[9] Richard T. Selden, "Monetary Velocity in the United States", in M. Friedman, ed., *Studies in the Quantity Theory of Money* (Chicago 1956).

[10] The phrase is Lawrence S. Ritter's. See his brief book, *Money*, (New York, 1970) p. 207.

*product markets, and fiscal policy. The monetary character of infla-
tion . . . is an empirical generalization backed by a wide range of
evidence which suggests that substantial changes in the demand for
money seldom occur except as a reaction to a sequence of events set
in train by changes in the quantity of money. It follows that the only
effective way to stop inflation is to restrain the rate of growth of the
quantity of money".*[11]

Despite the above, Friedman has argued that income velocity is
"extra-ordinarily" stable, and is well known for conclusions which
only necessarily follow if velocity is constant and causality is "left to
right". Regarding the stability of velocity, Friedman wrote:

*"One of the chief reproaches directed at economics as an allegedly
empirical science is that it can offer so few numerical "constants",
that it has isolated so few fundamental regularities. The field of money
is the chief example one can offer in rebuttal; there is perhaps no
other empirical relation in economics that has been observed to recur
so uniformly under so wide a variety of circumstances as the relation
between substantial changes in the stock of money and in prices . . .
There is an extraordinary empirical stability and regularity to such
magnitudes as income velocity that cannot but impress anyone who
works extensively with monetary data."*[12]

In one of his recurring denials of the reality of "cost-push" inflation he
writes:

*"Suppose . . . upward pressure on prices – ultimately of course re-
flecting an increase in the stock of money . . . History offers ample
evidence that what determines the average level of prices and wages
is the amount of money in the economy and not the greediness of
business men and workers."*[13]

Friedman, however, refuses to face squarely the contention that the
"greediness" of businessmen and workers determines the amount of
money in the economy and that, if the push for higher money incomes
is checked by the bankers, "near moneys" all too readily turn into
moneys.

---

[11] Milton Friedman, "What Price Guideposts?" in G.P. Schultz and R.Z. Aliber
eds., *Guidelines: Informal Controls and the Market Place,* (Chicago: The
University Press, 1966) p. 18.

[12] Milton Friedman, "The Quantity Theory of Money – A Restatement," in M.
Friedman, ed., *Studies in the Quantity Theory of Money,* pp. 20, 22.

[13] Milton Friedman, *Capitalism and Freedom,* (Chicago, 1962) pp. 134-5.

Income Distribution in Canada and
The Wage Cost Mark-Up (WCM) Equation

Let us return to the first simple theory of the price level we wished to explore, that holds that inflation is caused by too much money income for too little real output. As we have seen, Keynes subscribed to such a theory for all cases but open inflation, generally in wartime, when excess demand and monetary overexpansion were taken to the culprits. For further demonstration of this point see Chapter Three, footnotes 21 and 23 and accompanying text.

This insight of Keynes' was made use of by Sidney Weintraub to construct the "Wage Cost Mark-Up (WCM) Equation" we have used above in contrast to Fisher's Equation of Exchange (EOE), thus $P = k(W/Q)$.[14] Weintraub demonstrated that k has been far less variable than V_1 in the U.S. from 1929 through 1958 and invited the economist to substitute the WCM for the EOE as his price level theory, and wage restraints for control of the money supply as his chief reliance in anti-inflationary policy. I have since carried the comparison back to 1899 in the United States, and demonstrated that k is less variable than V_1 in 15 out of 16 nations surveyed,[15] the exception being the immediately post-war period in Japan.

As preparation for development of the WCM relationship in Canada, let us look at the facts of income distribution from 1926 through 1974. Figure 2.1 presents the distribution of Net National Income as Factor Cost (NI).[16] Here we see that wages and salaries rose as a percentage of national income during the Great Depression of the 1930's, fell in World War II, and has risen since. Clearly, however, military pay and allowances should be considered a "wage type" income. Their inclusion with wages and salaries make the total variation in the "wage bill" range from 58% of NI in 1926 to 77.1% in 1933. In 1974 the "wage bill" equalled 70.9% of NI. Farm income has swung violently over the course of the business cycle, but with an unmistakably downward trend. By 1931 farm income had fallen from its 1926 share of 14.9% of NI to 2.8%. During the war and for several of the postwar years, farm income hovered around 10% of NI before beginning its descent to its all-time low, to date, of less than 2.2% of NI in 1970. With the recent tripling of food prices, farm income as a percentage of NI rose to 3.3% in 1973 and 1974. Income of non-farm unincorporated business has likewise suffered a marked relative decline, from a high of 23.7% in 1930 to a low of 3.3% in 1974. Interest, rent and miscellaneous investment income has risen in relative importance from its low of less than 2% in the late 1930's to 6.8% in 1974. The rise has been particularly marked since the mid 1950's, a point we shall return to in later discussions of "interest push". Corporate profits before taxes were about 9% of NI in the late 1920's, fell to a miserable 1.3% of depressed NI in 1931 and then rose with recovery to vary between 10 and 15% in the postwar decades.

Figure 2.1 provides us with information on changes in the contractual income distribution in Canada. This is not quite the information we would wish to have to assess the functional distribution of

---

[14] Sidney Weintraub, *A General Theory of the Price Level, Output, Income Determination, and Economic Growth* (Philadelphia 1959).

[15] John H. Hotson, *International Comparisons of Money Velocity and Wage Mark-Ups,* (New York: Kelley 1968); also "Monetary and Wage Mark-Up Theories of the Price Level: Some Data", *International Economic Review II:* February 1970, pp. 53-76.

[16] Percentages calculated from figures supplied by Statistics Canada based on the 1968 revision of *National Accounts: Income and Expenditure.*

income between "labour" and "property", or between the theoretical triad of "wage", "rent" and "profit" income. The difficulty is centered in the "mixed income" accounts of Farm and Non-Farm unincorporated income. Clearly, much of the income of a farmer is a return to his labour, but some is a return to his property, or non-human capital. Similarly, unincorporated businesses return both labour and property incomes to their owners. Here we merely follow Gérald Marion's estimate that 81% of net income of farm operators and 68% of the income of unincorporated non-farm enterprises represents labour return and the remainder a return to property.[17] The result of this allocation is the "Labour Income" line running through the Farm income component of Figure 2.1. Our "Labour Income" allocation indicates that a roughly 80-20 split prevailed between labour and non-labour income throughout the period for which we have data, except for the depression era when labour income rose to a peak of 89.4% of the depressed income of 1933. Since the depression, virtually no trend and but little fluctuation is to be seen in the labour/non-labour shares in NI.

---

[17] Gérald Marion, *Répartition Fonchionalle des Revenus: Analyse de la part du travail au Canada* (Montreal 1965) pp. 73-7.

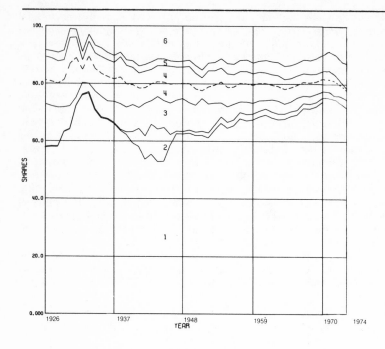

**Figure 2.1
Distribution of
National Income in
Canada 1926-1974**

1) Wages, salaries
   and supple-
   mentary labour
   income
2) Military pay and
   allowances
3) Accrued net
   income of farm
   operators from
   farm production
4) Net income of
   non-farm
   unincorporated
   business
   including rent
   Labour Income - -
5) Interest, and
   miscellaneous
   investment
   income
6) Corporation
   profits before
   taxes

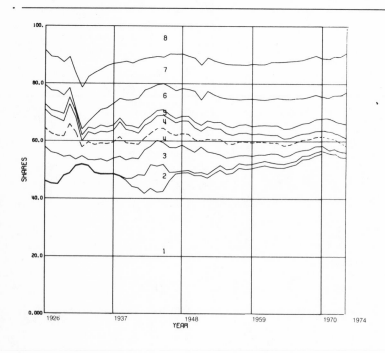

**Figure 2.2
Distribution of
GNP in Canada
1926-1974**

1) Wages, salaries
   and supple-
   mentary labour
   income
2) Military pay and
   allowances
3) Accrued net
   income of farm
   operators from
   farm production
4) Net income of
   non-farm
   unincorporated
   business
   including rent
   Labour Income - -
5) Interest, and
   miscellaneous
   investment
   income
6) Corporation
   profits before
   taxes
7) Indirect taxes
   less subsidies
8) Capital
   consumption
   allowances and
   miscellaneous
   valuation
   adjustments

Shares in Net National Income are not necessarily of greatest interest or relevance in our study of inflation. Shares in Gross National Product are of greater interest both because the model developed from Keynes in Chapter One stresses the gross (of capital consumption) proceeds of firms, and because indirect taxes affect prices by driving a "wedge" between prices and factor incomes. Figure 2.2 presents the relevant information. The upper bound of the area representing Corporation profits before taxes also represents NI as a percentage of GNP. Although in the past two decades NI has fluctuated narrowly around 75% of GNP, it equaled 79.4% of GNP in 1926 before falling to a low of 66.7% in 1933 with the collapse of profits. When net profits fell as a percentage of depression income, Capital consumption allowances rose. As a result, the contractual wage rose far less as a percentage of GNP than of NI in the depression. Including Military pay and allowances in the contractual wage share, we see that its total range of variation was from 45% of GNP in 1928 to 56% in 1971. Again, through the imputation of Farm and Non-Farm unincorporated income to labour and property, we obtained the "Labour Income" line which bisects the area labelled Farm income in Figure 2.2. Once more, the impression is of near invariance, with a roughly 60-40 split between labour and non-labour income in GNP, in comparison with the 80-20 split of NI. However, the changing relationship between NI and GNP causes the peak in labour income as a fraction of GNP to come in the war years rather than the depression period. The overall trend of the "labour share" in GNP is slightly downward. Interestingly, Indirect taxes less subsidies are not a markedly higher percentage of GNP now than they were in the 1920's (12.2% in 1926 vs 13.2% in 1970 with their peak percentage being 15.7% in 1933). Capital Consumption allowances likewise are of but little greater relative importance than in the initial period for which we have data.

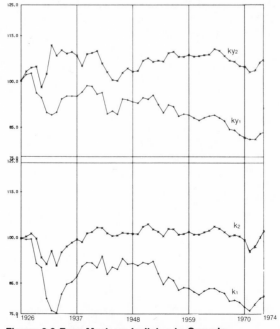

Figure 2.3 Four Mark-up Indicies in Canada

$$ky_2 = \frac{NI}{L} \qquad ky_1 = \frac{NI}{W} \qquad k_2 = \frac{GNP}{L} \qquad k_1 = \frac{GNP}{W}$$

Weintraub's "mark-up" measure is the reciprocal of the "wage share" in Business Gross Product, BGP, measuring gross output of the economy minus the government and foreign sectors. However, World War II was the only period in which the trend and variability of mark-up in the private economy differed greatly from that of the economy as a whole. Therefore, we shall confine ourselves to GNP and NI measures. Figure 2.3 presents our 4 variant measures of mark-up over wage costs in the Canadian Accounts. The upper section of Figure 2.3 contrasts the index of the ratio

$$k_{y1} = \frac{NI}{W} \text{ with the ratio } k_{y2} = \frac{NI}{L}$$

where W = the contractual wage bill and L = the contractual wage bill plus imputed wages of farm and non-farm unincorporated enterprises. The lower section graphs the index of the ratio k_1,

$$k_1 = \frac{GNP}{W}$$

against the index of the ratio

$$k_2 = \frac{GNP}{L}.$$

Appendix Table 1 presents the 4 Mark-up indices. It is clear that k_1 and k_{y1} have distinct downward trends (i.e. rising contractual wage share) while k_2 has, if anything, a slight upward trend and k_2 and k_{y2} have considerably narrower ranges than their contractual mark-up counterparts. Thus k_1 ranges between 102.5 and 82.3, or 20 index points, while k_2 varies between 110.5 and 97.9, or less than 13 index points, while k_{y1} and k_{y2} vary about 25 and 14 index points respectively. Thus, just as the monetarist found a greater degree of regularity when he broadened the definition of money, the "incomist" finds the stability of labour income to be greater than that of the contractual wage share. Since our preference is for gross rather than net income comparisons, we shall leave k_{y1} and k_{y2} out of further comparisons.

The EOE and WCM "Constants" in Canada

Let us compare the "constants" of the simple EOE and WCM approach to the price level directly. Figure 2.4 brings together k_1, k_2, and V_2 series for Canada from 1926 through 1974. Appendix Table 2. presents the derivation of these indices. Our velocity measure is labeled V_2 in recognition that the official Canadian definition of the money supply is the broad definition including time deposits in commercial banks, that Friedman prefers:[18]

$$V_2 = \frac{GNP}{M_2}.$$

As is immediately evident in Figure 2.4, V_2 is considerably more variable than k_1 and far more variable than k_2. Overall, the V_2 index ranges from a low of 69.4 in 1946 to 125.1 in 1966. Velocity fell drastically with the beginning of the depression, rose to late 1920's levels with the recovery to 1940 and then fell drastically and remained at depression levels throughout the remainder of the prosperous 1940's. Late 1920's velocity levels were reached by 1951 and then exceeded that of the initial period until 1970. If V_2's performance is to be accepted as being an "extraordinary empirical stability", as Friedman termed it, what superlatives can we reserve to apply to k_1 and k_2? Clearly they are among the "constants" or, at least, near constants of economics.

[18] No unfairness to the monetarist position is involved in switching the discussion from the "net income velocity" usually computed to the "gross product velocity" here used. As I have shown elsewhere, gross product velocity is considerably less variable than income velocity. See, J.H. Hotson, *International Comparisons of Money Velocity and Wage Mark-Ups*, pp. 7-13.

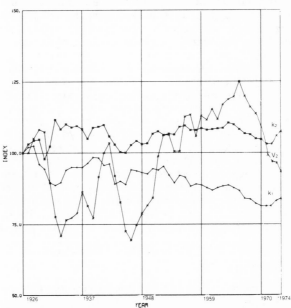

Figure 2.4 Gross Mark-Up and Velocity in Canada

$$k_1 = \frac{GNP}{W} \qquad V_2 = \frac{GNP}{M_2} \qquad k_2 = \frac{GNP}{L}$$

The EOE and WCM as Price Level "Laws"

An alternative mode of comparison of the rival EOE and WCM "constants" is to set up the rival formulations as price level equations and see how closely the ratio they focus upon "tracks" and supposedly "determines" the price level. Thus we have $P = V_2 (M_2/Q) = k_1(W/Q) = k_2(L/Q)$. Let us designate the money to goods ratio as "r_2", the contractual wages to goods ratio as "R_1" and the labour income to goods ratio as "R_2".

Figure 2.5 presents the indicies of the EOE components in Canada. The EOE "Law" of the price level states that the price level varies as does the ratio (r_2) of money to goods. If V_2 were truly constant, P and r_2 would be the same series. Because V_2 is not constant, the fit between the money supply and the price level is, as Lawrence Ritter puts it, "rather loose and a bit baggy. Like a 32A girl wearing a 36C, things tend to jiggle around quite a bit."[19] Several points might be made concerning Figure 2.5, but let us defer the discussion until we have developed further Canadian and United States series.

The WCM price level equation is graphed in Figure 2.6. The much tighter conformity between P and R_1 than P and r_2 is immediately evident. Except for an increasing divergence of level, from k_1's downward trend, and a somewhat more "saw toothed" pattern of R_1; P and R_1 are virtually the same series.

In Figure 2.7 the "labour income" variant of the WCM price level equation is graphed. The still greater conformity between P and R_2 because of the rigidity of k_2 is most evident.

A further comparison between the EOE and WCM can usefully be made by comparing the frequency and size of exceptions to the alternative price level "laws". Table 2.1 carries out this comparison for r_2, R_1 and R_2. An exception occurs when either P and the explanatory ratio move in opposite directions, or one series moves and the other does not. In all we have data on 48 year-to-year changes from 1926 to 1974. In 19 of these changes, or in 40 per cent of the cases, exceptions to the EOE "Law" occurred, i.e. P and r_2 moved in opposite directions. The entire depression era in Canada from 1930 through 1941 is one long exception to the Fisher equation: in every year in which the ratio of money to goods rose the price level fell and in every year in which the ratio of money to goods fell the price level rose! Is it any wonder that by 1941 the belief in the efficacy of monetary policy was at a low ebb? Presumably Friedman would account for these results by "long and variable lags",[20] that it took a three year rise in the r_2 ratio from 1930 to 1933 to brake and then reverse the fall in P, and then it took a four-year fall in r_2 to reverse the path of P again, and so on. Alternative explanations such that P and r_2 are inversely related to each other, either coincidently or with a short lag, are not directly considered by Friedman.[21] We have already touched on this disturbing thought in our Harrod's Dichotomy discussion which we will return to in Chapter Six.

---

[19] Lawrence S. Ritter, *Money*, p. 35.

[20] See his discussion in Chapters 11 and 12 of *The Optimum Quantity of Money and Other Essays*.

[21] However, he does consider, and eventually reject, the possibility that rather than the rate of change of money leading the peak (and trough) of general business by a long lag, it follows the prior trough or peak on an inverted basis and with a short lag: that is, he rejects the inference that the influence of business on money is stronger than the influence of money on business. *Ibid*, pp. 268-71.

**Figure 2.5 Equation
of Exchange (EOE)
"Law" of the Price
Level in Canada**

$P = V_2 r_2$

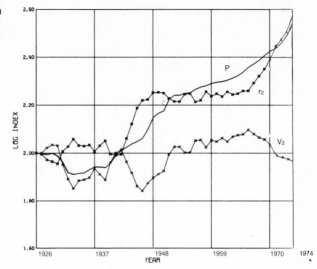

**Figure 2.6 Wage
Cost Mark-Up
(WCM) "Law" of
the Price Level
in Canada**

$P = k_2 R_1$

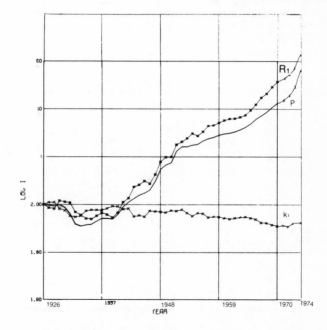

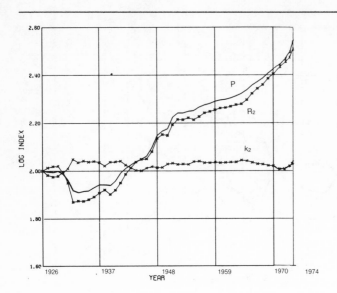

Figure 2.7 WCM "Law" of the Price Level in Canada
$P = k_2R_2$

Table 2.1
Exceptions to Alternative Price Level "Laws"
1) P and r_2 move in the same direction as V_2 is constant
2) P and R_1 move in the same direction as k_1 is constant
3) P and R_2 move in the same direction as k_2 is constant

Canada 1926-1974 – 48 Changes

(1) $P = V_2r_2$			(2) $P = k_1R_1$			(3) $P = k_2R_2$		
Year $\%\triangle P$ $+ \%\triangle r_2 =$ Exception %			Year $\%\triangle P$ $+ \%\triangle R =$ Exception %			Year $\%\triangle P$ $+ \%\triangle R_2 =$ Exception %		
28-9	+ 1.2% – 1.7%	2.9%				29-0 –2.8%	+4.0%	6.8%
30-1	– 5.9 +12.9	18.8						
31-2	– 9.4 + 4.4	13.8						
32-3	– 1.8 + 7.6	9.4				32-3 –1.8	+1.4	3.2
33-4	+ 1.4 – 6.0	7.4	33-4	+1.4% –3.3%	4.7%	33-4 +1.4	–0.3	1.7
34-5	+ 0.5 – 0.6	1.1	34-5	+0.5 –0.5	1.0			
36-7	+ 2.9 – 6.1	9.0						
37-8	– 0.2 + 5.8	6.0				37-8 –0.2	+3.0	3.2
38-9	– 0.6 + 4.8	5.4						
39-0	+ 4.6 –11.9	16.5						
40-1	+ 7.8 – 1.3	9.1						
			45-6	+0.3 –2.6	2.9			
49-0	+ 2.2 – 0.8	3.0				49-0 +2.3	–0.8	3.1
50-1	+11.7 – 4.8	16.5						
51-2	+ 4.2 – 3.0	7.2						
52-3	0.0 + 0.2	0.2	52-3	0.0 +3.4	3.4	52-3 0.0	–0.4	0.4
			54-5	+0.6 –2.2	2.8	54-5 +0.7	–1.9	2.6
55-6	+ 3.4 – 7.7	11.1						
58-9	+ 2.1 – 4.4	6.5						
60-1	+ 0.6 – 2.7	3.3						
62-3	+ 1.9 – 2.6	4.5						

Number of Exceptions	19			5			7
Largest Exception	18.8%			4.7%			6.8%
Average Exception	8.0%			3.0%			3.0%
Percentage of Exceptions	39.5%			10.2%			14.6%

In contrast with a simple EOE price level "Law", which is contradicted almost as often as it is confirmed in Canada, the simple WCM "Law" holds up very well indeed. We note only 5 contradictions in the 48 changes, or 10.2 per cent. The largest contradiction occurred in 1933-34 when P rose by 1.4 per cent and R fell by 3.3 per cent for an exception of 4.7 per cent (1.4 +3.3). By way of contrast, the largest EOE exception, that of 1930-31, was of 18.8 per cent, and 13 of the 19 EOE exceptions were larger than the largest exception to the $P = k_1 R_1$ law. Indeed the average EOE exception (8 per cent) is considerably larger than the largest exception to either "law 2" or "law 3".

Finally we turn to the alternative formulation of the WCM using contractual plus imputed labour income to calculate k_2 and R_2. The results are shown in section 3 of Table 2.1. Here we count 7 exceptions to the "Law" that P and R_2 move together, or 15 per cent exceptions. The largest exception of 6.8 per cent occurred in 1929-30. Evidently, the introduction of a portion of unstable agricultural income into wage income is responsible for increasing the number of exceptions notable in the 1930's.

It is interesting that there were no exceptions to either WCM price law variant between 1955 and the end of the period surveyed, while 4 EOE exceptions occurred between 1955 and 1974. We conclude from the data summarized in Table 2.1 that exceptions to a simple EOE price level "Law" are frequent and large in Canada while exceptions to the variant WCM "Laws" are few and small.

Income Distribution in the U.S. and the WCM.

Let us turn to the United States data for further insights. Figure 2.8 presents the facts on the distribution of U.S. National Income from 1929 to 1974. The all-over pattern is quite similar to that of Canada in that the contractual wage share has risen slowly over the decades (from 58.9 per cent of NI in 1929 to 75.3 per cent in 1970), farm income has declined (from 7.1 per cent in 1929 to 2.0 per cent in 1971 before recovering somewhat to 3.6 in 1973) and income of unincorporated enterprises has also decreased, but less drastically, (from 10.4 per cent to 5.4 per cent). Investment income (rental income of persons plus net interest) was a large fraction of national income in the depression (reaching 17 per cent of NI in 1932) and then dwindling during World War II (to 4.2 per cent of NI in 1944). It has since increased to 7.7 per cent in 1974, with rental income of persons a falling percentage and net interest a rising one. Corporate profits before taxes, which were negative for several years in the early 1930's, since World War II have fluctuated between 9 and 14.7 per cent of NI. 1970 was the first year since 1939 that they fell below 10 per cent of NI.

Again we carry out the operation of imputing farm and unincorporated income to "labour" and "capital". Here we have allocated these "mixed incomes" as non-farm, non-incorporated income is divided. The result is shown in Figure 2.8 in the line labelled "Labour income." In 1929, 69 per cent of income was contractual plus imputed wages. This rose to 81.9 per cent in 1933 and then fluctuated between 72.4 and 81.4 in the remaining decades.

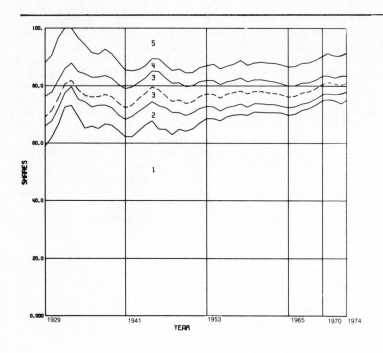

**Figure 2.8
Distribution of
National Income in
the United States
1929-1974**

1) Compensation of
   employees
2) Income of farm
   proprietors
3) Business and
   professional
   income
   Labour income - -
4) Rental income of
   persons plus net
   interest
5) Corporate profits
   and inventory
   valuation
   adjustment

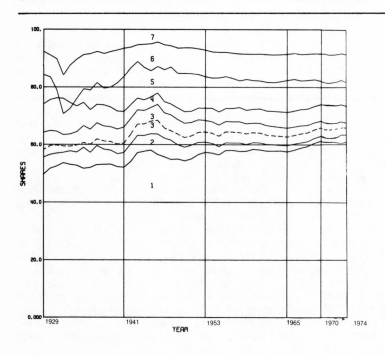

**Figure 2.9
Distribution of
Gross National
Product in the
United States**

1) Compensation of
   employees
2) Income of farm
   proprietors
3) Business and
   professional
   income
   Labour income - -
4) Rental income of
   persons plus net
   interest
5) Corporate profits
   and inventory
   valuation
   adjustment
6) Indirect
   business tax
   and adjustments
7) Capital
   consumption
   allowances

Figure 2.9 presents the distribution of GNP in the United States. The upper bound of the area representing Corporation profits marks the changing relationship between NI and GNP. It is interesting that Indirect business taxes are not a notably greater fraction of GNP in the 1960's than they were in 1929, while they grew from 8 per cent in 1929 to 15.1 per cent in 1933 as the economy collapsed. Capital consumption allowances likewise rose relatively in the depression as profits fell, but are only a slightly larger percentage of GNP in 1970 (8.8%) than in 1929 (7.6%). Again, contractual plus imputed labour income (L) displays a high degree of regularity, but with some upward trend, the lowest value occurring in 1929 (58.1%), the highest in 1946 (68.6%), and the final figure of 66.1% in 1974.

Figure 2.10 displays the indicies of the four variant mark-up series (reciprocal of wage shares), $k_1 = GNP/W$, $k_2 = GNP/L$, $ky_1 = NI/W$, and $ky_2 = NI/L$. It is readily evident that k_1 and ky_1 display somewhat more downward trend than do k_2 and ky_2, but that otherwise their movements are quite similiar. Appendix Table 3 gives the numbers.

Figure 2.10 Four Mark-Up Indicies in the United States

$$k_2 = \frac{GNP}{L}$$

$$k_1 = \frac{GNP}{W}$$

$$ky_2 = \frac{NI}{L}$$

$$ky_1 = \frac{NI}{W}$$

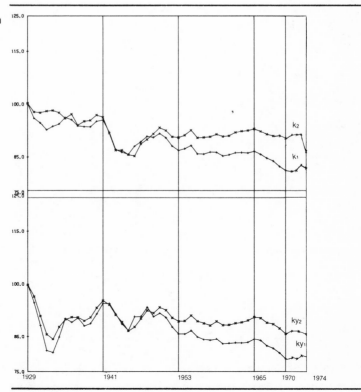

EOE and WCM in the United States

Next we wish to contrast the mark-up term from the WCM equation with the velocity term from the EOE. Figure 2.11 carries out the comparisons, and Appendix Table 4 presents the numbers. The upper section of Figure 2.11 contrasts k_1 and V_1, while the lower section presents the indicies of k_2 and V_2. $V_1 = GNP/M_1$, where M_1 is the official U.S. definition of the Money Supply; currency, coin, and demand deposits. It is readily apparent that V_1 is much more variable than is k_1, tending sharply downward with the onset of the Great Depression, reviving sharply in 1937, falling again to one-half its 1929 index in 1946, then trending continuously upward until 1970, but with setbacks in each recession year (1946, 1949, 1954, 1958, 1967, 1970, 1971).

When the definition of money is broadened to include time deposits in commercial banks (M_2) the result is to reduce considerably the fluctuations in velocity, as can be seen in the lower section of Figure 2.11. The year-to-year movements of V_2 are somewhat greater than are those of V_1, but the long downward trend ending in 1946 is much reduced, as is the upward trend since. While V_1 has an index value of 130.9 in 1974, V_2 stood at 103.7. However, V_2 is clearly considerably more variable than either k_1 or k_2.

Again we express our variant price level "Laws", looking for a close correspondence between the price index (P) and the ratio (r, R etc) which is supposed to determine it, given the "constancy" of V or k. Figure 2.12 is the graph of the equation $P = V_1r_1$. Is it any wonder that the quantity theory fell into disrepute, given that P and r_1 ($r_1 = M_1/Q$ i.e. the ratio of money to goods) moved in opposite directions

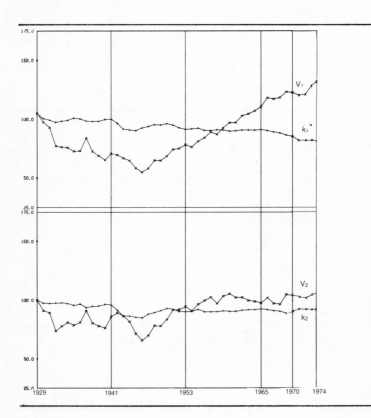

Figure 2.11 Mark-Up and Velocity in the United States

$$k_1 = \frac{GNP}{W}$$

$$V_1 = \frac{GNP}{M_1}$$

$$k_2 = \frac{GNP}{L}$$

$$V_2 = \frac{GNP}{M_2}$$

**Figure 2.12 EOE
"Law" of the
Price Level in the
United States**

$P = V_1 r_1$

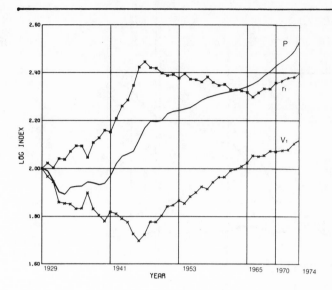

**Figure 2.13 EOE
"Law" of the
Price Level in the
United States**

$P = V_2 r_2$

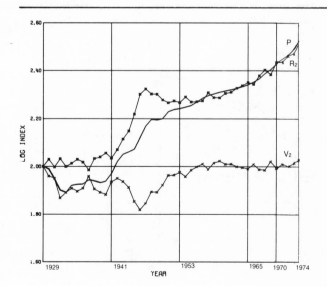

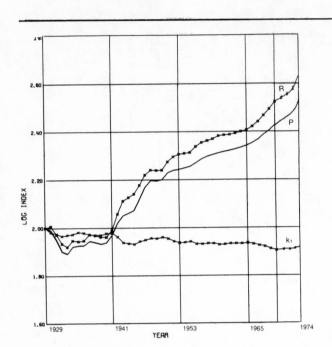

Figure 2.14 WCM "Law" of the Price Level in the United States

$P = k_1R_1$

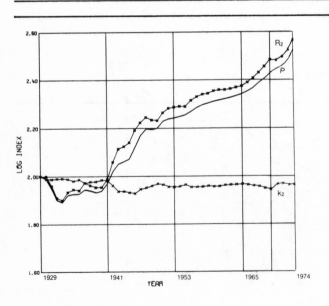

Figure 2.15 WCM "Law" of the Price Level in the United States

$P = k_2R_2$

through so much of the depression, that r_1 rose so much more rapidly than did P in the recovery, war, and early postwar years, and that r_1 fell steadily from 1947 to 1966, while P even more steadily rose? From the late 1940's the Federal Reserve authorities pushed in on the area of the "balloon" labelled "M_1" and the balloon bulged elsewhere, as time deposits and "near moneys" provided the liquidity necessary to pay rising wages and prices.

The quantity theory relationships look much more persuasive when we turn, in Figure 2.13, to the equation $P = V_2r_2$. Although the relationship is not particularly close during the depression, war, and early postwar period, since the early 1950's P and r_2 "track" very well as V_2 fluctuates narrowly around its 1929 value.

In Figure 2.14 we chart the WCM equation $P = k_1R_1$, where R_1 = W/Q, or wage to output ratio. Here we see a very close correspondence in direction and degree of year to year movement in P and R_1, but with increasing divergence because of the slight downward trend of k_1. In Figure 2.15 the alternative WCM formulation employing "labour income" is used, thus $P = k_2R_2$, where $R_2 = L/Q$. Here the same close correspondence between the direction and degree of year-to-year movement in P and R_2 is evident. Furthermore, as k_2 declines only to an index of 91.4 in 1974, versus a final value of 80.2 for k_1, the R_2 series exceeds P by less than it does the R_1 series. (In contrast, the Canadian k_2 series rose above its initial value, causing R_2 to rise more slowly than did P).

Before repeating the calculation of the frequency and seriousness of exceptions to the EOE and WCM price level "Laws", let us make use of the U.S. data on "net public and private debt"[22] to test our third theory of inflation; that inflation is caused by "too much debt for too little real output."

Net public and private debt of a country is one of the "biggest numbers" in its economic accounts, exceeded only by such magnitudes as "total wealth" or "total capital". In 1929, when United States GNP was $103.1 billion, Net Debt was $191.9 billion. Of this total, private debts were $161.8 billion, Federal government debt a mere $16.5 billion and State and local governments owed $13.6 billion. Of the private debts, corporate debt totalled $88.9 billion and individual and non-corporate totalled $72.9 billion. By 1969, when U.S. GNP had reached $931.4 billion, debt had also increased mightily, reaching $1,699.5 billion. Of this total, private debts were $1,247.3 billion, Federal $289.3 billion and State and local $132.4 billion. Of the private debts, corporate debt was $692.2 billion and individual and non-corporate was $555.1 billion. Thus the relative importance of components had changed, but it is interesting that the GNP/B ratio, which we have dubbed "h" is virtually the same in 1969 as it was in 1929. Thus, in 1929 h = .537 so that for every dollar of debts there was a GNP of 53.7¢ (or alternatively, for every dollar of GNP there existed $1.86 of debt), while in 1969 h = .548.

---

[22] Council of Economic Advisors, *Economic Report of the President,* (Washington: February 1972) Table C-62.

Net Debt and the Price Level

As mentioned earlier, the possible relationship between excess debt creation and a rising price level has been but little considered by economists. In a way, this is strange since the proximate cause of wartime open inflation is so clearly the government sector financing its large demands by deficits, which either take the form of interest bearing debt, or non-interest bearing paper money. Even when the deficits are financed by bonds, this quite regularly results in the banking system creating new money to purchase the new debt. Yet for all the discussion of "national debt" at *Reader's Digest* and more sophisticated levels of discourse, there is little recognition of the magnitude of private debts, of the essential role they play in the capitalistic process, and of the regularity of their growth relative to the money value of output. There is perhaps no other important economic relationship about which the public is less informed, or in which the instincts of the uninstructed individual are more likely to be in error than on the subject of "debt". The individual instinct is that debt is to be avoided and therefore the "national debt", and if he is aware of them, private debts, "ought to" be paid off. Nothing, of course, would be more ruinous than any such attempt.

The depth of ignorance of the public of this relationship might best be illustrated by recalling some recent U.S. history. The Kennedy administration proposed in 1962 to "get the country moving again" and reduce the level of unemployment, then running over 6 per cent, by means of a tax cut. The Gallup Poll asked the, perhaps loaded, question, "Would you favor a cut in taxes if it meant a rise in the national debt?" Only 18 per cent of those polled gave the affirmative response that an over-whelming majority of economists agreed was correct, under the circumstances.

A personal note might not be amiss. At about this time a national columnist, who shall be here nameless, denounced the folly of the "New Economics" proposals and supported instead the attempt of Senator Tower to enact a constitutional amendment to prevent any further rise in the national debt. I was then a Penn graduate student and eager to give the world the benefit of my knowledge. What most struck me was the columnist's innocent belief that the public debt, indeed, the federal debt, was the only debt which existed, or at least was of any magnitude. I wrote the Philadelphia *Bulletin* to point out the plain facts: that private debts are over twice as large as the public debt, that they grow continuously in every reasonably prosperous year, that in sum they are never "paid off", that there are sound reasons for the government as well as General Motors to borrow money, and that, unlike General Motors, the government could not go bankrupt as he seemed to fear it would. The *Bulletin* published my piece, and I was rewarded for my effort with the most thorough-going denunciation, by the columnist and his readers, that has been my lot since I played with matches as a child and nearly burned down the east end of Colorado Springs. I went a second round with the columnist and his readers, only to see myself denounced, coast to coast, as a purveyor of the "economic hogwash of Keynes" and the soundness of the Wharton School called into question for sheltering me. I regretfully came to see I had failed to win the hearts and minds of the people and had let down the side, even though I was wholly right – well, almost wholly right, I should not have been so sarcastic.[23] Fortunately, the tax cut ultimately passed, despite my attempts to help it

---

[23] I learned my lesson though and I've never been sarcastic since.

**Figure 2.16
Debt/Output Ratio
(DOR) "Law" of the
Price Level in the
U.S.**

$P = hr_3$

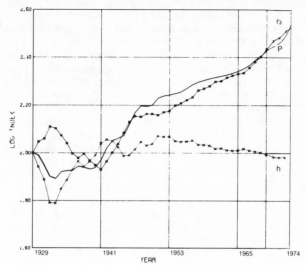

along, and Penn awarded me my doctorate despite the fact I'd doubt-less cost it some alumni contributions.

Unfortunately, no series on the total of all debts public and private exists for the Canadian economy. Therefore, we can only study the U.S. series, speculate as to what the Canadian series might reveal if we had it, and urge Statistics Canada or the Bank of Canada to devote sufficient resources to constructing it. As Marshall Robinson was the first to point out,[24] not only does total debt tend to grow with total output, in the U.S. it has tended to grow in equal ratio with GNP and by a larger absolute amount. As Robinson showed, on the average from 1916 to 1957, a one-dollar rise in GNP was accompanied by one-dollar and eighty-four cents of increased debt. The only period in which this ratio changed markedly was during the Great Depression when income fell much more than did the debt load. Appendix 4 presents the index of "Net Public and Private Debt" in the U.S. from 1929 through 1973, together with the indices of the components of the equation $P = h(r_3)$ where h = GNP/B, or the gross product to total debt ratio, and r_3 = B/Q, or the debt to real output ratio. The only years in which net debt fell in the U.S. were years of major or minor set-back to output, 1931-1933, 1938, and 1946.

Figure 2.16 is the graph of our Debt/Output Ratio (DOR) equation, $P = hr_3$. We see that the DOR components combine some of the characteristics of the EOE and WCM series. Thus the relationship between P and r_3 was not close during the Great Depression, when h

---

[24] M.A. Robinson, "Debt and Economic Growth", *Proceedings of the Fifty-First Annual Conference on Taxation,* National Tax Association, (1959) Reprinted in Lawrence Ritter ed., *Money and Economic Activity, 2nd Edition* (Boston: Houghton 1961).

fell considerably, as did V_1 and V_2. In the recovery and wartime period, h rose to equal and then exceeded its initial value. After falling in the early postwar years, h reached its peak in the Korean War years and has since trended steadily downward to equal its 1929 value by 1969. The visual impression of Figure 2.16 is of the debt/output ratio, r_3, "pushing up" the P index, as credit of all sorts expanded faster than real output. Thus, while real output in 1970 stood at 353.3 on a 1929 base, GNP was 944.8 and debt (B) an almost identical 958.9. Thus, those who believe that the direction of causation is from financial matters to the price level, might do well to look at the "whole balloon" instead of merely the M_1 and M_2 segments. Perhaps control over the money supply is not a sufficient lever to control the price level, but perhaps debt control could control P.[25]

But how good is even this expanded quantity theory relation as a "law of the price level" in comparison with the WCM equation? For a partial answer we turn to Table 2.2 where are tabulated the number and size of exceptions to the various "Laws". The first three sections of the table present the exceptions to the "Law" that P moves with r_1, r_2, or r_3. Here we see a steady diminution of the number of exceptions (22, 17, 14) as the key component changes from M_1 to M_2 to B. Also we note that exceptions to the DOR "Law" are heavily concentrated in the "ancient history" of the Great Depression, when output fell rapidly and debts fell slowly. However, although exceptions to the DOR "law" are fewer, they have also tended to be larger than the EOE exceptions. Thus the average exception to the V_1 law was of 7.3%, of the V_2 law, 7.7% and of the h law, 9.4%. Thus the V_1 law was contradicted 49% of the time, while the h law was contradicted "only" 31% of the time, but the h exceptions were larger when they did occur. Friedman's preferred law, or generalization, lies between these two. It was contradicted in 38% of our 46 observations.

The fourth and fifth sections of Table 2.2 catalog the exceptions to the WCM price level law. The job is quickly accomplished as there are only 3 exceptions to either the k_1 or k_2 variant, or 7% exceptions. Moreover, these few exceptions are very small, averaging only 2.7% with k_1 and 1.6% with k_2. Further, given the degree of error present in economic observation, it is quite possible that a very small exception, such as in section 4 in 1939-40, or section 5 in 1935-36 and 1954-55 were not exceptions at all. We may conclude, as we did in Canada, that exceptions to all variations of EOE relations tried were frequent and large, while exceptions to WCM variants were very few and small. Both price "Laws" appear to be less frequently contradicted in the U.S. than in Canada (V_2 38% vs 40%; k_1 7% vs 10.4%; k_2 7% vs 15%). The average exception is the same in the V_2 case at 8% in both countries, while the average k_1 exception was 2.7% in the U.S. and 3% in Canada vs 1.6% and 3% for k_2.

It might be reasonably argued that the Great Depression and World War II years were uniquely unstable and that a more "normal" period would give us a better insight into the relative stability of the EOE, DOR, and WCM "constants". If we confine ourselves to the period from 1946 to 1974, we have 27 year-to-year changes to review. The results are summarized in Table 2.3

---

[25] Hyman R. Minsky has argued that in the last decade the financial system became increasingly "fragile" as borrowing has increased quicker than cash flow. Thus the fall in h from 1953 through 1974 is ominous for the economy. See his article "Financial Resouces in a Fragile Financial Environment", *Challenge* July/August 1975, pp. 6-13.

Table 2.2 Exceptions to Alternative Price Level Laws

1) P and r_1 move together as V_1 is constant
2) P and r_2 move together as V_2 is constant
3) P and r_3 move together as h is constant
4) P and R_1 move together as k_1 is constant
5) P and R_2 move together as k_2 is constant

United States 1929-1974 – 45 Changes

(1) $P = V_1 r_1$

Year	%ΔP	+%Δr	= Exception %
29-0	− 2.6%	+ 5.3%	7.9%
31-2	−10.3	+ 9.3	19.6
35-6	+ 0.2	− 0.2	0.4
36-7	+ 4.0	−10.4	14.4
37-8	− 1.3	+15.4	16.7
38-9	− 1.6	+ 4.6	6.2
40-1	+ 7.5	− 1.7	9.2
47-8	+ 6.7	− 5.5	12.2
49-0	+ 1.4	− 4.6	6.0
50-1	+ 6.7	− 2.2	8.9
52-3	+ 0.9	− 3.3	4.2
54-5	+ 1.4	− 5.0	6.4
55-6	+ 3.5	− 0.5	4.0
56-7	+ 3.7	− 2.2	5.9
58-9	+ 1.6	− 5.0	6.6
59-0	+ 1.7	− 2.9	4.6
61-2	+ 1.2	− 4.7	5.9
62-3	+ 1.3	− 0.3	1.6
63-4	+ 1.6	− 0.9	2.5
64-5	+ 1.9	− 1.6	3.5
65-6	+ 2.6	− 4.2	6.8
68-9	+ 4.8	− 0.2	5.0
Number of Exceptions			**22**
Largest Exception			**19.6%**
Average Exception			**7.3%**
Percentage of Exceptions			**48.9%**

(2) $P = V_2 r_2$

Year	%ΔP	+%Δr₂	= Exception %
29-0	− 2.6%	+ 7.0%	9.6%
31-2	−10.3	+ 8.3	18.6
35-6	+ 0.2	− 2.7	2.9
36-7	+ 4.1	− 7.2	11.3
37-8	− 1.2	+11.8	13.0
38-9	− 1.6	+ 1.4	3.0
40-1	+ 7.5	− 4.8	12.3
47-8	+ 6.7	− 4.8	11.5
49-0	+ 1.4	− 5.3	6.7
50-1	+ 6.7	− 2.7	9.4
52-3	+ 0.9	− 1.7	2.6
54-5	+ 1.4	− 4.7	6.1
58-9	+ 1.6	− 4.5	6.1
59-0	+ 1.7	− 0.2	1.9
65-6	+ 2.6	− 1.8	4.4
67-8	+ 3.9	− 1.9	5.8
68-9	+ 4.8	− 0.1	4.9
Number of Exceptions			**17**
Largest Exception			**18.6%**
Average Exception			**7.7%**
Percentage of Exceptions			**37.8%**

(3) $P = h r_3$

Year	%ΔP	+%Δr₃	= Exception %
29-0	− 2.6%	+11.3%	13.9%
30-1	− 9.1	+ 3.0	12.1
31-2	−10.3	+12.2	22.5
33-4	+ 7.3	− 6.6	13.9
34-5	+ 1.0	− 7.2	8.2
35-6	+ 0.2	− 9.4	9.6
36-7	+ 4.2	− 4.1	8.3
37-8	− 1.2	+ 4.0	5.2
39-0	+ 1.6	+ 4.4	6.0
40-1	+ 7.5	− 4.2	11.7
47-8	+ 6.7	− 0.6	7.3
48-9	− 0.6	+ 2.9	3.5
49-0	+ 1.4	+ 0.1	1.5
50-1	+ 6.7	− 1.2	7.9
Number of Exceptions			**14**
Largest Exception			**22.5%**
Average Exception			**9.4%**
Percentage of Exceptions			**31.1%**

(4) $P = k_1 R_1$

Year	%ΔP	+%ΔR₁	= Exception %
29-0	− 2.6%	+ 1.7%	4.3%
34-5	+ 1.0	− 1.0	2.0
39-0	+ 1.6	− 0.1	1.7
Number of Exceptions			**3**
Largest Exception			**4.3%**
Average Exception			**2.7%**
Percentage of Exceptions			**6.7%**

(5) $P = k_2 R_2$

Year	%ΔP	+%ΔR₂	= Exception %
35-6	+ 0.2%	− 1.0%	1.2%
49-0	+ 1.4	− 0.6	2.0
54-5	+ 1.4	− 0.2	1.6
Number of Exceptions			**3**
Largest Exception			**2.0%**
Average Exception			**1.6%**
Percentage of Exceptions			**6.7%**

Table 2.3
Exceptions to Alternate Price Level Laws in the United States and Canada 1946-1974 – 27 Year to Year Changes

United States	(1) $P=V_1r_1$	(2) $P=V_2r_2$	(3) $P=hr_3$	(4) $P=k_1R_1$	(5) $P=k_2R_2$
Number of Exemptions	14	10	4	0	2
Largest Exemption	12.2%	11.5%	7.3%	0	2.0%
Average Exemption	5.7%	6.0%	5.1%	0	1.8%
Percentage of Exemptions	51.9	37.0%	14.8%	0	7.4%
Canada					
Number of Exemptions		8		2	3
Largest Exemption		16.5%		3.4%	3.1%
Average Exemption		6.5%		3.0%	2.0%
Percentage of Exemptions		29.6%		7.4%	11.1%

Since World War II, if the official U.S. definition of the money supply is adhered to, the EOE is refuted in 52% of our observations, while over the entire period from 1929 it was refuted in "only" 49% of the observations. When "M_2" is substituted to calculate "r_2" the EOE is refuted in only 37% of the U.S. and 30% of the Canadian post-war observations, a slightly better showing than over the entire period.

In the U.S. post-war period, the DOR price level law was refuted only 4 times or in 14.8% of the observations, a very substantial improvement over the finding of 31% exceptions over the entire period. Thus in "normal" years, it might be argued that the DOR price law would be contradicted only one-half as frequently as the r_2 EOE "Law", and that the exceptions will tend to be smaller.

There were no exceptions to the WCM law in the post-war U.S. data using "R_1" and only 2 exceptions in Canada in the same period, or 7.4% exceptions. There were 2 post-war exceptions in the U.S. and 3 in Canada when "R_2" is used. The WCM exceptions were invariably small, reflecting the near invariance of wage cost mark-up.

Conclusion and Further Argumentation

A simple wage cost mark-up theory of inflation is quite in accord with the facts of experience in the U.S. and Canada, while a simple money velocity theory is not. However, although monetarists must concede that the price level moves closely with the R ratio and is only loosely connected to the r ratio, they remain committed to the proposition that movements in the r ratio are the *cause* of both the P and R ratio. This is because they maintain that the wage level is determined, *as is any other price,* by the money to goods ratio, thus that it is wholly endogenous, while the money supply is an exogenous variable determined "outside" the economy by the central bank. There the matter rests with the "Keynesians" taking the wage level as the largely exogenous determinant of the price level[26] while the monetarists maintain that the central bank can, and should, make the money supply any magnitude it wants to carry out its policy goals. Given the errors of human foresight, however, the authorities should not try to "fine tune" the economy, so goes the argument, but expand the money supply constantly at a steady slow rate.

Keynesians generally deny that such a policy is compatible with either full employment or price level stability. It is not compatible with full employment because it may be necessary from time to time to use very expansionary monetary policy to aid fiscal policy in preventing depression or rescuing the *inherently unstable* economy from depression. And it is not compatible with either goal as long as vigorous "cost push" forces are at work. Thus, they argue that the central bank is a "constitutional monarch" in modern times and that only in theory does it have the power to make "M" any magnitude it likes. If it should expand "M" so slowly as to seriously inconvenience economic transactors either one or the other, or both, of two reactions will start to happen: 1. political pressures will build up to "make the money bags relent", 2. transactors will find ways to economize on cash, *i.e.* by holding "near" money instead of money a larger fraction of the time, so that they can carry out more transactions with a given volume of "M". In most countries, the central bank is so much a part of the government that reaction number 1 is the more important escape hatch from monetary pinch, while in the U.S. with its "independent" Federal Reserve, reaction number 2 is relatively more important. Reaction 1 fosters more inflation and reaction 2 fosters more recession, but either way, M becomes en endogenous, rather than an exogenous magnitude, the supply becoming a function of the demand for it. This dispute concerning the exogeneity or endogeneity of the money supply is central to the difference between monetarism and Keynesianism, and we shall return to the discussion in Chapter 8 on inflation control.

A recent statement of Milton Friedman's indicates the "self-sealing gas tank" quality of the monetarist ideology – that inflation is "always and everywhere" *caused* by too rapid growth of the supply of money and can be *cured* by Friedman's 5 per cent, or 3 per cent, or 2 per cent, rule for non-inflationary growth of M. No matter how many times this notion is punctured by historical experience, the ideology remains strangely intact. In his *Newsweek* column of August 27, 1973,

---

[26] Thus as Joan Robinson recently put it, ". . . the extraordinary vogue . . . of an argument so implausible as the Quantity Theory of Money was due to a refusal to accept the fact that the main influence on the general price level . . . is the level of money wage rates and the level of wage rates at any moment is more or less an historical accident, depending on conditions in the labour market over a long past." "The Second Crisis in Economic Theory". p. 5.

Friedman castigates "The Inflationary Fed" for allowing M_1 in the U.S. to rise at rates of 6 to 8 per cent per annum from January 1970 and maintains that,[27]

"That rate of monetary growth, probably even now, and certainly if long continued, implies that inflation in consumer prices will reach something like 7 per cent per year after full adjustment."

Curiously, Friedman turns to the M_1 data surveyed above to make his point, although it demonstrates that even a 2.4 per cent rate of growth of M_1 *over an 18 year period* still entailed "creeping" inflation.

"In not a single one of the 216 months from January 1948 to January 1966 did the year-to-year growth in the narrowly defined money supply (M_1) exceed 6 per cent. These eighteen years included the Korean inflation, yet M_1 rose at the average rate of only 2.4 per cent per year; consumer prices, of 1.7 per cent; wholesale prices, of 1.2 per cent."

As we saw above, Figure 2.12, from 1947 through 1966 the money to goods ratio (r_1) fell steadily while the price level even more steadily rose, and even in 1974 the ratio was lower than in 1949. If we give the 1947 magnitudes the value of one hundred, r_1 fell to 71 in 1966, 86 in 1972 and reached 92 in 1974, while the price level rose from one hundred in 1947 to 152 in 1966, 195 in 1972 and 228 in 1974. If we broaden the definition of money to M_2 the results are as follows: r_2 1947 = 100, 1966 = 105, 1972 = 136, 1974 = 154.

We all know of the "long and variable lags" with which the money supply moves "its wonders to perform," but was the rise in P in 1965 really only a lagged response to the excessive growth in M_1 in World War II, some 20 to 25 years earlier? If so how much longer should we have been prepared to wait for Friedman's most restrictive rule to cure inflation? Into that blessed long run, where even money doesn't matter because we are all dead?

Post numberless scoldings from Friedman, *ergo propter* these scoldings, the "Fed" in January 1970 dropped its sinful "Keynesian" attention to interest rate "targets" and adopted an (almost) virtuous monetarist goal of a steady "5 to 6 per cent" growth rate of M_1, as Chairman Arthur F. Burns then testified. For two decades prior to his 1969 "Optimum Quantity" essay, Friedman promised us a new golden age (*sans* gold "backing") of stable prices, full employment, and rapid real growth if, and only if, the money supply would grow with blessed regularity at 5 per cent per annum. Now he informs *Newsweek's* readers that 5 per cent is too much, but that "3 or 4 per cent" will usher in the millenium.

"The two years 1966 and 1967 set the stage for the subsequent burst of inflation. Yet the year-to-year growth in M_1 exceeded 6 per cent in only four out of 24 months. M_1 rose at the average rate of 4.3 per cent; consumer prices, of 3.4 per cent; wholesale prices, of 1.3 per cent. The evidence therefore supports a '3 or 4 per cent range' rather than Burns' "5 or 6 per cent range."

The evidence, if it supports anything at all, supports the contention that the rate of growth of the money supply had very little to do with the world-wide inflation since World War II – that inflation is due to

---

[27] Copyright 1973 by Newsweek, Inc. all rights reserved. Reprinted by permission.

more fundamental causes than mere monetary manoeuvres. What is, or are, the fundamental causes of both inflation and the growth of the money supply?

As we have seen above, and will see again below, Keynes' answer amounts to, "The cause of inflation is the inflated ego of the average man." We all think we should be paid far more than we are, and inflation is the result of our attempts to raise our incomes faster than output can increase. Paper, or credit money, facilitates inflation, but does not cause it. Indeed, we see the essence of this theory in Adam Smith's tart observation that, "The greater part of men have an over-weening conceit of their abilities."[28]

By this explanation, cultural differences account for the varying rates of inflation in money and prices. South Americans have for many decades been known for rapid inflation and for "machismo" egoism. North Americans have had considerably more willingness to live within the, more comfortable, limits of their economic possibilities, but increasingly we appear doomed also to do things the South American way. Unless we solve the problem of matching money income growth rates to real income growth rates we face a wage explosion. The price of food was up in 1973, and again in 1974, some 15 to 30 per cent because of crop shortages the world over. Petroleum products, copper, zinc, and other materials are in increasingly short supply. If we all now demand 15 per cent or so higher wages we shall convert what could have been a temporary inflationary surge into an inflation of truly Latin American magnitudes.[29]

---

[28] *Wealth of Nations,* New Canaan Edition, Chapter 10, p. 107.

[29] For cogent commentary on these pressing matters, see P. J. Wiles, "Cost Inflation and the State of Economic Theory," *Economic Journal,* June 1973, pp. 377-98. See also G.C. Means, A. Nove, S. Weintraub, P. Wiles, "Cost Inflation and the State of Economic Theory: An Interchange", *Economic Journal,* June 1974, pp. 375-86, and M. Chatterji, P. Wiles, "Cost Inflation and the State of Economic Theory: An Interchange," *Economic Journal,* March 1975, pp. 151-3.

Sources for Tables 1 to 4
Canada
1) *Economic Review,* April 1975, Table 8 (p. 109), Table 43 (p. 150).
2) *National Accounts: Income and Expenditure,* 1926-56, Table 5 (p. 36), Table 6 (p. 37).
3) *Canada Year Book, 1973* Table 19.5 (p. 788).
4) *Canadian Statistical Review,* May 1975, Table 3 (p. 109).
5) *Historical Statistics of Canada,* 1965, Series H 1-10 (p. 230).

U.S.A.
1) *Economic Report of the President,* February 1975, Table C-15 (p. 266), C-14 (p. 265), C-3 (p. 252), C-63 (p. 323).
2) M. Friedman and A.J. Schwartz, *Monetary Statistics of the United States,* New York 1970, Table 1 (pp. 4-53, esp. 24-53).

Note
For the calculation of the M_1 and M_2 indices, the estimates for the base year 1929 made by Friedman and Schwartz are used.

For the years 1968 to 1974 the figures for M_1 and M_2 given in the 1975 Report of the President are used.

During the overlap years of these two series (1960-1968) the figures for M_1 in the Presidential Report were on average 2.7% higher than those given by Friedman and Schwartz, for M_2 they were higher by 1.4%.

For the purpose of calculating the index figures 1968-1974, the base was adjusted in each case accordingly.

Table 1
Alternative Mark-Up Measures: Canada

Year	k_1	ky_1	k_2	ky_2
1926	100.00	100.00	100.00	100.00
1927	102.04	99.61	103.07	100.61
1928	102.49	99.81	104.32	101.59
1929	96.03	91.65	104.72	99.94
1930	94.41	90.27	97.86	93.57
1931	89.57	80.07	102.27	91.42
1932	88.69	76.06	111.75	95.83
1933	89.66	75.28	108.24	90.88
1934	94.00	81.49	110.07	95.42
1935	94.99	84.86	108.93	97.32
1936	94.97	85.54	109.46	98.59
1937	94.89	87.33	108.27	99.64
1938	96.32	90.32	104.86	98.75
1939	98.44	92.02	108.77	101.68
1940	98.21	91.85	109.17	102.10
1941	95.62	90.24	109.82	103.64
1942	96.15	94.10	105.71	103.45
1943	89.08	88.08	102.86	101.71
1944	90.07	90.50	100.29	100.77
1945	88.89	89.71	100.01	100.93
1946	94.06	93.32	102.66	101.85
1947	93.69	91.44	104.12	101.62
1948	93.06	91.69	103.01	101.49
1949	92.62	90.95	103.30	101.43
1950	94.45	92.01	106.63	103.87
1951	93.92	91.52	107.49	104.74
1952	95.30	92.38	106.24	102.98
1953	92.17	88.32	106.66	102.20
1954	89.44	84.73	106.34	100.73
1955	92.10	87.10	109.11	103.19
1956	91.48	86.05	109.57	103.06
1957	88.27	82.84	107.88	101.25
1958	89.03	83.72	107.90	101.47
1959	88.66	83.46	108.54	102.17
1960	87.70	82.30	107.95	101.30
1961	86.87	81.36	108.16	101.30
1962	87.78	82.61	108.46	102.07
1963	88.36	83.47	108.64	102.63
1964	88.68	83.46	110.49	103.98
1965	87.72	82.45	109.89	103.29
1966	86.73	81.86	108.17	102.10
1967	83.92	79.25	106.69	100.75
1968	83.65	79.56	106.33	101.13
1969	83.65	79.14	103.15	97.59
1970	82.88	77.52	103.24	96.57
1971	82.25	77.36	101.65	95.60
1972	82.25	77.09	102.20	97.03
1973	84.07	80.06	104.61	99.63
1974	84.54	81.10	106.51	102.18

Table 2
Derivation of Mark-Up and Velocity Ratios: Canada

Year	GNP	P	Q	Wages	Lab	R_1	R_2	k_1
1926	100.0	100.0	100.0	100.0	100.0	100.0	100.0	100.0
1927	108.1	98.8	109.4	105.9	104.8	96.8	95.9	102.0
1928	117.6	98.4	119.5	114.7	112.7	96.0	94.3	102.5
1929	119.3	99.6	119.8	124.2	113.9	103.7	95.1	96.0
1930	111.2	96.8	114.8	117.7	113.6	102.5	98.9	94.4
1931	91.2	91.1	100.0	101.8	98.2	101.7	89.1	89.6
1932	74.1	82.5	89.8	83.6	66.3	93.0	73.8	88.7
1933	67.9	81.0	83.8	75.7	62.7	90.3	74.8	89.7
1934	77.1	82.1	93.9	82.0	70.1	87.3	74.6	94.0
1935	83.6	82.5	101.3	88.0	76.7	86.9	75.7	95.0
1936	90.1	85.1	105.8	94.8	82.3	89.6	77.7	95.0
1937	101.8	87.5	116.4	107.3	94.1	92.2	80.8	94.9
1938	102.4	87.3	117.4	106.4	97.7	90.6	83.2	96.3
1939	109.2	86.7	126.0	111.0	100.4	88.1	79.7	98.4
1940	130.5	90.7	143.8	132.8	119.5	92.4	83.1	98.2
1941	160.9	97.8	164.6	168.3	146.6	102.3	89.1	95.6
1942	199.5	102.2	195.2	207.5	188.7	106.3	96.7	96.2
1943	214.8	105.8	203.0	241.1	208.8	118.8	102.9	89.1
1944	230.2	109.1	211.0	255.6	229.6	121.1	108.8	90.1
1945	230.5	111.7	206.4	259.3	230.5	125.7	111.7	88.9
1946	231.0	115.2	200.7	245.6	225.0	122.4	112.1	94.1
1947	255.9	125.2	204.4	273.2	245.8	133.6	120.2	93.7
1948	294.0	140.5	209.2	315.9	285.4	151.0	136.4	93.1
1949	316.8	146.2	216.7	342.0	306.6	157.8	141.5	92.6
1950	348.9	149.6	233.2	369.4	327.2	158.4	140.3	94.5
1951	409.2	167.1	244.9	435.7	380.7	177.9	155.5	93.9
1952	467.2	174.2	268.2	490.2	439.7	182.8	164.0	95.3
1953	492.2	174.2	282.5	534.0	461.5	189.0	163.3	92.2
1954	490.3	177.0	277.0	548.2	461.1	197.9	166.4	89.4
1955	542.1	178.2	304.2	588.6	496.8	193.5	163.3	92.1
1956	609.7	184.3	330.8	666.5	556.4	201.5	168.2	91.5
1957	639.5	188.1	340.0	724.4	592.7	213.1	174.4	88.3
1958	662.5	190.7	347.4	744.2	614.0	214.2	176.7	89.0
1959	704.7	194.8	361.8	794.9	649.3	219.7	179.5	88.7
1960	734.1	197.2	372.2	837.0	680.0	224.9	182.7	87.7
1961	759.4	198.4	382.8	874.3	702.1	228.4	183.4	86.9
1962	823.0	201.2	409.1	937.6	758.8	229.2	185.5	87.8
1963	883.5	205.0	431.0	999.9	813.2	232.0	188.7	88.4
1964	967.4	209.9	460.9	1090.9	875.5	236.7	190.0	88.7
1965	1066.8	217.3	490.9	1216.1	970.7	247.7	197.7	87.7
1966	1193.6	227.2	525.3	1376.2	1103.3	262.0	210.0	86.7
1967	1277.1	234.9	543.7	1521.9	1197.0	279.9	220.2	83.9
1968	1387.3	243.1	570.7	1658.4	1304.7	290.6	228.6	83.7
1969	1549.2	254.0	609.6	1852.0	1501.9	303.8	246.3	83.7
1970	1663.1	265.6	626.2	2006.7	1611.0	320.4	257.2	82.9
1971	1811.1	274.2	661.0	2201.9	1781.6	333.1	269.5	82.3
1972	2008.8	287.3	699.2	2442.3	1965.5	349.1	280.9	82.3
1973	2307.9	309.1	746.7	2745.3	2206.1	367.6	295.4	84.1
1974	2707.6	349.7	774.3	3202.7	2542.1	413.3	328.1	84.5

Table 2
Derivation of Mark-Up and Velocity Ratios: Canada

Year	k_2	M_2	r_2	V_2
1926	100.0	100.0	100.0	100.0
1927	103.1	108.0	98.8	100.0
1928	104.3	111.9	93.7	105.0
1929	104.7	110.3	92.1	108.2
1930	97.9	103.5	90.2	107.3
1931	102.3	101.9	101.8	89.5
1932	111.7	95.5	106.3	77.6
1933	108.2	95.7	114.3	70.9
1934	110.1	100.9	107.4	76.5
1935	108.9	108.1	106.7	77.3
1936	109.5	114.2	108.0	78.8
1937	108.3	118.0	101.4	86.3
1938	104.9	125.9	107.3	81.4
1939	108.8	141.7	112.5	77.1
1940	109.2	142.5	99.1	91.6
1941	109.8	160.9	97.8	100.0
1942	105.7	193.0	98.9	103.4
1943	102.9	233.6	115.1	91.9
1944	100.3	278.7	132.1	82.6
1945	100.0	317.9	154.0	72.5
1946	102.7	332.9	165.9	69.4
1947	104.1	342.3	167.5	74.8
1948	103.0	373.6	178.6	78.7
1949	103.3	388.4	179.3	81.6
1950	106.6	414.5	177.7	84.2
1951	107.5	414.3	169.2	98.8
1952	106.2	440.3	164.2	106.1
1953	106.7	463.1	163.9	106.3
1954	106.3	487.9	176.1	100.5
1955	109.1	539.1	177.2	100.5
1956	109.6	541.1	163.6	112.7
1957	107.9	564.0	165.9	113.4
1958	107.9	626.6	180.4	105.7
1959	108.5	624.1	172.5	112.9
1960	107.9	658.2	176.8	111.5
1961	108.2	658.6	172.1	115.3
1962	108.5	736.6	180.1	111.7
1963	108.6	755.6	175.3	116.9
1964	110.5	814.9	176.8	118.7
1965	109.9	891.5	181.6	119.7
1966	108.2	954.5	181.7	125.0
1967	106.7	1065.2	195.9	119.9
1968	106.3	1195.5	209.5	116.0
1969	103.2	1381.9	226.7	112.1
1970	103.2	1533.2	244.8	108.5
1971	101.7	1825.3	276.1	99.2
1972	102.2	2072.9	296.5	96.9
1973	104.6	2394.1	320.6	96.4
1974	106.5	2902.3	374.8	93.3

Table 3
Alternative Mark-Up Measures: U.S.A.

Year	k_1	ky_1	k_2	ky_2
1929	100.00	100.00	100.00	100.00
1930	95.74	94.85	97.51	96.60
1931	94.39	88.31	97.28	91.01
1932	92.43	81.02	97.76	85.69
1933	93.41	80.42	97.94	84.32
1934	94.07	84.96	97.29	87.86
1935	95.94	90.28	95.70	90.05
1936	95.31	89.20	96.89	90.67
1937	93.54	90.46	93.69	90.61
1938	93.29	88.18	94.82	89.63
1939	93.25	88.86	95.12	90.63
1940	94.85	91.64	96.63	93.36
1941	95.23	94.67	95.99	95.43
1942	91.75	94.62	91.39	94.26
1943	86.72	91.56	86.48	91.31
1944	85.92	88.70	86.48	89.28
1945	85.32	86.80	85.24	86.72
1946	87.65	90.83	84.81	87.88
1947	88.94	90.89	88.31	90.24
1948	90.49	93.54	89.57	92.60
1949	90.16	90.81	91.20	91.86
1950	91.30	91.81	92.99	93.51
1951	90.08	90.57	92.17	92.68
1952	87.68	87.84	90.31	90.47
1953	86.42	85.79	90.11	89.44
1954	86.93	85.79	90.78	89.59
1955	87.87	86.80	92.26	91.14
1956	85.47	84.95	90.04	89.49
1957	85.40	84.19	90.15	88.88
1958	86.00	83.99	90.36	88.25
1959	85.90	84.37	91.07	89.45
1960	82.94	84.88	90.40	88.36
1961	85.19	83.13	90.62	88.43
1962	85.82	83.27	91.66	88.93
1963	85.83	83.20	91.97	89.15
1964	85.71	83.40	92.22	89.74
1965	86.20	84.36	92.66	90.68
1966	85.34	83.89	91.92	90.36
1967	84.22	82.36	91.06	89.04
1968	83.39	81.61	90.57	88.63
1969	81.47	79.67	91.49	89.48
1970	80.19	78.04	90.53	88.10
1971	81.29	78.52	91.98	88.83
1972	81.17	78.80	91.81	89.14
1973	81.65	79.81	91.29	89.23
1974	80.90	78.58	91.35	83.73

Table 4
Derivation of Mark-Up, Velocity and Debt-Output Ratios: U.S.A

Year	GNP	P	Q	Wages	Lab	R₁	R₂	k₁
1929	100.0	100.0	100.0	100.0	100.0	100.0	100.0	100.0
1930	87.7	97.4	90.0	91.6	90.0	101.7	100.0	95.7
1931	73.5	88.5	83.1	77.9	75.6	93.8	91.0	94.4
1932	56.3	79.4	70.9	60.9	57.6	85.9	81.3	92.4
1933	53.9	77.7	69.4	57.7	55.1	83.2	79.4	93.4
1934	63.1	83.4	75.7	67.1	64.9	88.7	85.8	94.1
1935	70.0	84.2	83.2	73.0	73.3	87.8	88.1	95.9
1936	80.0	84.4	94.8	84.0	82.6	88.5	87.2	95.3
1937	87.7	87.9	99.8	93.7	93.7	94.0	93.9	93.5
1938	82.2	86.8	94.6	88.1	86.6	93.0	91.5	93.3
1939	87.8	85.4	102.8	94.1	92.3	91.6	89.8	93.3
1940	96.7	86.8	111.4	102.0	100.2	91.5	89.9	94.8
1941	120.8	93.3	129.4	126.8	125.9	98.0	97.3	95.2
1942	153.2	104.7	146.3	166.9	167.6	114.1	114.6	91.7
1943	185.8	112.3	165.5	214.3	215.0	129.5	129.9	86.7
1944	203.8	115.0	177.2	237.2	235.7	133.8	133.0	85.9
1945	205.5	118.0	174.2	240.9	240.7	138.3	138.2	85.3
1946	202.2	131.8	153.4	230.7	238.6	150.4	155.5	87.7
1947	224.3	147.4	152.2	252.3	254.3	165.7	167.1	88.9
1948	249.9	157.3	158.8	276.1	279.1	173.8	175.7	90.5
1949	248.8	156.3	159.2	275.9	273.0	173.4	171.5	90.2
1950	276.2	158.5	174.3	302.5	297.2	173.6	170.5	91.3
1951	318.5	169.2	188.3	353.6	345.7	187.8	183.7	90.1
1952	335.1	172.9	193.8	382.2	371.3	197.2	191.6	87.7
1953	353.6	174.5	202.7	409.2	392.5	201.9	193.7	86.4
1954	353.8	177.1	199.8	407.0	390.0	203.7	195.2	86.9
1955	386.0	179.6	214.9	441.3	418.7	205.3	194.8	87.5
1956	406.6	185.8	218.8	475.7	451.9	217.4	206.5	85.5
1957	427.8	192.7	222.0	501.0	474.8	225.6	213.8	85.4
1958	433.9	197.6	219.6	504.5	480.5	229.8	218.8	86.0
1959	469.2	200.8	233.6	546.2	515.5	233.8	220.6	85.9
1960	488.6	204.2	239.3	575.7	540.7	240.6	226.0	84.9
1961	504.5	206.7	244.1	592.2	556.9	242.6	228.2	85.2
1962	543.5	209.1	259.9	633.3	593.3	243.7	228.3	85.8
1963	572.7	211.9	270.3	667.3	623.0	246.9	230.5	85.8
1964	613.4	215.2	285.0	715.7	665.6	251.1	233.5	85.7
1965	664.3	219.2	303.1	770.6	717.4	254.3	236.7	86.2
1966	727.4	224.9	323.4	852.4	791.8	263.6	244.8	85.3
1967	769.6	323.4	331.2	914.7	846.1	276.2	255.5	84.1
1968	838.2	241.5	347.1	1007.1	900.0	290.2	259.3	83.2
1969	902.3	253,2	356.4	1107.6	986.3	310.8	276.0	81.5
1970	947.7	267.1	354.9	1181.8	1046.9	333.0	295.0	80.2
1971	1023.2	279.1	366.6	1258.5	1112.4	343.0	303.5	81.3
1972	1123.2	288.5	389.3	1383.8	1223.4	355.5	314.3	81.2
1973	1256.0	304.7	412.2	1538.2	1375.8	373.2	333.8	81.7
1974	1354.7	335.9	403.3	1674.6	1483.0	415.2	367.7	80.9

Table 4
Derivation of Mark-Up, Velocity and Debt-Output Ratios: U.S.A.

Year	k_2	M_1	M_2	r_1
1929	100.0	100.0	100.0	100.0
1930	97.4	94.8	96.3	105.3
1931	97.2	83.5	82.5	100.5
1932	97.7	77.9	76.2	110.0
1933	97.9	75.7	69.3	109.0
1934	97.2	89.1	78.0	117.7
1935	95.6	103.4	89.0	124.3
1936	96.8	117.6	98.7	124.0
1937	93.6	110.9	96.3	111.1
1938	94.8	121.3	102.2	128.2
1939	95.1	137.8	112.5	134.1
1940	96.5	160.7	126.8	144.2
1941	95.9	183.5	140.2	141.8
1942	91.4	237.1	171.9	162.1
1943	86.4	301.5	215.1	182.2
1944	86.4	341.9	249.5	193.0
1945	85.4	386.1	287.9	221.7
1946	84.8	406.0	307.3	264.6
1947	88.2	423.6	320.7	278.3
1948	89.5	417.6	318.8	262.9
1949	91.1	416.5	318.8	261.7
1950	93.0	435.2	330.5	249.7
1951	92.1	459.6	347.3	244.1
1952	90.3	477.2	364.1	246.2
1953	90.1	482.4	374.3	238.0
1954	90.7	495.5	390.1	248.0
1955	92.2	506.4	400.0	235.6
1956	90.0	512.7	407.8	234.3
1957	90.1	509.0	417.5	229.3
1958	90.3	528.5	446.2	240.7
1959	91.0	534.1	453.6	228.6
1960	90.4	530.7	463.5	221.8
1961	90.6	546.8	493.3	224.1
1962	91.6	554.7	531.1	213.4
1963	91.9	575.3	574.1	212.8
1964	92.2	601.1	620.1	210.9
1965	92.6	629.2	679.9	207.6
1966	91.9	643.1	712.7	198.8
1967	91.0	685.8	791.8	207.1
1968	93.1	735.6	813.8	211.9
1969	91.5	761.1	834.8	212.9
1970	90.5	807.4	905.3	227.5
1971	92.0	858.1	1007.1	234.1
1972	91.8	932.9	1119.0	239.7
1973	91.3	990.2	1218.0	240.2
1974	91.4	1035.0	1306.7	256.6

Table 4 continued

Year	r_2	V_1	V_2	DBT	r_3	h
1929	100.0	100.0	100.0	100.0	100.0	100.0
1930	107.0	92.5	91.0	100.2	111.3	87.5
1931	99.3	88.0	89.1	95.3	114.7	77.1
1932	107.6	72.2	73.8	91.2	128.7	61.7
1933	99.9	71.3	77.8	87.8	126.5	61.4
1934	103.0	70.8	81.0	89.4	118.1	70.6
1935	107.0	67.7	78.7	91.2	109.6	76.8
1936	104.1	68.0	81.1	94.1	99.3	85.0
1937	96.6	79.1	91.0	94.9	95.2	92.3
1938	107.9	67.7	80.4	93.7	99.0	87.6
1939	109.5	63.7	78.0	95.5	92.9	91.9
1940	113.8	60.2	76.3	98.9	88.8	97.8
1941	108.3	65.8	86.1	110.2	85.1	109.6
1942	117.5	64.6	89.1	134.8	92.1	113.6
1943	130.0	61.6	86.4	165.8	100.2	112.1
1944	140.8	59.6	81.7	193.0	108.9	105.6
1945	165.3	53.2	71.4	211.5	121.4	97.2
1946	200.3	49.8	65.8	206.7	134.7	97.9
1947	210.7	53.0	69.9	216.6	142.3	103.6
1948	200.7	59.8	78.4	224.8	141.5	111.2
1949	200.3	59.7	78.0	231.8	145.6	107.3
1950	189.6	63.5	83.6	253.4	145.4	109.0
1951	184.5	69.3	91.7	270.6	143.7	117.7
1952	187.9	70.2	92.0	286.7	147.9	116.9
1953	184.7	73.3	94.5	303.1	149.6	116.7
1954	195.2	71.4	90.7	315.7	158.0	112.1
1955	186.1	76.2	96.5	347.0	161.4	111.3
1956	186.3	79.3	99.7	363.9	166.3	111.7
1957	188.0	84.1	102.5	379.5	170.9	112.7
1958	203.2	82.1	97.2	401.0	182.7	108.2
1959	194.1	87.8	103.4	434.1	185.8	108.1
1960	193.7	92.1	105.4	455.5	190.4	107.2
1961	202.1	92.3	102.3	484.8	198.6	104.1
1962	204.3	98.0	102.3	519.3	199.8	104.6
1963	212.4	99.6	99.8	558.1	206.5	102.6
1964	217.6	102.0	98.9	600.1	210.5	102.2
1965	224.4	105.6	97.7	648.3	213.9	102.5
1966	220.4	113.1	102.0	699.0	216.1	104.1
1967	239.1	112.2	97.2	751.8	227.0	102.4
1968	234.5	114.0	103.0	828.1	238.6	101.6
1969	234.2	118.6	108.1	908.4	254.9	99.8
1970	225.1	117.4	104.7	973.9	275.6	97.3
1971	274.7	119.2	101.6	1066.1	292.0	96.0
1972	287.5	120.4	100.4	1189.7	305.2	95.0
1973	295.5	126.9	103.1	1326.8	321.9	94.7
1974	324.0	130.9	103.7	1447.3	358.9	93.6

3

Adverse Effects of Tax and Interest Hikes As Strengthening the Case for Incomes Policies – or A Part of the Elephant

Economists attempting to understand and control inflation are somewhat like the four blind Indian philosophers who each seized a part of an elephant, took the part for the whole, and then fell to quarreling rather than integrating their partial insights.

One proclaims that inflation is a matter of too much money and too few goods, another that it is excess demand from deficits, a third that it is a cost push, a fourth that it is a natural condition without beginning or end. Perhaps the monetarist is the one who has hold of the elephant's tail – the famous rope that you can't push on and that he now,[1] perhaps unwisely, is pulling on. In the thought that it concerns a somewhat different part of the inflationary beast's anatomy, and some integration, the following is offered.

In recent decades the public sector has increased relative to the private sector, with taxes per unit of output rising.[2] Since economists generally conclude that sales and excise taxes, probably corporate profits taxes, and perhaps the personal income tax as well, are shifted forward in higher prices, is not "tax-push" a partial explanation of our creeping inflation?[3] Also the nominal rate of interest has more than

---

[1] "Now" was June 1970. Soon after that he started pushing again with little effect as of June 1971.

[2] Current plus capital expenditures of the Canadian government sector increased from 18.6 per cent of GNP in 1952 to 21.4 per cent in 1969. However, total expenditures plus transfers increased from 30.0 per cent of GNP to 43.0 per cent over the same period. Taxes equalled 24.7 per cent of GNP in 1952 and 31.4 per cent in 1969. Indirect taxes less subsidies were 11.6 per cent of GNP in 1952 and 13.6 per cent in 1969. Government transfers to persons were 5.6 per cent of GNP in 1952 and 7.7 per cent in 1969. Source: Dominion Bureau of Statistics, *National Income and Expenditure,* First Quarter 1970, 14, 19-22, 38. I am indebted to the DBS for making as yet unpublished data on 1952 based on the recent revision available to me.

[3] *Ad hoc* statements attributing higher prices to higher taxes per unit of output are not lacking, as for example the following: "In Germany, the 1.4 per cent consumer price rise and the 5.6 per cent advance in wholesale prices of investment goods . . . were mostly attributable to . . . the . . . value added tax . . . In France, too, the extension of the value added tax to the consumer sector . . . caused consumer prices to increase." US Federal Reserve Board *Federal Reserve Bulletin* (Washington, Nov. 1968), 890-1. The importance of rising taxes in accounting for the recent inflation has been stressed by the Economic Council of Canada: "Indirect taxes per unit of output have risen by close to one third since 1960, and have been the most steeply rising component of costs per unit of output in the national accounts . . . The combination of increased indirect taxes and the introduction of the Pension Plans may have had a particularly pronounced and pervasive cost-push effect on prices in 1966 . . . conceivably accounted for somewhere in the vicinity of a quarter of the overall increase in prices in Canada over the past few years . . . Increases in direct taxes . . . may also tend to contribute to price increases – in the case of

Continued on P. 92

92   Adverse Effects of Tax and Interest Hikes As
Strengthening the Case for Incomes Policies – or
A Part of the Elephant

doubled in the last 20 years[4] while the ratio of debt to output is nearly
unchanged.[5] According to our theory of the firm, interest hikes raise
the cost level and thus the price level, just the opposite of the conclusion reached by our macro analyses. Should not we attempt to resolve
this conflict? Furthermore, increased interest payments become increased incomes to lenders. Does not their increased consumption
expenditure offset the decreased investment which we expect to
make interest hikes deflationary?[6]

Classical assumptions in Keynesian analysis?

E.R. Rolph theorized that excises are shifted backward in lower factor
incomes and thus tend to lower the price level. Most economists have,
however, followed R.A. Musgrave in concluding that Rolph's theory
only holds in the "classical" world of strict quantity theory with prices
fully flexible downward.[7] Musgrave concluded that in a world like
ours with varying velocity, imperfect competition and sticky wages,
forward shifting of excise taxes in the "typical case,"[8] and in his
well-known text he maintains: " . . . A potential inflationary gap . . .

Continued from P. 91

personal income taxes, perhaps largely through the route of increased wage
demands." *Third Annual Review* (Ottawa 1966), 223-224. For further insights
regarding "tax push" see the Economic Council's *Performance and Potential*
(Ottawa, 1970), 29-32. I have argued elsewhere that as much as 70 per cent of
the rise in the Canadian GNP deflator from 1965 to 1968 can be attributed to
"excess" net taxes, transfers, and interest incomes. See my, "Some Neglected
Factors in Inflation in the U.S. and Canada," *Waterloo Economic Series*, No. 9
(Waterloo, 1969).

[4] A few representative statistics: *Canada* government bond yields: 1948 2.9 per
cent, 1957 4.1 per cent, 1968 6.9 per cent, 1969 7.5 per cent; *United Kingdom*
1948 3.2 per cent, 1957 5.0 per cent, 1968 7.4 per cent, 1969 9.0 per cent.
International Monetary Fund, *International Financial Statistics*, supplement to
1962/63 issues and Sept. 1969 issue. (Washington, 1964, 1969); *United States*
average rate of interest on net debts public and private: 1948 2.9 per cent, 1957
4.6 per cent, 1968 6.7 per cent, 1969 7.2 per cent. US Council of Economic
Advisors, *Economic Report of the President* (Washington, 1970), 248; US
Department of Commerce, *Survey of Current Business* (Washington, July
1969), 45. *Canada:* interest and miscellaneous investment income was 1.6 per
cent of GNP in 1948, 2.9 per cent in 1957, 3.6 per cent in 1968 and 3.9 per cent in
1969. Interest, dividends and miscellaneous investment income (including
interest on public debts) was 5.1 per cent of GNP in 1948, 4.9 per cent in 1957
and 6.1 per cent in 1968. Source: Dominion Bureau of Statistics.

[5] Since figures on all debts public and private are not published in Canada, US
figures must be cited. Net debt/GNP ratio was 1.67 in 1948 and rose even as
interest rates rose. In 1968 it was 1.81 and about 1.79 in 1969. For an earlier
recognition of the near constancy of this ratio see M.A. Robinson, "Debt and
Economic Growth," *Proceedings of the Fifty-First Annual Conference on
Taxation*, National Tax Association (1959), 205-14.

[6] For some thoughts on these matters see John H. Hotson, *Guideposts, Interest
and Tax Push, and Amnesia* (Denver, National Council for Sound Monetary
Policy, 1967); "Neo-Orthodox Keynesianism and the 45⁰ Heresy," *Nebraska
Journal of Economics and Business*, 6 (Autumn 1967), 34-39.

[7] See E.R. Rolph, *The Theory of Fiscal Economics* (New York, 1954), or E.R.
Rolph and G.F. Break, *Public Finance* (New York, 1960); R.A. Musgrave "Gen-
eral Equilibrium Aspects of Incidence Theory," *American Economic Review*,
Proceedings, 43 (May 1953), 504-17. See also P. Davidson's arguments,
"Rolph on the Aggregate Effects of a General Excise Tax," *Southern
Economic Journal*, 27 (July 1960), 37-42; and P. Mieszkowski's review article,
"Tax Incidence Theory: The Effect of Taxes on the Distribution of Income,"
Journal of Economic Literature, 7 (Dec. 1969), 1103-24.

[8] Musgrave, "General Equilibrium Aspects of Incidence Theory", 43, 514.

may be closed by an increase in consumption taxes only while permitting some rise in the price level, reflecting the increase in cost due to tax. [Continuing in a footnote] This increase in price level cannot be avoided by raising consumption taxes further. It would only add to the increase in price level and, assuming money wages to be rigid in the downward direction, would make for a reduction in real income."[9]

Musgrave argues, however, that this tax push rise in the price level is a "once-and-for-all increase, to be distinguished from the continuous increase that results if the inflationary gap is not closed."[10] That this is more a difference of degree than kind is indicated by G. Brennan and D.A.L. Auld, whose analysis "demonstrates the possibility that the sales tax may be subject to cumulative shifting: first shifted forward to customers . . . then . . . back on firms in higher income claims to match the higher cost of living – then forward . . . and so on."[11] Moreover, Canada has not enjoyed full employment at which the "inflationary gap" is supposed to live since the second world war, but has experienced inflation. Further, Musgrave's analysis is in terms of the government taxing more but spending no more, when the usual reason for raising tax revenue is to spend it – and perhaps a bit more. Perhaps the most meaningful hypothesis is that a rise in the government share of GNP in a near fully employed economy is always inflationary to some extent. It is highly inflationary if the extra government spending and transfers are financed by deficits and new money creation. It is still inflationary if it is financed by indirect, or even direct, taxes, but much less so.[12] Musgrave is also co-author of the well known study which indicates that the US corporation profits tax is more than fully shifted in the short run,[13] which as

---

[9] R.A. Musgrave, *The Theory of Public Finance* (New York, 1959), 447-8. For recent empirical evidence of forward shifting see O. Brownlee and G.L. Perry, "The Effects of the 1965 Federal Excise Tax Reduction on Prices," *National Tax Journal,* 20 (Sept. 1967). They concluded, "On all commodities on which retail excise taxes were eliminated (except for admissions and club dues) and on most commodities on which excise taxes imposed at the manufacturers' level were cut, retail prices fell approximately the full amount of the tax . . . with no apparent time lag" (p. 235). See also F.O. Woodward and H. Siegelman, "Effects of the 1965 Federal Excise Tax Reduction upon the Prices of Automobile Replacement Parts," *ibid.,* 250-7. This finding is further confirmed by Evans and Klein who conclude, "A decrease in excise taxes thus lowers prices, while an increase raises prices and is therefore of dubious anti-inflationary benefit." Michael K. Evans and Lawrence R. Klein, *The Wharton Econometric Forecasting Model* (Philadelphia, 1968), 68.

[10] Musgrave, *Public Finance,* 447.

[11] G. Brennan and D.A.L. Auld, "The Tax Cut as an Anti-Inflationary Measure," *Economic Record* (Dec. 1968), 520-5.

[12] This hypothesis is close to R. Eisner's argument in "Fiscal and Monetary Policy Reconsidered," *American Economic Review,* 59 (Dec. 1969), 897-905. See my "Comment" and Eisner's "Reply," *American Economic Review* (June 1971). See also the recent pathbreaking article by William Krehm, "La stabilité des prix et le secteur public," *Revue Economique,* 21 (May 1970), 425-66. Krehm approaches the phenomena of tax push in terms of the concepts of the "*social lien,* the total accretion of all taxes upon price" and "an *aggregate shift function* determining the proportion of total taxation shifting into aggregate price" (p. 426).

[13] M. Krzyaniak and R.A. Musgrave, *The Shifting of the Corporation Income Tax* (Baltimore, 1963).

94   Adverse Effects of Tax and Interest Hikes As
                Strengthening the Case for Incomes Policies – or
                A Part of the Elephant

his critic R.J. Gordon points out implies the tax is inflationary.[14] However, Musgrave is reluctant to commit himself, professing ignorance of which "direction" shifting takes.[15]

A similar gap in our theories is detected by G. Horwich who writes that economists have failed to integrate their theories "of interest as a production cost, as a return to the claimants of capital, and as a variable in monetary policy."[16] Horwich, however, while stressing his "Keynesianism" solves the dilemma of "interest push inflation" in a thoroughly "classical" manner: showing that in such a world tight money will result in a fall in depreciation allowances thus "financing" the higher interest payments without a cost or price hike. Unfortunately, the real world does not appear to conform to Horwich's assumptions.

But Horwich is far from alone in using "classical" assumptions in "Keynesian" analysis. The "classical dichotomy" which Keynes complained of and sought to bridge is still very much with us. Keynes pictured economists as on "one side of the moon" in their theory of value, or micro theory, and on the other side in their macro theory of money and prices.[17] He sought "to escape from this double life and to bring the theory of prices as a whole back to close contact with the theory of value."[18] But in vain! Keynes' disciples perpetuate the classical schizophrenia – making use of a quantity and/or "excess" demand theory of the price level with little or no reference to their micro

---

[14] "An increase in corporation income tax rates is a perverse tool for short-run stabilization policy in inflationary periods, since corporations react immediately by raising prices and thus work against the attempts of policy makers to stabilize prices," R.J. Gordon, "The Incidence of the Corporation Income Tax in US Manufacturing, 1925-62," *American Economic Review,* 57 (Sept. 1967), 731-58. Gordon rejects Krzyaniak and Musgrave's finding that the corporate tax is shifted and accounts for the continued bouyancy of after-tax profits in the face of higher taxes by increased productivity of capital over time. Byron G. Spencer "The Shifting of the Corporation Income Tax in Canada 1926-65," *Can. Jour. Econ.,* 2 (Feb. 1969), 21-34 follows Krzyaniak and Musgrave in estimating technique and reaches similar results. Spencer answers many of the objections raised by Gordon and others in his "Reply" to Robert J. Levesque's "Comment." See *Can. Jour. Econ.,* 3 (Feb. 1970), 158-67 for this exchange. Krzyaniak and Musgrave's conclusions have also been attacked by Cragg, Harberger, and Mieszkowski who maintain that time series analyses of incidence can be all too easily made to "prove" anything and therefore actually prove very little. See J.G. Cragg, A.C. Harberger, and Peter Mieszkowski, "Empirical Evidence on the Incidence of the Corporation Income Tax," *Journal of Political Economy,* 75, 6 (Dec. 1967), 811-21; and M. Kryzaniak and R.A. Musgrave, "Corporation Tax Shifting: A Response," and J.G. Cragg, A.L. Harberger and Peter Mieszkowski, "Corporation Tax Shifting: Rejoinder," *ibid.,* 78, 4 (July-Aug. 1970), 768-77.

[15] M. Krzyaniak and R.A. Musgrave, "Incidence of the Corporation Income Tax in US Manufacturing: Comment," *American Economic Review,* 58 (Dec. 1968), 1358-60. Neither in this comment, nor in Gordon's Reply are the macro implications of forward shifting explored further.

[16] G. Horwich, "Tight Money, Monetary Restraint, and the Price Level," *Journal of Finance,* 21 (March 1966), 15-33. See my "Comment" and Horwich's "Reply," *Journal of Finance,* 26 (March 1971), 152-8.

[17] J.M. Keynes, *The General Theory of Employment, Interest and Money* (New York, 1936), 292. (GT henceforth.)

[18] *GT,* 293.

and tax incidence theory, regarding them merely as theories of relative prices."[19] Or as Weintraub puts the matter, economists embraced
Keynes' theory of income and employment, or Q and N theory, but
neglected or rejected his theory of the price level, or P theory:[20]

To Keynes the price level is determined by the wage level – or
more inclusively, by the "cost-unit," a weighted average of the rewards of the factors entering into marginal prime cost – and the scale
of output.[21] Changes in the money supply, interest rates, taxes and
government expenditures exert their influence on the price level
through their influence on the cost-unit and through the law of diminishing returns, always excepting, as Keynes did, conditions of
completely full employment where "true inflation" can occur.[22] Turning to the long run, Keynes adopted an almost solely "wage push"
explanation of the secular tendency for prices to rise.[23] Thus in terms
of $MV \equiv PQ \equiv kW$ truisms Keynes may be interpreted as being an
"ultra right-to-leftist" in holding that wage (W) increases cause PQ
increases and ultimately M increases – in fact impelling us to invent
paper, checkbook,and now the near monies and money substitutes
the "left-to-rightist" monetarists bring into the argument to explain
events.

Aggregate supply-demand versus 45⁰ Keynesianism

Keynes sketched an analysis of employment and prices in terms of
aggregate supply and aggregate demand in money terms (or deflated
by a wage index).[24] However, Samuelson and Hansen substituted the
45⁰ line analysis with all magnitudes in "real" or constant price level

---

[19] A near perfect example of the classical dichotomy is to be found in Charles E.
McLure Jr.'s "Tax Incidence, Macroeconomic Policy, and Absolute Prices,"
Quarterly Journal of Economics, 84 (May 1970), 254-67. McLure sets up a
Walrasian world of nine equations in which the first eight equations determine
relative prices and incomes and these are affected by taxes. However, the ninth
equation, which determines the absolute price level, is the quantity theory with
constant velocity.

[20] Sidney Weintraub, "Keynes and the Monetarists," *Can. Jour. Econ.*, 4 (Feb.
1971), 37-49.

[21] *GT*, 302, or, "In a single industry its particular price-level depends partly on the
rate of remuneration of the factors of production which enter into its marginal
cost, and partly on the scale of output. *There is no reason to modify this
conclusion when we pass to industry as a whole.* The general price-level
depends partly on the rate of remuneration of the factors of production which
enter into marginal cost and partly on the scale of output as a whole" (p. 294)
(emphasis mine).

[22] *GT*, 303. We approached, but at no time achieved such "full" employment in
the expansion of recent years. At all times there was a margin of unemployed
resources. A few figures: in 1969 382,000 of those in the labour force were
unemployed (4.7 per cent). 137,000 more would have to be employed before
Canada would have achieved the 3 per cent rate of unemployment set several
years ago by the Economic Council of Canada as a feasible and desirable goal
(a rate we haven't approached since 1956). Source: Bank of Canada, *Statistical
Summary,* March 1970 (Ottawa, 1970), 230.

[23] *GT*, 306-9, and in the following: "Experience since the age of Solon at least . . .
indicates what a knowledge of human nature would lead us to expect, namely,
that there is a steady tendency for the wage-unit to rise over long periods of
time and that it can be reduced only amidst the decay and dissolution of
economic society. Thus, apart altogether from progress and increasing population, a gradually increasing stock of money has proven imperative" (p. 340n).

[24] *GT*, chaps. 3, 4, and Book 5, entitled "Money Wages and Prices," contain his
development of the aggregate supply side.

96   Adverse Effects of Tax and Interest Hikes As
Strengthening the Case for Incomes Policies – or
A Part of the Elephant

terms, and this diagram has been presented to a generation of
economists as the essence of Keynes' thought. More recently, Weintraub has re-emphasized the supply side and wage bill focus of the
general theory.[25] Coupling the aggregate supply and demand functions to a fact also noted by Keynes, that the wage share is close to
constant,[26] Weintraub arrived at an analysis which I believe to be true
to Keynes' intent and highly enlightening regarding inflation causes
and control measures. Figure 1 presents a sketch of Weintraub's
model adapted to our question of the expected and the adverse
effects of tax or interest hikes to prevent inflation.

---

[25] Sidney Weintraub, *An Approach to the Theory of Income Distribution*
(Philadelphia, 1958); *A Keynesian Theory of Employment, Growth, and Income
Distribution* (Philadelphia, 1966).

[26] For a comparison of the stability of the wage share reciprocal (k) and money
velocity (V) see John H. Hotson, *International Comparisons of Money Velocity
and Wage Mark-Ups* (New York, 1968).

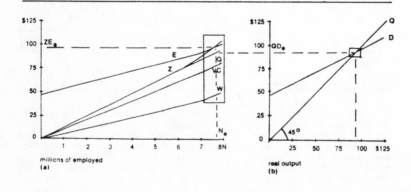

Figure 1
*(a) Aggregate supply (Z), aggregate demand (E), and employment (N) model;
(b) real output (Q), and real demand (D) model.*

The diagram on the right is the familiar 45⁰ line with real output *(Q)* and aggregate demand in constant prices *(D)* in equilibrium at QD_e. The marginal propensity to expend is 0.5. To the left of Figure 1 we have a model of the same economy in terms of aggregate supply *(Z)* and aggregate demand in current prices *(E)* as functions of the level of employment *(N)*.[27] The wage level is assumed to be constant unless more than 7 million are employed, thus the wage function *(W)* is linear up to this employment level. If employment exceeds 7 million the economy enters a "Phillips curve" region where increased employment is accompanied by some increases in the average money wage. Variable costs *(VC)* are taken to consist of wages, interest on short-term debts, imports, and indirect business taxes. It is assumed that variable interest payments and imports vary directly with the level of employment, given the level of interest rates, and that indirect business taxes vary proportionately with the wage function.[28]

The real output or production function *(Q)* is here drawn with constant returns as employment increases. Constant returns are here specified as a bow to the empiricists who detect little evidence of diminishing returns to labour over the swings of the business cycle. If anything they find increasing productivity with higher utilization. A number of cogent reasons[29] have been given for these results leading us to accept Bodkin's conclusion that "classical diminishing returns is probably confined in its operation to a range very close to full utilization of the labour (and capital) factors of production."[30] This finding is an encouraging one for it means that the attainment of full employment need not entail a fall in the real wage with consequent inflation, social friction and wage push.

---

[27] Martin Bronfenbrenner is fond of referring to the *IS = LM* diagram as "Islamic Keynesianism." Here we go further to the east for enlightenment to "*Zen* Keynesianism." Here rather than in the "Keynesian cross" of the 45⁰ diagram is to be found the true cross.

[28] Corporate profits taxes are omitted from variable cost to sidestep the controversy over the shifting of this tax as not essential to the present discussion. In analysing an open economy, such as that of Canada, it is appropriate to recognize the importance of the foreign sector explicitly rather than netting out exports against imports. Therefore aggregate supply is here defined as Gross National Product *plus* imports while aggregate demand in GNP plus *gross,* rather than net, exports. The aggregate supply function thus represents the total of goods and services which Canadian producers wish to make available from domestic production plus imports. The aggregate demand function is the total demand for Canadian output-domestic demand being a function of the Canadian employment, interest and tax level while demand for Canadian exports is treated as autonomous.

[29] Such as: that firms do not minimize short-run costs during slack periods, keeping on employees with little to do; that units of capital and labour are shut down or re-employed together; that given some degree of monopoly power firms may find themselves at a level of output where marginal cost falls as output expands; that in cyclical upswings the *Q* function is up-shifted from the new investment, and so on. See T.A. Wilson and O. Eckstein, "Short-Run Productivity Behavior in US Manufacturing," *Review of Economics and Statistics,* 46 (Feb. 1964), 41-59; Edwin Kuh, "Cyclical and Secular Labor Productivity in United States Manufacturing," *ibid.,* 47, (Feb. 1965), 1-12; Robert E. Lucas Jr., "Capacity, Overtime, and Empirical Production Functions," *American Economic Review,* Proceedings, 60 (May 1970), 23-7.

[30] Ronald G. Bodkin, "Real Wages and Cyclincal Variations in Employment: A Re-examination of the Evidence," *Can. Jour. Econ.*, 2 (Aug. 1969), 353-74.

98   Adverse Effects of Tax and Interest Hikes As
            Strengthening the Case for Incomes Policies – or
            A Part of the Elephant

Marginal cost pricing under pure competition is assumed so that the price level *(P)* is given by the change in variable cost divided by the (here constant) marginal product of the variable factors.[31] The aggregate supply function is the real output, or production *(Q)*, value of a given employment level multiplied by the price index. The *Q* function is thus constant dollar GNP plus real imports, while *Z* is current dollar GNP plus imports. Aggregate demand *(E)* in current prices is likewise derived from aggregate real demand *(D)* by multiplying real demand by the price index.

In the fairly happy world of near full employment in which we live, thanks to Keynes – or rather thanks to "military Keynesianism," we directly observe only the last 10 per cent or so of the entire, *Z, E, N, VC,* and *W* functions. Thus we only observe, or need to be concerned with, the area within the box in Figure 1. Here much is happening which is obscured in the simplistic 45° model. The intersection of *Z* and *E* determines the equilibrium level of GNP plus imports *(ZE_e)*, employment *(N_e)* and the price level *(P_e)*.

---

[31] Thus $P = MC = \triangle VC / \triangle Q$. It may be objected, however, that it is inconsistent to assume *(a)* pure competition in product markets, and *(b)* that wages are not flexible downward. Pure competition is assumed for simplicity and to demonstrate that the perverse effects of interest and tax hikes shown do not depend upon mark-up pricing or other non-maximizing non-competitive behavior. If these real world imperfections are added to the model the conclusions are re-enforced, at some cost in complexity and, I believe, persuasiveness.

Downward inflexibility of the average wage is the foundation upon which post Keynesian economics have been built – its very reason for being, so no apology for the assumption is offered.

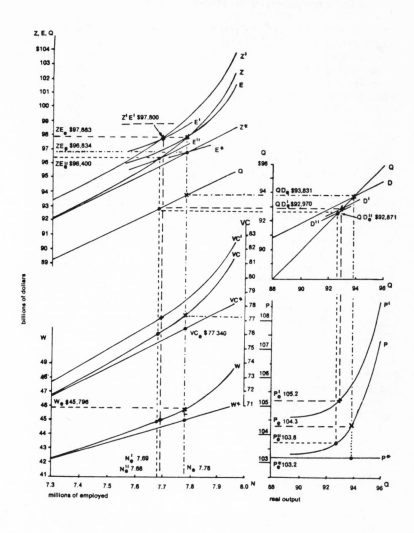

Figure 2
*Canada 1969 aggregate supply (Z), aggregate demand (E), and the price level
(P). Actual equilibrium (ZEe, Pe, QDe etc.); hypothetical response to indirect
tax (Z'E'e, P'e, QD'e); to direct tax (ZE''e, P''e); and to incomes policy (ZE*e, P*e).*

100   Adverse Effects of Tax and Interest Hikes As
Strengthening the Case for Incomes Policies – or
A Part of the Elephant

1969 in Canada – policy alternatives

Figure 2 is a "blow-up" of the boxed areas of the ZEN and 45^0 diagrams together with a separate diagram for the price index. Let us use Figure 2 to examine anti-inflation policy alternatives. The equilibrium values $(ZE_e, Q_e, N_e$ etc.$)$ are those actually attained by the Canadian economy in 1969; thus current dollar GNP was $78,537 million, imports totalled $19,346 million, for a ZE_e total of $97,883 million, and 7,780,000 out of the labour force of 8,162,000 were employed.[32] Since the price level rose in 1969 to 104.3 on a 1968 base, real output was only $93,831 million " in 1968 dollars."[33] Labour income,[34] (W) totalled $45,796 million, and indirect taxes less subsidies, (T_i) were $10,647 million. Interest, and miscellaneous investment income was $3042 million, but not all of this represented interest on short-term borrowing by business. By my calculation short-term business debt totalled $18,255 million.[35] Applying the prime rate of 8.5 per cent which obtained during the second half of 1969 to this total yields the calculation that business-interest payments on short-term debt (i_v) totalled $1551 million, or about one-half of the total. Thus variable cost totalled $77,340 million $(VC = W + i_v + M + T_i)$. By how much would these figures have differed if instead of 7,780,000 Canadians being employed in 1969, 7,600,000 or 7,900,000 were working? For guidance we turn to the Phillips curve theorists and find not one, but several estimates of the determinants of the trade-off between unemployment and wage and price level change in Canada.[36] The trade-offs of Figure 2 amount to the estimate that with the US wage level increasing 7 per cent in 1969, and with the Canadian price level increasing 4.3 per cent over 1968, the Canadian wage level would have increased by 7.2 per cent over 1968 even if some 10 per cent of the labour force had been unemployed, rather than the 8.7 per cent increase actually recorded with 4.7 per cent unemployment. I believe this to be a good "ball-park" estimate of the actual situation, but those

---

[32] Dominion Bureau of Statistics, *National Income and Expenditure Accounts* (first quarter, 1970); Bank of Canada, *Statistical Summary,* 16 (May 1970), 396.

[33] The GNP deflator in 1969 was 104.7 on a 1968 base while the import prices deflator was 102.8. GNP and imports were thus deflated separately and summed for the composite index of 104.3.

[34] Sum of wages, salaries, and supplementary labour income, military pay and allowances, and accrued net income of farm operators from farm production.

[35] Sum of loans from chartered banks to farmers and business, other business loans, short-term, sales, finance and consumer loan companies and other commercial paper, wholesale and retail finance and net new issues of corporate bonds. Bank of Canada, *Statistical Summary,* 16 (March 1970), 176-8, 205, 212.

[36] Reference is to R.G. Bodkin, E.P. Bond, G.L. Reuber, and T.R. Robinson, *Price Stability and High Employment: The Options for Canadian Policy,* Economic Council of Canada, Special Study No. 5 (Ottawa, 1966).

who do not like it are urged to substitute their own – our results do not depend crucially upon these particular estimates.[37]

Once the particular shape of real output *(Q)* and wage *(W)* functions are chosen the other functions are derived very simply. Marginal product along the *Q* function was determined and divided into unit changes in *VC* to determine the profit-maximizing price function.[38] The price level function is graphed in the lower right quadrant of Figure 2 and labelled *P*. The price level at each level of employment is multiplied by the corresponding real output level to determine the aggregate supply *(Z)* function. Appendix Table I gives the figures for all of this.

In the upper right of Figure 1 we have the 45⁰ equilibrium *(QDₑ)* at $93,831 million. Real demand magnitudes were multiplied by the price index corresponding to output magnitudes to derive current dollar demand *(E)* shown intersecting *Z* in the upper left of Figure 2 at $97,883 million, employment level 7.78 million.

Tax hikes – deflationary?

Suppose that before the inflationary implications of these *ex ante* 1969 functions had hardened into actual wage hikes, price boosts and output decisions, the federal government had recognized the inflationary potential of the economy and determined to thwart it by raising taxes while not increasing expenditures. Suppose the new tax became effective on January 1, 1969 and was designed to increase tax receipts by $1 billion at employment level 7.78. This is a fairly large

---

[37] The wage adjustment curve in Figure 2 is derived from the Bodkin *et al* steady state wage adjustment relationship 5.7e with the percentage change in wage equal to 8.68 per cent when 4.7 per cent of the labour force is unemployed. *Ibid.*, 164.

Unemployment (per cent)	Wage change per year (per cent)
2.5	12.65
3.0	10.90
4.0	9.25
4.7 actual	8.68
5.0	8.40
6.0	7.90
7.0	7.60
8.0	7.45
9.0	7.30
10.0	7.22

Curve 5.7e was the "worst" trade-off curve estimated for wage increases as unemployment dropped, and the "best" for decreased wage hikes as unemployment increased. Thus Figure 2 is based on highly favourable assumptions for "demand suppression" policy.

[38] The marginal product of the variable factors was set equal to $9531 per annum since the change in variable cost when one more man is employed at equilibrium was calculated to be $9941 and this divided by $9531 yields the equilibrium price index of 104.3. This marginal product was assumed constant at all employment levels. Those who accept the rest of my argument, but deplore this departure from neoclassical rectitude are invited to modify Appendix Table I by choosing any degree of diminishing returns they wish. It takes a considerable degree of diminishing returns to reverse the main point of the paper – that increased indirect taxes, even if unmatched by increased government outlay, will *raise* the price level. Thus if it is assumed that the 7,690,000th Canadian employed had a MP of $9940 vs $9531 for the 7,780,000th, raising taxes as below would leave the price level unchanged, and a higher degree of diminishing returns would cause demand reduction to *reduce* the price level. However, this is a larger degree of diminishing returns, one assumes, than could escape the net of our econometric colleagues.

102

Adverse Effects of Tax and Interest Hikes As
Strengthening the Case for Incomes Policies –or A Part
of the Elephant

fiscal policy move, comparable to the US surtax of 1968. Suppose, however, that the new tax was a sales tax which is fully shifted, raising variable cost from VC to VC' while leaving money incomes at an employment level unchanged. As the result of this tax shifting, aggregate supply moves upward to Z' so that at every employment level the price level is higher, as indicated by the price function labelled P'. At the initial income level the price level rises to 105.7.

How much will the tax hike reduce real demand? Because the sales tax hike is passed forward in higher prices it does not reduce real private income dollar for dollar. Real private income (Y_r) at a level of employment (N) with indirect taxes (T_i) at their initial level is given by $Y_r = Z - T_i/P$. Real private income after the tax hike (Y_r) at each N level is thus given by $Y'_r = Z' - T'_i/P'$ and the change in real private income is given by $Y_r - Y'_r$ at each N level. Appendix Table II gives the figures. Real demand is reduced by one-half the fall in real income.[39] The new demand function D' intersects the $45°$ line at \$92,970 million, thus the effect of the tax is to reduce the real output of the economy by \$861 million, cost about 90,000 Canadians their jobs, raise the percentage unemployed from 4.7 to 5.8, and *raise* the price level. As can be seen in the lower right quadrant of Figure 2, the equilibrium price on P' with $Q \approx$ \$93 billion is 105.2 as against 104.3 along P when our actual 1969 real supply of \$93,831 million was produced.

Was the 'incidence'' of the tax on consumers or workers? On the one hand we can say that the tax was fully shifted forward to consumers in higher prices and that it raised the price level at $N = 7.69$ million from 103.9 to 105.2. However, since in the absence of the tax the price level would have risen to 104.3 anyway, we can argue that the tax was partially shifted backward on the workers by holding down the pace of wage increases. Since 90 per cent of consumption is out of labour income we can also argue that the burden is almost wholly on the same persons whether as consumers or workers. Clearly, the unemployed get hurt both as consumers and by loss of income. Clearly too, Canada was better off without this tax.

Let us contrast this unhappy result with the effects of raising the personal income tax. Suppose the income tax collects the same amount of revenue at each level of N as does the sales tax but that it is not shifted. In order to calculate the fall in real income we divide the tax receipts by the initial price function (P) and real demand falls by one-half this amount to D''. Thus real demand falls slightly more with an income than with a sales tax. The effects on real output and employment are therefore somewhat larger, \$960 million and 100,000 respectively and since the aggregate supply function does not shift as when the sales tax is imposed, the equilibrium price level is lowered to 103.8 and ZE''_e is \$96,400 million. See Appendix Table III. The burden on an unemployed individual is somewhat less than in the case of indirect taxes but there are about 10,000 more of them. To argue that Canada is better off because of this tax is to argue that is worth about \$960 million in lost output per year to reduce inflation by one-half of an index point.

---

[39] It may be that a marginal propensity to spend of 0.5, and resulting multiplier of 2, is too small. If the MPE should be 0.6 or 0.7 tax hikes would have a greater demand reducing effect than those shown in Figure 2. However, given the shape and location of P' in Figure 2 even greatly decreased real demand entails a higher equilibrium price if the demand suppressant is an indirect tax. The multiplier in the US appears to be in the 2-2.5 range. (See Council of Economic Advisors, *Economic Report of the President* (Washington 1963, 1964, 1965).) The large import "leak" in Canada makes for a small multiplier.

Eisner has argued, however, that the actual fall in real demand occasioned by a rise in taxes will be much smaller than the above analysis would suggest.[40] Eisner states that the US surtax was advertised as a temporary tax and households and firms expenditures are based on their permanent income estimates. Since a temporary tax does not change these estimates it has very little effect on aggregate demand, but instead the savings function falls, as happened in the US in 1968-9. If Eisner is correct, we must change our conclusion and hold that the sales tax increase would raise the price level beyond 105.8 and the income tax increase would depress the price level but little below the actual equilibrium of 104.3.

Interest hikes – deflationary?

Let us turn to monetary policy. Clearly, it would take a very large increase in the interest rate to shift up variable cost by $1 billion. What would be the effects upon real income of such an increase in interest rates? Here we recognize an important difference between fiscal and monetary policy. In theory, at least, the "anti" inflationary tax receipts will not be respent. However, those receiving higher interest incomes presumably spend more, offsetting part or all of the fall in investment spending which was supposed to make the interest hike depressionary and presumably deflationary.[41] Indeed, if firms' plans are as little affected by "transitory" changes as Eisner maintains, the result may be only a very slight fall in real demand and a considerable rise in the price level. Certainly there is little evidence that doubling the rate of interest the world over in recent years has decreased investment as a percentage of GNP.[42] Thus there is even less justification for the idea that interest hikes will stop inflation than for indirect tax hikes.

Incomes policies – deflationary?

Let us contrast tax and interest hikes, which we have argued are of "doubtful sign" relative to the price level, although depressionary, with an incomes policy. Suppose that in 1969 Canada had an incomes policy which was successful in holding the pace of wage gains to 7.1 per cent, rather than the 8.7 per cent gain actually recorded. This is about 2/3rds of the effectiveness achieved by the US "Guideposts" in 1966,[43] before they were abandoned in the face of the inflationary

---

[40] Eisner, "Fiscal and Monetary Policy Reconsidered," 898.

[41] Interest incomes of persons will rise more rapidly than does the interest on short-term business debt, because of the existence of the national and other governmental debt. In addition, if the higher rates are adhered to, an ever increasing fraction of long-term debts come due and are refinanced at the higher rate. W.E. Weber, "The Effect of Interest Rates on Aggregate Consumption," *American Economic Review,* 60 (Sept. 1970), 591-600, concludes that consumers "increase current consumption in response to the interest rate increase" (p. 600).

[42] Thus in Canada in 1947-9 Investment averaged 21 per cent of GNP while in 1967-9 it averaged 23 per cent of GNP.

[43] G.L. Perry, "Wages and the Guideposts: Reply," *American Economic Review,* 59 (June 1969), 365-70. Perry estimates that during 1966 the guideposts reduced the pace of wage increases by an average of 2.53 per cent below their historical relationship from 1947-60 and that upon their abandonment the wage increases went back to their historical level (p. 369). See also G. Perry, "Wages and Guideposts," *ibid.,* 57 (Sept. 1967), 897-904; and P.S. Anderson, M.L. Wachter, and A.W. Throop, "Comment," *ibid.,* 59 (June 1969), 351-8.

104   Adverse Effects of Tax and Interest Hikes As
          Strengthening the Case for Incomes Policies – or
          A Part of the Elephant

enemy. If the wage function could have been held linear, as in Figure 2 *(W*)*, the variable cost function also becomes linear, denoted *(VC*)*, and the price function *(P*)*, becomes horizontal at $P = 103.2$. The aggregate supply function *(Z*)*, likewise becomes linear, and unexpected bonus, the aggregate demand function *(D*)*, intersects it at the initial employment level[44], so everyone employed in 1969 remains employed and the price index rises to only 103.2.

Having approached the Economic Council's price goal of a rise in the price index of less than 2 per cent, the country would have been in an excellent position to go for the Council's second goal of a 3 per cent unemployment level. According to our model this employment level could have been achieved with no additional rise in the price deflator provided the wage level did not rise more than 7.1 per cent – again assuming away diminishing returns. The model suggests further that if the necessary nudge to aggregate demand took the form of interest and indirect tax cuts to lower the price level function we could have done somewhat better than this on the price front. However, simultaneous achievement of both goals would seem to require an incomes policy with real "teeth" and conventional wisdom concerning the shape of the elephant, excuses such that Canadian inflation is "made in America" where so many of our unions have their head offices, and constitutional difficulties in obtaining provincial-federal cooperation, stand in the way.

Implications and conclusions

Economists must strive mightily to integrate their micro and macro price theories, and develop the macro implications of their micro theories, in order to arrive at a general theory of the "elephant."

By taking account of the adverse cost effects of present "anti" inflation policies we could develop workable policies which minimize or eliminate these effects.[45] Thus lower interest rates to stimulate investment, *combined* with consumer credit controls might be indicated. Or if it is deemed necessary to make home construction the "goat" of credit contraction this could be accomplished by requiring higher down payments and shorter mortgage amortization periods rather than by higher interest rates. For decades we have moved in the opposite direction; with each hike in interest rates we have stretched out the mortgage contract to keep the monthly payment within people's means.

---

[44] On the assumption that aggregate real demand is not affected by reducing the path of money wage increases. Whether reducing the rate of wage increases would raise or lower real demand is an interesting question. Certainly, an end to "inflationary psychology" would lower real demand from consumers and investors. On the other hand, a lowered price level with a given nominal money supply increases the real money supply, lowers interest rates, and increases demand.

[45] Sir Roy Harrod has expressed similar views. He writes "It is to be remembered that some of the weapons of 'deflation' for example high interest rates and indirect taxes tend to raise costs. I would not go so far as to affirm that these measures of 'deflation' usually have a price inflationary effect. I will rather maintain the neutrality of a strict agnostic . . . What is now happening in the United States may be an important test case. The stern deflationary measures undertaken by the US authorities in 1969 seem indeed to have had an effect in reducing the rate of increase of demand during that year. But at the close of that year they had still had no effect in reducing the rate of price increases." Roy Harrod, "Reassessment of Keynes' Views on Money," *Journal of Political Economy,* 78, 4 (July-Aug. 1970), 617-25.

If the public sector is to continue to expand relatively to the private sector, so that Krehm's "social lien" grows, a rising price index can only be prevented if wage and other incomes grow more slowly than does average productivity. Since "tax shift" inflation is in part an "illusory" element in rising prices resulting from a "growing package of government services being embedded in the rising prices of goods and services purchased by consumers and business,"[46] it might be better to adjust our indices than attempt to offset it fully.

The more "direct" taxes are the better they are for demand reduction without price hikes from attempts to shift their burden. However, in the absence of an incomes policy with some ultimate legal sanction, even the personal income tax might trigger a wage push to restore take home pay. Sanctions should be no less thinkable here, nor more frequently invoked, than those penalties which compel us to pay taxes, or which induce bankers to maintain legal reserves. Thus we come to the crucial point: with control over the pace of income changes, especially wage changes, we can simultaneously attain "full" employment and stable prices. Without this "essential element"[47] of Keynes' system we cannot.

Space will permit no discussion here of the mechanics of incomes policy administration, beyond the usual observation that they are only necessary within the industrial sector where firms and unions exercise considerable discretion and that even there they need not be very elaborate to have important price reducing effects, – for as Galbraith puts it, "it is relatively easy to fix prices that are already fixed."[48] A fresh approach designed to increase the incentive of employers to use their "countervailing power" to resist excessive wage hikes has recently been suggested by Weintraub.[49]

This is not to argue that "incomes policies" are the be-all-and-end-all of inflation control and that we can neglect fiscal and monetary moves. Paul Samuelson is fond of his "Neoclassical Synthesis" argument that "mastery of the modern analysis of income determination genuinely validates the basic classical pricing principles."[50] Perhaps in addition a "grand neo-orthodox synthesis" argument may be proposed – that price and wage restraints can validate Samuelson's assumption that monetary and fiscal policies have their impact on income and employment rather than the price level so long as care is taken not to exceed the "full employment ceiling."

Thus the "incomist" approach takes the elephant by the nose which is, after all, the best way to lead the beast – aided from time to time by "fiscalist" pokes in the sides and "monetarist" kicks in the rear.

---

[46] Economic Council of Canada, *Third Annual Review*, 224.

[47] Joan Robinson, *Economics: An Awkward Corner* (London, 1969), 19. Keynes implied an incomes policy would be necessary to reconcile full employment and stable prices and sketched every element of such a policy save one – how to get people to comply. See *GT*, 270–1.

[48] J.K. Galbraith, *A Theory of Price Control* (Cambridge, 1952), 17. This little book, based on Galbraith's experiences as head of OPA during the second world war, is highly relevant to present concerns.

[49] Sidney Weintraub, "An Incomes Policy to Stop Inflation," *Lloyd's Bank Review*, 99 (Jan. 1971), 1–12.

[50] P.A. Samuelson, *Economics*, 6th ed. (New York, 1964), 361.

106   Adverse Effects of Tax and Interest Hikes As
Strengthening the Case for Incomes Policies – or
A Part of the Elephant

Addendum – June 1976

At the time (June 1970) that I gave an earlier version of the above
chapter as a paper at the Canadian Economics Association Meetings,
I thought of myself as being rather daring. Although I had presented
the basic argument in the *Nebr. Jour. of Econ.* two and one half years
earlier, and had not been attacked for it, I was still uneasy. There was
always the chance that no one had read the earlier article – or at least
no one who knew how to "write economics" – despite the fact that I
had mailed out three hundred copies to every "big name" that I could
think of.

But I need not have worried. The paper was "well received,"
discussant Ron G. Bodkin politely steered me away from a couple of
errors I had made in the draft and to top it all off, *Globe and Mail*
reporter David Crane gave my paper a three-column spread on June
9th. His piece contains the following passage which rather neatly
reverses the economists' pecking order and direction of inspiration.

*"Support for an incomes policy to get a wage and salary settlements
was voiced by a number of economists at the Canadian Economics
Association. Joan Robinson, a Cambridge University economist, took
the same basic position as Mr. Hotson, as did Sidney Weintraub of the
University of Waterloo."*

As a result of Crane's article I was contacted by William Krehm, a
journalist, businessman, and student of economics who had long
been frustrated by economists' inability to see what any businessman
knows – that higher taxes and interest rates means higher, not lower
prices. Our resulting friendship and intellectual interaction has cul-
minated in his dedicating his newly published book, *Price in a Mixed
Economy,* (Thornwood, Toronto 1975) to me as follows. "To John
Hotson, a beacon of open-mindedness in the ranks of the dismal
science."

Since 1970 tax and interest "push" inflation, which I feared might
be dismissed as "Hotson's heresy" have become increasingly established, as a few citations will indicate.

Jump and Wilson[51] analyzed the effects on price levels and unemployment in Canada of three policy options: a 10% reduction in
personal income tax, a 50% reduction in building materials tax, and a
50% reduction in all federal sales taxes, with the aid of the University
of Toronto TRACE econometric model. The resemblance between
their 65 behavioral equations and 79 identities model simulation results and of my own french curve and desk calculator methods increases my faith in econometrics.

Where I "guestimate" above that a $1 billion hike in excise taxes
in 1969 would reduce real output $861 million, raise the unemploy-
ment rate from 4.7 to 5.8% and raise the price level from 104.3 to 105.2
on 1968 base; Jump and Wilson estimate that a 50% decrease in
Canadian federal sales taxes would reduce revenues $986 million the
first year (but increase the deficit by only 70% of this), increase real
output by $856 million, reduce unemployment from 6.02 to 5.64%
while reducing the general price level by 1.4%.

The close fit of our estimates of the effect of a change in the income tax is also remarkable, given that my work was simple comparative statics (with no adjustment for the increase of the labour force) and I was trying to be "conservative" while Jump and Wilson were aiming for an accurate simulation. The figures are as follows:

Mine   T + $1,000,   Q + $960   P + .5%   U + 1.1
Theirs   T − $1,000,   Q − 700   P − .2%   U − .3

Two articles by Robert Eisner[52] have contributed greatly to the willingness of the profession to concede that our "anti-inflationary" policies may have been inflationary, both for the reasons I have advanced and several others.

Several other articles should be cited for completeness, but my sense that tax and interest push have now become establishment come from their endorsement by Blinder and Solow[53] and W.W. Heller.[54].

As Blinder and Solow put it,

"The basic remark is so obvious that it is almost embarrassing that it does not appear in textbook expositions of the analytics of fiscal policy.[55]. It is simply this: most taxes are, in the short or long run, incorporated into business costs, and therefore (at least partially) passed on to the consumer in higher prices. Therefore, if the contractionary fiscal medicine administrated to cure inflation takes the form of higher taxes it may well have the desired deflationary impact on aggregate demand, but also an unintended cost-push inflationary impact on aggregate supply. The net result is, in many cases, unclear on purely theoretical grounds ... The clearest example of an inflationary tax hike is probably an increase in excise taxes ... A similar argument can be made with respect to the corporate income tax ... an analogous argument applies to increases in the personal income tax as a tool to cure inflation ... We conclude then that tax raising may not be the best way to curb inflation ... For the sake of symmetry we should also note that tight money as a cure for inflation runs into analogous objections. Restrictive monetary policies generally imply high interest rates and interest payments are a significant component to cost of many firms."[56]

---

[52] Robert Eisner, "Fiscal and Monetary Policy Reconsidered," *Am. Econ. Rev.* 59, (December 1969) 897-905; "What Went Wrong?" *Jour. Pol. Econ.*, 79 (May/June 1971) 629-41. See also comments by Bent Hansen, John H. Hotson, Barbara Henneberry and James G. Witte, Keith M. Carlson and reply by Robert Eisner *Am. Econ. Rev.*, 61, (June 1971) 444-61.

[53] Alan S. Blinder and Robert M. Solow, "Analytical Foundations of Fiscal Policy," *The Economics of Public Policy,*(©by the Brookings Institution, Washington, D.C.), 3-115. See also Christopher Green, "Recent Inflation: Its Causes and Implications for Public Policy," *Canadian Public Policy II*, (Winter 1976.)

[54] Walter W. Heller, "What's Right With Economics?" *Am. Econ. Rev.*, 65, (March 1975) 1-26.

[55] It is beginning to: See Nancy S. Barrett, *The Theory of Macroeconomic Policy*, (Englewood, Prentice, 1972) 275-6 for brief development of this point; John Lindauer, *Macroeconomics*, 2nd. ed., (New York, Wiley, 1971) 378-82; G. Brunhild and R.H. Burton, *Macroeconomic Theory*, (Englewood, Prentice, 1974) 439-40. Thus "policy push" becomes "practically immortal."

[56] Blinder and Solow, 98-101.

108.   Adverse Effects of Tax and Interest Hikes As
        Strengthening the Case for Incomes Policies – or
        A Part of the Elephant

In Walter W. Heller's Presidential Address to the American Economic Association with the heads-up title "What's Right With Economics?" the following belated recognition of the cost effects of tax hikes – but not, interestingly enough, interest hikes – occurs:

"Further work is needed to measure the cost-push effects of anti-inflationary tax increases that offset part of their demand damping effect. In recession, the cost-easing and demand-push effects work in happy harmony. They work at cross purposes in tax increases (though not in expenditure cuts) to curb inflation. The question of how large the offsetting cost-push effects, or aggregate supply effects, may be, is unresolved. In a high inflation economy, this is a serious gap in our fiscal policy knowledge."[57]

What it takes to embarrass one or "almost embarrass" one is a matter of personal constitution and it takes a tough-hided, unflapable person indeed to stand up in December 1974 and speak on "What's Right With Economics?" Blinder, Solow and Heller evidently have such a constitution: I do not. For close to a decade now I have been almost continuously blushing to be part of a profession which could advocate, as good macroeconomic policy, suppressing aggregate demand by tax and interest hikes, when we know, in the microeconomic part of our minds, that these moves boost prices by reducing supply. Now after tens of millions of man years of unemployment and perhaps $600 billion of GNP has been sacrificed to appease the inflationary gods, the priests discover they've been feeding the idols the wrong meat! Almost embarrassing!

That we've still plenty of unfinished work is indicated by Aaron Gordon when he says:

". . . . 'the forecasters fell flat on their faces when predicting price changes because they didn't have any way of estimating sectoral supply scarcity" and adds that we have not "even started to develop a theory of aggregate supply'."[58]

That economists remain slow learners may be seen from the fact that as of September 1974 the majority of the two dozen leading lights summoned to the White House "summit conference" on inflation advised President Ford on "the advisability of resisting popular demands for reimposing full-scale wage and price controls."[59]

Yet there is some progress. One of the basic anomolies obscuring the answer to the questions of incidence of various taxes, is that neo-classical models are being used to answer Keynesian questions. However, A. Asimakopulos and J.B. Burbidge[60] have recently remedied this defect in our approach to these important matters.

---

[57] Heller, 14.

[58] As quoted by Heller, p. 15.

[59] Heller, p. 4.

[60] A. Asimakopulos and J.B. Burbidge, "The Short Period Incidence of Taxation," *Economic Journal*, 84, (June 1974) 267-88. See also J.B. Burbidge, *The Short Incidence of Profits Taxes*, Working Paper No. 75-07, McMaster University. Hopefully, Burbidge's doctoral thesis, *The Incidence of Profits Taxes* will shortly be published.

Appendix Table 1

Numerical Values of Figure 2: Initial Equilibrium Functions

1 N	2 w	3 W (1) x (2)	4 iv	5 M	6 Ti	7 VC (3) ÷ (4) + (5) + (6)	8 ΔVC
7.3	$5806	$42,384	$1455	$18,147	$ 9859	$71,845	$ 9841
7.4	5809	42,987	1475	18,398	9987	72,847	9846
7.5	5817	43,628	1495	18,650	10,147	73,920	9854
7.6	5829	44,300	1515	18,901	10,296	75,012	9868
7.7	5852	45,060	1535	19,153	10,477	76,225	9902
7.78e	5886	45,796	1551	19,346	10,647	77,340	9941
7.8	5895	45,981	1556	19,404	10,690	77,631	9951
7.9	5985	47,282	1574	19,636	10,988	79,480	10,061
7.96*	6120	48,715	1587	19,791	11,328	81,421	10,227

9 ΔQ	10 P (8) ÷ (9)	11 Q	12 Z (10) x (11)	13 D	14 E (10) x (13)
↑	103.3	$89,259	$ 92,202	$ 91,503	$ 94,523
	103.3	90,210	93,187	91,992	95,028
	103.4	91,163	94,263	92,480	95,624
	103.5	92,116	95,340	92,966	96,220
	103.9	93,069	96,699	93,448	97,092
$9531	104.3	93,831	97,883	93,831	97,883
	104.4	94,022	98,159	93,926	98,059
	105.6	94,975	100,294	94,400	99,686
↓	107.3	95,547	102,520	94,867	101,792

e = initial equilibrium – actual figures in Canada in 1969.
*2.5 per cent unemployment – analysis not attempted beyond this point.
(1) N = millions of employed persons; (2) w = average labour income (dollars); (3) W = labour income (wages, salaries, and supplements + military pay + farm income (millions); (4) iv = interest on short-term business debts (i_{ve} x N/N_e) (millions); (5) M = imports of goods and services (M_e x N/N_e) (millions); (6) T_i indirect taxes less subsidies (T_{ie} x W/W_e) (millions); (7) VC = variable cost ($W + i_e + M + T_i$)(8)$ΔVC$ = change in variable cost when one additional man is employed (w x VC/W) (dollars); (9)$ΔQ$ = change in real output when one additional man is employed (marginal product of the variable factors) (dollars); (10) P = implicit deflator ($P = MC = ΔVC/ΔQ$) index; (11) Q = real supply (GNP + imports in 1968 prices) (millions); (12) Z = aggregate supply function (GNP + imports at current prices) (millions); (13) D = real demand (aggregate demand in 1968 prices) ($46,915.5 + 0.5Q$) (millions); (14) E = aggregate demand function in current prices ($E = PD$) (millions).

Note
columns 12 and 14 will not check as P was carried to further decimal places.

110   Adverse Effects of Tax and Interest Hikes As
                       Strengthening the Case for Incomes Policies – or
                       A Part of the Elephant

Appendix Table 2

Figure 2 Functions: Indirect Tax Increased $1 Billion at Initial Equilibrium

1 N	2 w	3 W	4 i_e	5 M	6 T_i	7 T_i	8 VC'	9 ΔVC'
7.6	$5829	$44,300	$1515	$18,901	$10,296	$967	$75,979	$ 9,997
7.69e'	5849	44,979	1532	19,134	10,455	982	77,082	10,023
7.7	5852	45,060	1535	19,153	10,477	984	77,209	10,024
7.78e	5886	45,796	1551	19,346	10,647	1000	78,340	10,071
7.8	5895	45,981	1556	19,404	10,690	1004	78,635	10,080

10 Q	11 P'	12 Q	13 Z'	14 ΔY_r	15 D'	16 E'
↑	104.9	$92,116	$96,630	$788	$92,572	$97,108
9531	105.2	92,970	97,800	809	92,970	97,800
	105.2	93,069	97,909	810	93,043	97,881
	105.7	93,831	99,179	828	93,417	98,742
↓	105.8	94,022	99,475	830	93,511	98,934

e'= equilibrium with indirect tax.
e = initial equilibrium
New functions: (7)ΔT_i=increase in indirect tax ($1000 x W/W_e) (millions); (8)
VC'= variable cost when increased indirect tax is shifted forward ($VC'= W + i_v +$
$M + T_i + \Delta T_i$) (millions); (9)$\Delta VC'$= change in variable cost (W x VC'/W') (dollars);
(11) P'= price index with increased indirect tax ($P'= MC' = \Delta VC'/\Delta Q$); (13)
Z'= aggregate supply function with increased indirect tax ($Z'= P'Q$) (millions);
(14)ΔY_r=change in real private income because of increased indirect tax
$(\Delta Y_r = Y_r - Y'_r) = (Y'_p/P)$; where $Y'_p = Z' - T'_i$, $Y_p = Z - T_i$, P'= price index with
increased indirect tax, P= initial price index; (15) D'= aggregate real demand
$(D' = D - 0.5\Delta Y_r)$ (millions); (16) E'= aggregate demand with increased indirect
tax $(E' = P'D')$ (millions).

Appendix Table 3

Figure 2 Functions: Direct Tax Increased by $1 Billion at Initial Equilibrium

1 N	2 w	3 W	4 iv	5 M	6 Ti	7 VC	8 △VC	9 △Q
7.6	$5829	$44,300	$1515	$18,901	$10,296	$75,012	$9868	↑
7.68e''	5847	44,905	1531	19,095	10,439	75,970	9893	9531
7.7	5852	45,060	1535	19,153	10,477	76,255	9902	
7.78e	5886	45,796	1551	19,346	10,647	77,340	9941	
7.8	5895	45,981	1556	19,404	10,690	77,631	9951	↓

10 P	11 Q	12 Z	13 △T	14 △Y'r	15 D''	16 E''
103.5	$92,116	$95,340	$967	$934	$92,499	$95,737
103.8	92,871	96,400	980	944	92,871	96,400
103.9	93,069	96,699	984	947	92,713	96,599
104.3	93,831	97,883	1000	959	93,351	97,365
104.4	94,022	98,159	1004	962	93,443	97,557

e'' = equilibrium with direct tax.
e = initial equilibrium.
New functions: (13) $\triangle T$ = increase in direct tax ($\triangle T$ = $1000 x W/W_e) (millions);
(14) $\triangle Y'_r$ = decrease in real income from increase in direct tax ($\triangle Y'_r = \triangle T/P$)
(millions); (15) D'' = aggregate real demand ($D'' = D - 0.5\triangle T'_r$) (millions); (16)
E'' = aggregate demand with increased direct tax ($E'' = PD''$) (millions).

112   Adverse Effects of Tax and Interest Hikes As
Strengthening the Case for Incomes Policies – or
A Part of the Elephant

Appendix Table 4

Figure 2 Functions: Income Policy Holds Wage Level Constant

1 N	2 w*	3 W*	4 iv	5 M	6 T*i	7 VC*	8 △VC*	9 △Q
7.6	$5800	$44,080	$1515	$18,901	$10,264	$74,760	↑	↑
7.7	5800	44,660	1535	19,153	10,393	75,740		
7.78e	5800	45,124	1551	19,346	10,500	76,521	$9837	$9531
7.8	5800	45,240	1556	19,404	10,530	76,730	↓	↓

10 P*	11 Q	12 Z*	13 E*
↑	$92,116	$95,064	$95,941
	93,069	96,047	96,383
103.2	93,831	96,834	96,834
↓	94,022	97,031	96,932

e   initial equilibrium (also equilibrium with incomes policy).
New functions: (2) $w*$=average wage ($w*$= $5800 at all employment
levels=1.071 x $5416 (average wage in 1968)) (dollars); (3) $W*$= labour income with average wage held constant (millions); (6) $T*_i$=indirect taxes with average wage constant ($T*_i = T_{i7.4}$ x $W*/W*_{7.4}$); (7) $VC*$= variable cost with average wage constant ($VC*= W* + iv + M + T*_i$) (millions); (8)$△VC*$= change in variable cost when one additional man is employed ($△VC*= w*$ x $VC*/W*$) (millions); (10) $P*$=price index with average wage constant ($P*= MC*=△VC*/△Q$); (12) $Z*$= aggregate supply function with wage constant (millions); (13) $E*$= aggregate demand function with wage constant (millions).

4 Inflation and the Rise of The Government Sector: Some Alternate Approaches

Introduction

As we saw briefly in Chapter One, economists have failed to analyze fully the price level implications of a rising government sector. Table 4.1 sets forth the figures on the rise of government expenditures in Canada and the United States.

Table 4.1

Government Expenditures as a Percentage of Gross National Product in Canada and the United States – Selected Years

Canada						United States
Year	Current Expenditures	Gov't Investment	Subsidies & Trans.	Interest On Pub. Dt.	Total	Total
1929	7.6%	2.9%	1.5%	3.8%	15.8%	10.0%
1933	11.2	2.4	5.4	8.1	27.1	19.2
1944	41.6	.7	4.4	3.5	50.2	49.0
1947	10.1	2.3	7.7	4.2	24.3	18.3
1956	14.1	3.6	6.0	2.2	25.9	24.8
1961	16.2	4.2	9.3	2.9	32.6	28.6
1968	16.9	4.4	10.6	3.6	35.5	31.3
1971	19.7	4.0	9.7	3.8	37.7	32.2
1974	19.5	3.9	11.6	3.8	39.3	33.0

Source:
Canada: *Economic Review,* April 1975, Tables 2, 52.
United States: *Economic Report of the President,* Feb. 1975, tables C-1, C-67.

As Table 4.1 indicates, government expenditures and transfer payments were more than twice as large a percentage of GNP in Canada in 1974 than they were in 1929, while the U.S. governments' share of GNP more than tripled. Within the broad movement of a rising government sector there are some ebbs and flows. Thus the government sector became as large as the private sector in World War II and decreased sharply at the end of hostilities. The increase in the relative importance of the government sector from 1929 to 1933 does not reflect an increase in government spending. Rather it reflects the great fall in GNP from $6,139 millions to $3,492 millions and the lesser fall in the government sector (from $469 million to $392 million). All categories of government expenditures were a larger percentage of GNP in 1974 than in 1929 except, interestingly enough, Interest on Public Debt. The greatest rate of increase is in the category of Subsidies and Transfers. These represent tax, or loan, monies raised from the private sector and then transferred back to the private sector,

rather than expended on goods and services in the government sector. United States government expenditures plus transfers parallel the
Canadian pattern although the percentages are somewhat lower.

The causes of the relative rise of the government sector are an
often told tale which need not detain us unduly here. The pattern is
world wide and reflects basically the high income elasticity of demand
for services, and thus government services, together with the increasing acceptance of the philosophy that the government sector must
protect individuals from the financial exigencies of unemployment,
old age, and illness. Additional factors usually cited as helping to
account for the faster growth of government include: increased urbanization and consequent complexities of urban life, increased need
for higher education in our highly technical civilization, increased
cost of military preparedness (more important in the U.S. than in
Canada), and, more cynically, "Parkinson's Law" which purports to
show that the government expands whether its actual functions
expand or contract.

That a rising government sector and a rising general level of
prices are characteristics of our times is evident to all. That the first
rise is at all the cause of the second has, however, occurred to few
except within familiar contexts. Thus, "excess demand" or 45^0
theorists would consider it true, but trite, that a rise in government
spending financed by deficits might well drive the economy against
its full-employment ceiling and set off an inflationary spiral. A
"monetarist" surveying the same familiar landscape would focus on
the excessive growth of the money supply occasioned by government
deficits as the inflation cause. Both schools would urge that as the
economy approaches "full employment" fiscal policy should become
more "restrictive" with tax receipts rising more rapidly than expenditures. The "excess demand" theorist would stress the "balanced
budget multiplier" theorem – that a balanced increase in government
spending and taxation is still expansionary as a portion of taxation is
paid out of savings. Monetarists might note the increased "velocity"
occasioned by increased taxing and spending.

Both schools, however, tend to overlook important aspects of an
increased government sector which fall outside the small slice of
economic reality they focus upon. Suppose an economy with
"reasonably full" employment and a government sector which is
growing relatively to the economy as a whole. Suppose further that
taxes are regularly increased sufficiently to offset the "balanced
budget multiplier" effect and that Friedman's "steady as she grows"
rule governs the rate of increase of the money supply. Would such an
economy suffer from a "tax, or government push" inflation? There
are several reasons for contending that it would. Let us organize our
thinking regarding these matters by means of the concepts developed
in Chapter One and brought together in Figure 1.5 Higher taxation
and expenditure will raise the price level if it causes aggregate supply
and aggregate demand to intersect so that the Z/Q ratio is increased.
We are used to such intersections during expansions, here we wish to
see why they might occur at a constant level of employment.

Taxation and the Supply of Factors

An increased level of taxation coupled with increased government
expenditures "should" not be seen by a "rational" individual as decreasing his real income. At least this should follow if the individual
approves of the expenditures as benefiting him. Because of the
higher taxes he can consume fewer individually distributed goods,

but he receives more collectively consumed goods and services, and if the increased spending was socially beneficial he receives greater utility from the collectively provided "bundle" than from the bundle he could have bought with the tax money. However, it is open to an individual faced with increased taxation to reduce his tax payments by reducing his taxed activities or purchases without at the same time decreasing the collectively provided goods available to him. Indeed, he may thus increase the socially provided resources available to him – by "going on welfare" or retiring early. Reducing his economic contribution may be the only way in which the individual can "get his money's worth" out of social goods, *i.e.*, taking a longer vacation to see the national parks or a new museum in Ottawa. Also, taxes may induce a shift from market to non-market activities – an M.D. in a high tax bracket might prefer to see fewer patients and paint his own house, or a drinker might make his own beer and wine to avoid the alcohol excise. All of these tax effects tend to raise the price level by reducing the supply of labour, or by reducing its efficiency.

In addition to reducing the supply of labour, taxation may also reduce the supply of savings for capital formation and lessen the willingness of entrepreneurs to employ their capital in risky undertakings. Personal taxes and sales taxes are partially paid out of income which would otherwise be saved. To the extent that the corporate profit tax reduces the after-tax rate of profits it reduces one of the chief sources of savings for private capital formation. A larger government sector could thus prove inflationary by reducing the pace of capital formation and thus the availability of final products.

The effect of governmental expansion is not all on the side of reducing labour supply and capital formation, however. Government employment is particularly free from the cyclical wastes of unemployment. In addition, the government's role in damping down cyclical instability in the private sector has contributed to increasing and stabilizing labour demand – and as many studies of the "labour force participation rate" have shown, labour supply is itself a function of labour demand. Furthermore, the government also "saves" and invests in many kinds of "social overhead capital". Still further, the modern "Keynesian" state by guaranteeing that great depressions shall never recur induces private investment on a greater scale than was possible in the old days of "boom and bust."

Finally, not all of the effects of taxation operate to reduce the supply of factors available to the economy. In the above discussion we have concentrated on the substitution effects of higher taxation. The income effect of taxation has the opposite effect, inducing a person to supply more factor units in an attempt to maintain his pre-tax income. Thus, heavier taxation may induce workers to "moonlight" by taking a second job, or induce an M.D. to maintain his practice longer before retiring. Similarly, high taxes may induce persons to save more to achieve a given retirement income. Economic theory provides no basis for concluding whether the income or substitution effect are more powerful. It is interesting that a survey of the evidence by Brown and Dawson[1] concludes that it is a virtual standoff as regards the

---

[1] C.V. Brown and D.A. Dawson, *Personal Taxation, Incentives and Tax Reform*, (London, Political and Economic Planning, 1969). See also, Edward Shapiro, "The Surtax Labor Supply Reaction, and the Rate of Inflation," *Nebr. Jour. of Econ. and Bus.*, XI, Summer 1972, pp. 49-56. Shapiro sees tax hikes as increasing labor supplies somewhat and thus damping inflation.

In a later study, C.V. Brown and E. Levin, "The Effects of Income Taxation on Overtime: The Results of a National Survey," *Economics Journal*, 84, December 1974, also conclude that the net result is a slight increase in hours worked.

labour supply. Therefore we must conclude that we cannot form a clear inference regarding the inflationary or non-inflationary effect of higher taxation upon labour supply.

Tax "Push" as a Struggle for Net Income Shares

The Economic Council of Canada has recently argued that an imperfect perception of the cost and benefits of a rising government sector can contribute to inflation. If people feel more keenly the pain of increased taxation than they do the pleasure of increased government services, or if they look on the taxes as an imposition and the services as "manna from heaven" they may demand higher wages "to pay the higher taxes" with inflation the result. As the Council puts the matter:

". . . an increasing role of government may result in an inflationary bias in the economy. In our opinion, this danger originates in the adjustments in nominal incomes induced by tax increases. Traditionally, this adjustment has been largely neglected by economists . . . Experience throughout the world seems to show that . . . desired incomes are adjusted . . . to maintain disposable income . . . In short, people want to obtain increases in nominal incomes that will be sufficient to compensate them for both increases in price and increases in taxes, and so protect their real disposable incomes." [2]

The Economic Council's insight may be illustrated by a model similar to one developed two decades ago by Holzman[3].

The Model
$Y_t = V_t + F_t + T_t$
$V_t = anY_{t-1}$
$F_t = F_o$
$T_t = \beta Y_{t-1}$
$P_t = Y_t/Q_o$

Consider the current dollar income (Y_t) of a country to be the sum of the disposable incomes of those receiving variable incomes (V_t), fixed incomes, (F_t), and net tax receipts (T_t). Suppose that

$V_t = anY_{t-1}$, $T_t = \beta Y_{t-1}$, and $F_t = F_o$;

where a equals the desired (= initial) income share of those who are able to vary their incomes in response to changed prices and taxes, and n represents the ratio of variable income rise to price (income) rise or

$$\frac{V_t/V_o}{Y_t/Q_o}$$

---

[2] Economic Council of Canada, *Ninth Annual Review, The Years Ahead*, (Ottawa 1972). p. 101.

[3] F.D. Holzman, "Income Determination in Open Inflation," *Review of Economics and Statistics*, 32, May 1950, pp. 150-58. Holzman's model involves a struggle over income shares, thus "Type II" inflation in Abba Lerner's parlance. See Abba Lerner, "Three Kinds of Inflation," *Policy Formation Canada* (Waterloo 1974). In Holzman's model, the struggle is between labour (the aggressors), profit (the, largely successful, defenders) and the fixed income victims. The inflation, set off by a rise in the wage share, comes to an end when the fixed plus profit shares are so reduced that the three shares sum to 100 percent.

Thus n represents the ability of the variable income group to recapture income lost through price increases.

Suppose, for simplicity, $n = 1$ and the rate of taxation is increased[4] to β'. If, again for simplicity, real income (Q) remains constant, the price level ($P_t = Y_t/Q_o$) must increase until the fixed income share has decreased by $\beta' - \beta$. Thus if $Y_o = Q_o = 100$, $a = .5$, $n = 1$, $\beta = .2$, $F_o = \$30$ (.3 of Y_o), and in period 1 taxation increases to $\beta' = .3$, the price level will increase in successively smaller tax-income spirals until $F_t = .2Y_t$; thus until $Y_t = \$30/.2 = \$150$.

Since real output has remained constant it is clear that the price level has increased to $P = 1.5$, or, expressed as an index number, $P = 150$. Table 4.2 presents this model through five time periods.

[4] In a country with a progressive tax structure, the existence of inflation increases β as money incomes rise. Canada now removes this government inflation bonus through indexing of incomes.

Table 4.2

Tax Push Inflation in Hypothetical Economy.
Government share rises in period 1 from $T = .2Y_{t-1}$ to $T' = .3Y_{t-1}$.

Period	Variable Income	Fixed Income	Gov't Receipts	Y	$P = \frac{Y}{Q} \times 100$
	$V = .5Y_{t-1}$	$F = \$30$	$T = \beta Y_{t-1}$		
0	$50	30	20	100	100
1	50	30	30	100	100
2	55	30	33	118	118
3	59	30	35.4	124.4	124.4
4	62.2	30	37.3	129.5	129.5
5	64.75	30	38.95	133.6	133.6
.	.	.	.	.	.
.	.	.	.	.	.
∞	75.00	30	45	150	150

Clearly, if $n < 1$ the degree of inflation accompanying a given rise of the government share is lessened. Thus if $n = .9$ so that $an = .45$, inflation need only continue until $F_t = .25Y_t$, thus until $Y_t = \$120$. Table 4.3 illustrates this variant of the model through five time periods.

Table 4.3

Tax Push Inflation in Hypothetical Economy.
Tax "shift" factor for Variable Incomes, $n = .9$.
Other assumptions as in Table 4.2

Period	Variable Income	Fixed Income	Gov't Receipts	Y	$P = \frac{Y}{Q} \times 100$
	$V = .9 (.5) Y_{t-1}$	$F = \$30$	$T = \beta Y_{t-1}$		
0	$50	$30	$20	$100	$100
1	50	30	30	110	110
2	49.5	30	33	112.5	112.5
3	50.525	30	33.75	114.275	114.275
4	51.43	30	34.25	115.68	115.68
5	52.06	30	34.7	116.76	116.76
.	.	.	.	.	.
.	.	.	.	.	.
∞	$54	$30	$36	$120	$120

It may be asked, however, why, if the "variable income" group are able to recapture all or part of the income lost through tax increases, they fail to push their power to the full irrespective of what happens to taxes? An answer to this question was given by Adam Smith in his discussion of the motives of trade unions, but, despite the regard economists have for the "founder" of our discipline, the question is still considered a live one today. Trades unions are, as Smith pointed out, primarily defensive organizations, ordinarily coming into existence to resist a cut in the money, or real wage[5].

People will usually fight much harder to retain what is already "theirs" than they will to obtain further gains, that is, "to maximize." Thus a tax hike, which curtails take-home pay, may call forth more militancy than was involved in winning that level of pay initially. Indeed, there may be no aspect of economic life where the economist's facile assumption of simple maximizing behaviour is less relevant than in labour relations. The decisions of wage bargainers as much closer to those of military commanders than they are to economic men maximizing their "net advantage" under conditions of "full certainty".[6] A high degree of uncertainty attaches to the whole question, "What is the maximum rate of which "labour" can increase the money wage?" As in the military case, one never knows until one tries, and "trying" involves high and uncertain costs.

In such circumstances the rank and file may be much more ready to endure the hardships of a long strike to "repel aggression" than they would be to themselves aggress. Thus workers might be much more determined to "pass on" a tax hike in a wage hike than they would have been to obtain a wage hike in the absence of a tax hike.

In a progressive community people come to expect a gradual improvement in their money and real income. Thus the "defensive" expectations of a union's members might be that their money incomes will grow five per cent a year and that their real incomes will grow somewhat more slowly because of inflation and higher taxes – say at three per cent. These expectations, if strongly held, are among those things the membership consider "theirs," things to which they are entitled, and any shortfall will be strongly resisted. (The membership would, of course, like to see incomes grow much more rapidly than five per cent and would support the leadership in demanding ten

---

[5] "Such combinations [of masters to lower wages] are frequently resisted by a contrary defensive combination of the workmen; who sometimes too, without any provocation of this kind, combine of their own accord to raise the price of their labour. Their usual pretences are sometimes the high price of provisions; sometimes the great profit which their masters make by their work." Adam Smith, *An Inquiry into the Nature and Causes of the Wealth of Nations*, [1776] Modern Library Edition, New York, 1937, p. 67.

[6] It is possible, and useful, to go much further in rejecting this central concept of conventional economics. To assume "full certainty" is to assume away the human condition. Conventional theory is in the ridiculous position of ascribing truly god-like knowledge to its "powerless" competitive businessman-worker-consumer economic man. If any one person has such powers he would soon rule all others. If all men had such powers they would quickly put an end to all mere economic problems and turn to more important matters. For many important insights regarding this central point see G.L.S. Shackle, "Keynes and Today's Establishment in Economic Theory: A View," *Journal of Economic Literature*, XI, June 1973 , pp. 516-19. As Shackle sees it, Keynes escaped from the "invented world" of economic theory "where knowledge of circumstance is (miraculously, impossibly, unexplainedly) *sufficient,*" to explore "our real predicament. We are not omniscient, assured masters of known circumstance via reason, but the prisoners of time." p. 519

per cent of fifty per cent wage hikes if they believed that such gains could be won at little cost and at little risk of losing present levels of income and employment. However, in Canada at any rate, if not in Latin America, they believe that any such gains could be wrung from management, if at all, only at the cost of frighteningly expensive strikes.) In such a situation, if an "anti-inflationary" tax of, say, ten per cent is imposed, it may provoke a militant demand for fifteen per cent pay boosts and the union may settle for twelve per cent with as little grace as it formerly settled for two per cent.

The situation of corporations is not too dissimilar in this regard. Corporate managers lack the information regarding marginal costs and revenues not only now but over the distant future necessary to "maximize" their profits. They do, however, know what their costs and revenues have been in the recent past and whether or not they are receiving "satisfactory" profits. A hike in the corporate profits tax may reduce net profits below the "satisfactory" level and induce "defensive" price hikes which would not have been assayed in the absence of the tax. All of this is the tritest of common sense and observation, and is well confirmed by econometric tests cited in Chapter Three showing that the corporate profits tax is promptly shifted to consumers. However, it is stoutly resisted both by fiscalists who look only at demand management and monetarists who care only about the pace of the growth of the money stock.

The struggle over shares model is capable of considerable elaboration; as by allowing real incomes to grow, but it is beyond our purpose to do so here. Clearly, also, this model assumes that the product of money supply and velocity increases are permissive of this inflationary tax shifting game. As we saw in Chapter Two, velocity did increase considerably in U.S. and Canada in recent decades concurrently with the increase of the government sector. This "weakened the grip" of the monetary authorities over the economy as they sought to stop inflation by stabilizing or reducing the money to goods ratio. Thus, Figure 2.12 of Chapter Two indicates that the ratio of money to goods (r_1) in the U.S. fell steadily from 1947 to 1966, while V_1 as steadily rose. When the definition of money is broadened to Friedman's M_2 the rise in velocity (V_2) is much attenuated and r_2 in Canada and the U.S. merely rises more slowly than does P. (See Figures 2.5 and 2.13 in Chapter Two).

Our argument at this point may be seen to shade into the familiar "dilemma model". Suppose an increase in the price level occurs, the ultimate cause of which is the tax push postulated by the Economic Council. The monetary authority is now faced with an unpleasant range of options; from reducing the money supply in an attempt to drive the price level back down, to increasing the money supply rapidly enough so that no avoidable unemployment accompanies the inflationary spiral.

The first extreme is not a realistic policy, as any major reduction in the money supply would plunge the economy into politically intolerable depression. The only post World War II years in which M_2 in Canada fell even marginally were 1951 and 1959 and in both of these years P and Q rose. The U.S. Federal Reserve reduced M_1 and M_2 in 1948, 1949, 1957 and 1960, but in every one of these years except 1949 P and Q rose. Moreover, in a world of very imperfect competition in labour markets and long term contracts, any damping effect on wages and prices through contractionary monetary policy must be slow while the effect on unemployment and output will come quickly.[7]

Therefore, whatever the anti-inflationary instincts of central bankers, and whatever monetarists might wish them to do, it is not possible for central bankers to reduce the money supply more than marginally in an attempt to drive down prices. The monetary authority is a "constitutional" rather than an absolute monarch which reigns over the process of money creation but is not free to make M, or even $\triangle$ M any number it might wish[8].

The central bank may be depended upon, however, to shy away from the opposite extreme of an expansion of M sufficient to avoid all unemployment accompanying the inflation. It is not that bankers are malevolent souls who like to see their fellow men unemployed. However, they like inflation even less. As Joan Robinson once put it,

". . . a lively sense of the horrors of inflation is sucked up with the milk of the mothers of bank presidents, and, indeed, the process of checking a rise in money wages is usually set to work long before the point of full employment is actually reached. In the imagination of monetary reformers the ideal banking system controls its policy in such a way as to avoid unemployment. But in reality the first duty of banking authorities imposed upon them alike by law, tradition and sentiment, is to prevent full employment from being attained. And in the normal course they carry out their duties with devotion and success."[9]

The post World War II concern of governments to maintain "high" employment has weakened, but not eliminated the power of the bankers to sabotage prosperity. The weakening is most marked in the European countries where the central bank is an integral part of the government and least marked in the United States, where the Federal Reserve System still is able to maintain a semi-independent, "in but not of", relationship to the federal government.

A Two-Party Politics Approach to Public Sector Inflation

D. Auld and C. Southey have recently suggested an indifference curve approach to the question of public sector inflation[10]. Their analysis posits an electorate which prefers a large fraction of total income in the form of private goods and services and a small volume of publicly

[7] See S. Weintraub and H. Habibagahi, "Money Supplies and Price-Output Indeterminateness, the Friedman Puzzle," *Journal of Economic Issues*, June 1972 for development of the argument that in the short run the growth of the money supply is a major determinant of growth of employment and output, but is neutral regarding price level changes. Price level change is here seen as the resultant of the price increasing impact of exogenously given wage gains and price reducing productivity gains. See also S. Weintraub and H. Habibagahi, "Keynes and the Quantity Theory Elasticities," *Nebraska Journal of Economics and Business*, X, Spring 1971, pp. 13-25.

[8] Such a "constitutional monarch" view of the central bank is urged by Nicholas Kaldor in his scathing rejection of Friedmanism. See Kaldor, "The New Monetarism," *Lloyd's Bank Review*, July 1970, pp. 1-17. For Friedman's Comment and Kaldor's Reply see *Lloyd's Bank Review*, October 1970, pp. 52-5. Also in the same issue see A.B. Cramp, "Does Money Matter?", pp. 23-37.

[9] Joan Robinson, *Essays in the Theory of Employment* (Oxford: Blackwell, 1947), p. 19.

[10] D.A.L. Auld and C. Southey, "A Theory of Public Sector Inflation," presented at the Canadian Economic Association Meetings, Queens University, Kingston, June 2, 1973.

provided goods and services and a government with the reverse preferences. Auld and Southey show that the attempts of government and the electorate to impose their mutually inconsistent social preference functions can lead to inflation under a wide variety of assumptions (full, or less than full, employment; lump sum, proportional, and progressive taxes). Auld and Southey do not explain why a "small government" electorate would vote in a "big" government.

R.C. Bellan maintains that in recent decades lower income, low status, high risk or high physical strain, groups of workers have become increasingly unwilling to accept the prevailing degree of income inequality and that their attempts to reduce traditional differentials coupled with the attempts of those more favorably situated to maintain these differentials accounts for much of the world-wide inflation since World War II.[11] Thus Bellan's view fits well into the Holzman model developed above, with the "lower orders" the aggressors seeking a rise in their share and the variable and fixed income "uppers" cast as the successful and unsuccessful defenders of their piece of the income pie. Additionally, Bellan's contention can be adapted to Auld and Southey's analysis. Thus we may picture the "lower orders" supporting a programme of "big government" as a means of raising their relative and absolute incomes, and the "upper orders" attempting to offset the growing political success of the "lowers" by using their market and non-market power to raise their own money incomes.

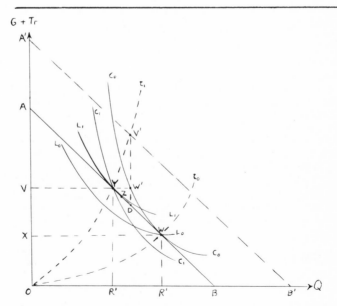

Figure 4.1.
Tax Inflation at Full Employment

[11] R.C. Bellan, "Taxation of Increases in Incomes to Prevent Inflation," presented at the Canadian Economic Association Meetings, June 2, 1973. Bellan's vision is similar to Krehm's concept of "Social Revalorization," *Price in a Mixed Economy,* pp. 99-106.

Figure 4.1. brings together these concepts into a model of two-party inflation at full employment. On the vertical axis of Figure 4.1 are government expenditures and transfers (G – Tr) while on the horizontal axis are privately purchased and consumed goods and services. The line AB represents the real consumption (also production) possibilities of this society. Thus they may consume OA of G and Tr, with no private goods; or OB of private goods, or any combination along AB. Here we accept the concept of a social preference or social indifference curve undeterred by Arrow's theorem that such a social preference function could only be imposed on individual preferences by a dictator.[12] The two sets of indifference curves represent the summed preferences of two groups, Bellan's aggressive lower income groups (the LL curves) and the share defending middle to upper income groups (the CC curves). The lower income groups prefer high taxation – soak the rich – coupled with massive transfer and public services for themselves, while the "rich", quite understandably, prefer taxation limited to the provision of those government goods which they value highly (education, police protection, etc.) and, perhaps, a minimum social welfare programme.

Suppose initially the economy is at full employment, that the conservative middle to upper income party has been in power and has maximized the satisfactions of its supporters at point W by taxing and spending OX and leaving OR of privately consumed goods. Here the conservatives have enacted a progressive tax structure indicated by the dotted curve t_0. This initial situation does not maximize the satisfactions of the lower income supporters of the liberal or labour party, however. They prefer point Y, with OV of government taxing and spending the only OR' of private goods.

Assume that in time 1 the downtrodden assert themselves, the big government liberals win the election and carry out their programme. "Arise ye prisoners of starvation! Arise from W to Y!" They raise the government sector to OV and raise the rate of taxation from t_0 to t_1 to finance the increased G –Tr without any (initial) increase in the money supply. We assume with Auld and Southey that the balanced budget multiplier is zero, and that the income velocity of circulation is constant and unitary. Therefore, the programme of the low income "attackers" is not, in itself, expansionary or inflationary. The response of the conservative "defenders", however, is. The new government's programme drives them from group preference function C_0 to C_1 as the winners rise from L_0 to L_1. If the conservatives respond by demanding and getting higher money incomes sufficient to remain on C_0 at W, inflation will ensue.[13] Real output cannot increase, but the money value of GNP will increase to A'B', where the government budget again balances. In real terms the economy will be at point Z, rather than at point Y, desired by the liberals. Thus the conservative "tax push" inflation has won back for them some of the ground they lost in losing the election. What happens next will be much affected by the politics of the situation. Will the liberal government persist in its determination to raise real G – Tr to OV – thus stepping up the inflation, or will it attempt to reduce inflation by not spending all of its

---

[12] Kenneth J. Arrow, *Social Choice and Individual Values*, 2nd edition, 1963.

[13] They are able to do this, under the assumption of the model, only because the "passive" banking system creates money equal to AA'. Thus we have an example of Keynes' concept that the thirst for higher money incomes is the cause of increasing money supplies, rather than an increased money supply being itself the root cause of inflation. As noted previously, the wide variability of income velocity over time has allowed considerable scope for prices to rise without a corresponding rise in the money supply. Thus the "constant and unitary" assumption is adopted for analytical convenience rather than reality.

"inflation bonus" of W'V', thereby perhaps producing some unemployment? Will the inflation strengthen the conservative party so that it can soon return to power and dismantle at least some of the "welfare state"? Who knows? Note, however, that re-establishment of sound conservative principles would not necessarily end the inflation if the losing liberals are in a position in their turn to play the loss-minimizing game of gaining higher incomes as compensation for, say, a cut in family allotments.

Bellan proposes a special anti-inflationary tax and subsidy programme to tax away the additional money income A'A (or equivalent V'D) and using it to subsidize producers not to raise their prices and thus to keep the economy at AB rather than A'B'. Thus in addition to the "inflation bonus" rise in tax receipts of V'W', Bellan would also tax away W'D. Since W'D is equal to YW' this is just the amount of additional taxation necessary to drive the losers' back to their group curve C_1 and carry out the winners' programme without inflation. Alternatively, and I would argue much better, the country might institute an incomes policy to keep the disgruntled losers, of whatever party, from regruntling themselves with money income increases which exceed the all-over gain in productivity. The Auld-Southley-Bellan model does, however, inject a new dimension into the inflation dilemma model – that it is the middle to upper income tax payer who is the chief instigator and beneficiary of "tax push" inflation. Who, after all, owns the banks and corporations? Also, the model possesses the merit of focusing on the struggle over relative incomes which Keynes saw as critical, but which his disciples have ignored – other than its use in the "relative income hypothesis" regarding the determinants of the consumption function.

Let us employ the model to examine the even more interesting question of tax-push inflation with unemployment. Figure 4.2. explores such a scenario. Here the initial situation is a depressed economy, where the equilibrium level of real output of A'B' is considerably below the full employment level AB. Initially a conservative government is in power and again they have maximized the satisfaction of their supporters with the allocation of *employed* resources at point W , producing OX of government and OR of private goods. In time 1, the big government liberals come to power with the promise of full employment, social justice and (why not?) stable prices. Let us assume that the new government is highly intelligent and hires scores of fine economists – men who know all about balanced and unbalanced budget multipliers, income velocity, deflationary gaps and how to plug them – the works. They know everything except the new matters our model focuses upon.

Obviously, this intelligent government is not concerned merely to change the allocation of employed resources to point Y' , but rather to achieve the allocation of fully employed resources desired by their supporters. Suppose they know this point to be at Y , along AB , where the liberal "reaction function" R_1 cuts through the highest attainable liberal indifference curve.[14] As I have drawn R_1, liberals wish a somewhat smaller government sector when there is full employment than in depression, as there is less necessity for transfer payments there being no unemployment. The line L cutting through Y represents the government expenditure plus transfer function. Clearly, since in this model the balanced budget multiplier is zero, it would not do to raise taxes by as much as expenditures are to be increased. Part of the expansion is to be deficit financed by new money creation. But how

---

[14] Thus the "reaction function" is completely analogous to the "income consumption line" of the individual consumer.

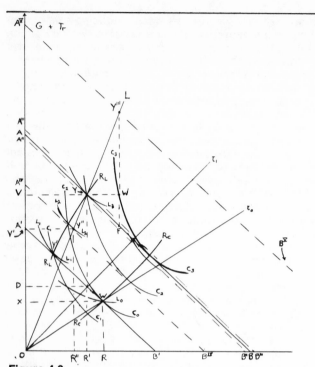

Figure 4.2.
Tax Inflation with Unemployment

much should taxes be raised and how much should the money supply
be increased? Given our constant velocity of 1 assumption, it is clear
that the money supply should be increased by AA' and the remainder
of the government expenditure increase should be tax financed.
Thus, the total increase in government spending is VX, of which VD
(VD = AA') is financed by new money creation and only DX by higher
taxation. Thus T_1 is the optimal tax function (proportional for
simplicity) to replace the conservative's t_0 function.

The liberal's "textbook Keynesian + redistribution" programme
should be a real improvement for our model economy, but will it really
give "full employment, social justice (as liberals would define it) and
stable prices?" Enter the problems Auld, Southey and Bellan focus
upon. Let us suppose that the conservatives' "reaction function" R_c
has some increasing slope – they are willing to see a relatively larger
government sector at full employment because their income elasticity
of demand for government services is greater than 1, but they are
unwilling to see government expenditures plus transfers as large as
the liberals have enacted and they are unwilling to pay taxes along the
t_1 function.

Here a very interesting and vital question emerges. Do these
conservatives react only to the tax increase, which is perhaps Auld
and Southey's view, or do they react to the erosion of their relative
income position caused by all those transfers to the poor, which is
Bellan's contention? (Or are they quantity theorists, who panic at the
sight of all that money creation?)

If it is merely higher taxes which rile conservatives into inflating
the problem will be minor as there is little divergence between R_c and
t_1 at full employment. When the government spends and transfers OV
and finances it by DO of taxes plus VD of new money, the result will be

an increase of *money* GNP to AB, but real GNP will be somewhat less; here A"B". Part of the increase in M has been used up in the higher prices exacted by the "conservatives" and only the remainder has resulted in increased Q. In this case a small addition to the money supply will raise real GNP to AB and money GNP to A" 'B" '.

However, if conservatives react to the increased relative importance of government expenditures and transfers, rather than to the taxes they pay, the result is not so happy. If the government creates enough money to raise money GNP to AB much of the money will merely finance higher goods and factor prices rather than the expansion of real output. Here, creation of AA' of money increases real income only to $A^{IV}B^{IV}$ The economy is at point Y" in real terms, with OV' of government goods and OR" of private goods. Conservatives are only slightly better off (marginally above C_0) than initially while liberal supporters are not as well off as they expected to become, and as the economy is capable of making them.

The government is in a cruel dilemma. The monetary expansion and deficit finance has gone about one-half to raise prices and one-half to raise real income and employment. If they attempt to make good their pledge of full employment, inflation will become yet more severe. If real output is raised to AB by expansion along L conservatives will demand money incomes of W', which can only be reconciled with full employment by expanding the money supply to make money income equal $A^{V}B^{V}$, which runs us off the page with a rate of inflation of BB^{V}/OB.

The liberals could compromise their sense of social justice by abandoning L for some expenditure programme closer to conservative preferences and achieve full employment with a correspondingly lower rate of inflation. As matters stand, however, they can make good on at most two out of their three campaign pledges, and may well make good on only one, or none.

What should be done? Again Bellan suggests that the entire excessive monetary expansion AA^{V} (or equivalently Y" 'F) be taxed away and be used to subsidize producers to keep prices at their initial levels. This enforces the liberals' social preference function and makes the system work. At least it works if they can pass the law, enforce it and keep in power! Further trouble looms, moreover, because unless this was an economy of secular stagnation a resurgence of investment demand may soon require a more nearly balanced budget with consequent further tax hikes.

The above model is, of course, limited by its comparative statics approach and it could not be used to analyze the complex horse trading of actual politics, for example the uneasy alliance by which for a time the Liberals held power with NDP support. However, it is a large step away from the reigning, but inadequate, ideas of "textbook Keynesianism" – or what Joan Robinson tartly dismisses as "Bastard Keynesianism" – to take a realistic look at real-world problems in the spirit of Keynes. Keynes *was* concerned with the inequality of income distribution as a great fault of the capitalist system and he did see the struggle for higher money incomes as the basic cause of inflation. Higher wages cause higher prices compelling new money creation if the system is to function. To the best of my knowledge, he never wrote of tax (or interest) push inflation, or sought to reduce income inequality in order to reduce inflation, but these ideas are logical extensions of his "cost-function" theory of prices. Keynes did propose a policy of driving down interest rates with the dual objective of maintaining full employment in an economy rapidly approaching "capital saturation" and in order to bring about a "euthanasia" of high rentier incomes. As we have seen in Chapter Three, Keynes saw clearly that an incomes policy would be a necessary supplement to fiscal and monetary policy if we are to perpetuate full employment, achieve social justice and enjoy stable prices. All these points were lost in the bastardized version of Keynes we have in our textbooks and public policies.

To put the matter another way, the Auld-Southey-Bellan model provides an answer to a question which has much vexed Milton Friedman – although he might not care for the answer. Friedman writes:

"The general subject of the division of changes in money income between prices and quantity badly needs more investigation. None of our leading economic theories has much to say about it." [15]

The answer proposed is somewhat as follows: The division of changes in money income between prices and quantity depends upon social, or interpersonal factors. The price level is socially determined and among the social determinants which the economist must analyze are: the degree of social consensus, or lack thereof, regarding the optimum size of the government sector; the optimum, or at least tolerable, degree of income inequality; and the optimum division of the burdens of taxation and distribution of benefits of progress among individuals and social classes.

---

[15] Milton Friedman, *The Optimum Quantity of Money and Other Essays,* (Chicago, Aldine 1969) p. 279.

5 Government Inflation: Some Attempts at Measurement

Changes In Disposable Income Shares And Inflation[1]

In Chapter Two we expressed alternative inflation theories as truisms and in Chapter Four developed alternative approaches to a "struggle over shares" theory of inflation. Here we wish to explore the truism that in inflation net, or after tax and transfer, incomes increase more rapidly than gross real output, thus that

$$P = \frac{DPY + DBY + DGY,}{Q}$$

where DPY is Disposable Personal Income, DBY is Disposable Business Income, DGY is Disposable Government Income, and Q is Real Gross National Product. Whatever our theory of the cause of inflation the result is measurable as money income gains which are excessive relative to real output. Canadian GNP increased from $13,169 millions in 1947 to $84,468 millions in 1970 or 6.4 fold. The GNP deflator increased from 100 to 211.7 over the same period, however, so that the growth in "real" GNP was only to $39,900 millions, or 3.0 times the 1947 figure. Thus $44,568 millions of 1970 GNP was "excess" and it is a useful exercise to discover how the various net income categories shared in this "excess".

The accounting framework needed for our study of "who got what" is net, or disposable income of Persons, Business, and Government. These are easily found, or derived from the published figures. However, we wish to push the disaggregation a step further and examine the disposable income of wage, interest and profit recipients separately. Data on taxes payable by occupation (employees, farmers and fishermen, pensioners, and all others) as a percentage of total taxes payable by persons are published in *Canada Year Book* for 1947 through 1968. Appendix Table 5.1 presents the percentages, while appendix Table 5.2 uses this information to calculate total direct taxes of persons plus other current transfers from persons by occupation. Appendix Table 5.3 calculates employee direct taxes and other transfers as a percentage of employee income. Table 5.1 summarizes these percentages and indicates that within the 1947 to 1970 period the rise of direct taxes as a percentage of wage income occurred almost wholly after 1960 and that the pace of increase quickened from 1965.

---

[1] For an earlier study of these matters in the United States for the period 1947-1969 see John H. Hotson, "Changes in Sectoral Income Shares: Some Neglected Factors in Inflation." *Nebraska Journal of Economics and Business,* 10, Winter 1971, pp. 3-21.

Table 5.1. *Employee Taxes and Other Current Transfers From Persons as a Percentage of Employee Income, Canada Selected Years*

Year	Taxes as % of Wages
1947	9.6
1950	7.2
1955	10.2
1960	11.7
1965	13.1
1968	18.3
1970	21.7

Again, as in Chapter Two, we allocate the "mixed" income categories of farm and non-farm unincorporated enterprise income to "labour" and "capital". It is assumed that 81% of the net or disposable income of a farmer, and 68% of the net income of a non-incorporated business is a return to "labour" and the rest is a return to "capital". Appendix Table 5.4 presents our calculation of Gross National Product as Gross Disposable Income and Appendix Table 5.5 presents these dollar figures as percentages, with the above allocation of "mixed" incomes. Appendix Table 5.5 indicates the net contractual wage income was a virtually constant 45% of Gross Disposable Income from 1947 to 1970. However, when the net labour income of farmers and independent businessmen is added to net contractual wage income it may be seen that net "labour" income has fallen from 57.3% of GNP in 1947 to 48.4% in 1970. It is also readily evident from Appendix Table 5.5. that Personal Disposable Income fell from 73.1% of GNP to 63.5% over the same period while Business Disposable Income rose from 7.1% to 12.3% and Government Disposable Income rose from 17.6% to 23.9%. Table 5.2. presents the relevant figures for 1947, 1958 and 1970. The only personal disposable income categories to increase relatively to GNP were Interest and Dividends and Disposable Current Transfers. However, the remaining "capital" based income account, that for farm and enterprise property income, decreased so greatly that Disposable Property and Transfer Income fell from 15.9% of GNP in 1947 to 14.9% in 1970.

Table 5.2. *Changes in the Distribution of Gross Disposable Income of Canada – Assumption 1 – Selected Years*

	1947	1958	1970
Disposable Wage & Salary Income	44.5%	46.7%	44.5%
Disposable Farm & Enterprise Labour Income	12.8	7.3	3.9
Disposable Labour Income	57.3	54.0	48.4
Disposable Interest & Dividend Income	4.7	4.3	5.2
Disposable Farm & Enterprise Property Income	4.5	2.8	1.6
Disposable Current Transfers	6.7	8.0	8.1
Disposable Property & Transfer Income	15.9	15.1	14.9
Disposable Personal Income	73.1	69.1	63.5
Disposable Business Income	7.1	13.8	12.3
Disposable Government Income	17.6	15.2	23.9
Residual error of estimate	2.2	2.0	0.3
Gross Disposable Income	100.0	100.0	100.0

Source: Appendix Table 5.5.

Figure 5.1. is a graph of the changing shares in Gross Disposable Income in Canada from 1947 through 1970. The lower bound of Disposable Business Income marks the upper bound of Disposable Personal Income. The overall impression is one of a growing government sector (region 5), some increase in the business sector (mainly from a growth in capital consumption allowances as Appendix Table 5.5. makes evident) and a decline in the share of Disposable Personal Income.

According to the Holzman and Auld-Southey-Bellan inflation theories developed above, the rise in the government sector leads to inflation because it is resisted by some or all of the "losing" sector income recipients. But how much of Canadian inflation is attributable to this struggle over net income shares? As an aid to answering this question let us consider two alternative assumptions concerning the degree to which receiving inflationary income gains may be taken as synonymous with *causing* inflation. By the first assumption, "blame" for inflation is apportioned among the Gross Disposable Income categories according to the current relative size of the income category. In 1947 Canadian GNP was $13,169 million and it rose to $15,127 million in 1948. However, the GNP deflator, or price index, rose from 100 in 1947 to 112.2 in 1948, thus real GNP (Q henceforth) rose only to $15,127/112.2 = $13,482 million and $15,127–$13,484 = $1,645 million was "excess" GNP. Since in 1948 wage and salary income was 45% of GNP, we may impute 45% of the "excess" GNP to "excess" wages and "blame" excess wages for 45% of the rise in the P index (thus accounting for its rise from 100 to 105.5) and so on for the remaining disposable income categories. Appendix Table 5.6 carries

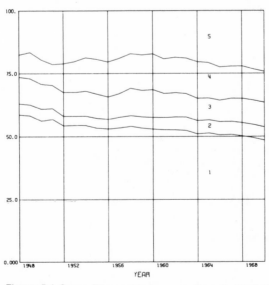

Figure 5.1 *Gross Disposable Income: Canada 1947-1970*
1) Disposable Labour Income (Disp. Wages – Disp. Farm Labour Income – Disp. Enterprise Labour Income)
2) Disposable Interest and Dividend Income
3) Disposable Farm and Enterprise Property Income – Disposable Current Transfer Income
4) Disposable Business Income
5) Disposable Government Income

out this operation for each year from 1947 through 1970 and the result is graphed in Figure 5.2. Note that in Figure 5.2. all farm and unincorporated business income is lumped together with wage income rather than being imputed to labour and capital. This technique fails to come to grips with the "struggle over shares" theory of inflation since the rise in net wages from 1947 to 1948 may have resulted in a larger or smaller share in GNP.

Whether Figures 5.1. and 5.2. yield us information on the *causes* of inflation or not, they certainly show us the *effects* of inflation. Each disposable income category actually received "excess" GNP in proportion to its share of GNP and thus shared proportionately in inflation. By the "struggle over shares" theory, inflation is caused by the rise of the "aggressor" shares and the resistance, successful and unsuccessful, of the defending and losing share receivers. Assumption 2 is an attempt to isolate the effect of shifting shares from 1947 in Canada and thus imputes "inflationary excess" disproportionately to the rising business and government sectors. Assumption 2 consists of treating as "excess" income any rise in personal, business, or government disposable income at a faster pace than the growth in real GNP. Since the Q index rose from 100 in 1947 to only 102.4 in 1948, net wages "should" have only increased from their 1947 level of $5,859.6 to $5,998.9 million in 1948, or $139.3 million. Instead they rose to $6,801.8 million in 1948, or a gain of $942.2 millions. Thus $942.2 – $139.3 million, or $802.9 million, becomes our figure for "excess" wages in 1948 which is 48.8% of "excess" GNP. Appendix Table 5.7. carries out the calculation of non-inflationary fixed (1947) weight shares of our disposable income categories by multiplying each 1947 disposable income category by the Q index in each year. When these

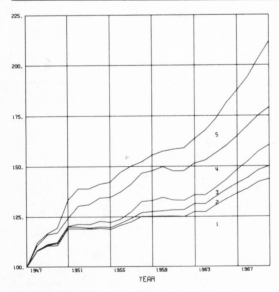

Figure 5.2. *The Rise of the GNP Deflator (P) in Canada 1947-1970 and Shares in Inflation Assumption 1: Rise in the Price Index "Caused" by Excess Disposable*
1) Participation Income (Sum of Wages, Farm, and Enterprise Income)
2) Interest and Dividend Income
3) Current Transfer Income
4) Business Income
5) Government Income

fixed-shares-in-real-GNP incomes are subtracted from the actual disposable incomes (Appendix Table 5.4.) the result is the "excess" income figures in Appendix Table 5.8. Appendix Table 5.8. indicates that the share losing farm sector had large "negative excess" in every year subsequent to 1954 as farm income fell absolutely and relatively to real GNP. The fall of the money and real income of the Canadian Farm sector over the postwar period is as familiar a tale as it is strange. In money terms disposable farm income in 1970 was little more than one-half that of the peak year of 1951 ($986.9 million vs $1,835.0 million) and in real terms it was only one-third ($466.2 million vs $1,375.6 million in 1947 dollars). It is familiar to all that farmers over produce and thus receive very little for the ever growing abundance they provide to the rest of us. It is strange, as no other sector of the economy could work that way; in no other sector is there such a fracturing of the equation real output equals real income. Can one picture General Motors producing more cars each year and receiving ever lower real receipts? Yet Real Domestic Product of Canadian Agriculture rose from an index of 100 in 1947 to a peak of 171.2 in 1971; thus real output of agriculture rose 70 per cent while the real income of farmers fell 60 per cent. Very recently there has been a dramatic shift in the "terms of trade" between farm and city and farmers have had some belated revenge. Accrued Net Income of Farm Operators from Farm Production (pretax) was strongly up in 1974 from the 1970 low ($3,561 vs $1,211 million in current dollars, or $1,271.3 vs $593.3 million 1947 dollars)[2] and all indications are that 1975 farm income will be much higher still. More on these matters in Chapter Eight on the current inflation and income policies. The other income category which contributed a large "negative excess" was "Other Business Income" which consists of dividends paid to non-residents, inventory valuation adjustments and transfers to and from business. In the earlier part of the 1947-1970 period two government accounts, Subsidies and Capital Assistance, and Interest on the Public Debt, contributed "negative excess" by growing more slowly than did Q, but since the late 1950s they have grown more rapidly than Q. All other net income categories usually contribute to excess income and are thus part of the inflationary excess of money income over real output. Appendix Table 5.9. presents the various excess income categories as percentages of excess GNP. The results are summarized in Table 5.3 and graphed in Figure 5.3.

---

[2] Department of Finance *Economic Review,* April 1975, pp. 109, 123, 151.

Table 5.3. *Changes in the Distribution of "Excess" GNP of Canada –*
Assumption 2 – Selected Years

	1948	1958	1970
Excess Net Wage and Salary Income	43.3%	51.6%	43.9%
Excess Net Farm Income	19.5	–6.0	–4.8
Excess Net Unincorp. Enterprise Income	4.0	2.6	0.1
Excess Net Participation Income	66.8%	47.2%	39.2%
Excess Net Interest & Dividend Income	1.7	3.6	5.7
Excess Net Current Transfers	0.4	10.6	9.3
Excess Disposable Personal Income	68.9%	61.4%	54.2%
Excess Disposable Business Income	20.4	26.9	16.7
Excess Disposable Government Income	9.3	10.7	29.2
Total Excess GNP	100.0*	100.0	100.0

*Contains residual "excess" of 1.3%

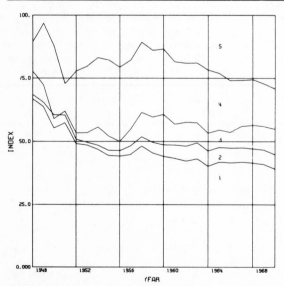

Figure 5.3. *Excess Disposable Income as a Percentage of Excess GNP in*
Canada 1948-1970 Assumption 2:
1) Excess Participation Income (Sum of excess Wages, Farm and Enterprise
   Income)
2) Excess Interest and Dividend Income
3) Excess Current Transfer Income
4) Excess Disposable Business Income
5) Excess Disposable Government Income

As Table and Figure 5.3. make evident, the percentage of "excess" GNP ascribable – under assumption 2 – to excessive growth of Net Participation Income has fallen greatly from 1947 to 1970. (Net Participation Income is defined as the sum of the Disposable Income of Wage, Farm, and Unincorporated Enterprise income recipients). This decline is largely because of the decline of "excess" farm income to negative values, but also reflects the slower pace of "excess" net wage and enterprise incomes. It is also evident that the percentage of the excess GNP ascribable to excess Disposable Personal Income has fallen as the fall in participation income outweighed the rise in net interest, dividends and transfer income. The "excess" growth of Disposable Business Income accounted for an increasing fraction of "excess" GNP from 1951 to 1955, when almost 30 per cent of excess GNP was excess DBY. In 1958 excess Government Disposable Income accounted for only 10.7 per cent of excess GNP. By 1971 this had increased to almost 30 per cent of excess GNP.

The figures on Appendix Table 5.9. may be used to "account for" the inflation in Canada by multiplying the GNP deflator by the "excess" incomes (positive or negative). The results of this operation are presented in Appendix Table 5.10. and graphed in Figure 5.4. As Figure 5.4. makes evident, we may increasingly ascribe inflation to the rise of the business and government sectors rather than to excessive personal income.

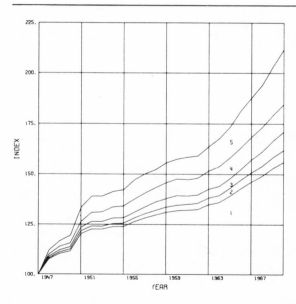

Figure 5.4 *The Rise of the GNP Deflator (P) in Canada From 1947 through 1970 Assumption 2: Rise in P "Caused" by Excess Disposable*
1) Participation Income (Sum of Wages, Farm and Enterprise Income)
2) Interest and Dividend Income
3) Current Transfer Income
4) Business Income
5) Government Income

Several disclaimers are, however, much in order. It will not do simply to equate the "excess" of an income share to its contribution in "causing" inflation. The Canadian economy could not forever remain locked in the sectoral mold of 1947. Increased industrialization and urbanization meant an inevitable relative decline in the farm sector and a rise in services and thus in government services. Also, modern industrial societies have considered it wise public policy to expand the percentage of income transferred to those who are unable to obtain "earned" or property income. Finally, personal interest and dividend income was an unusually small fraction of Personal Income in 1947 (6.8% compared with 8.6% in 1926) and some upsurge of interest rates and income would probably have occurred even in the absence of general inflation. It is also possible that we should have had even more inflation than we did experience if interest rates had not been allowed to increase.

However, for all its shortcomings, our excess income truism does point up some important and neglected matters. For increased taxes, interest payments, and pension contributions are costs to business which must be covered by selling prices.[3] Furthermore, not only is increased interest a cost to business, it is also increased income to lenders, and their increased consumption offsets, in whole or in part, the fall in investment which is expected to make interest hikes counter-inflationary.

The

$$P = \frac{DPY + DBY + DGY}{Q}$$

truism, like all truisms, remains inviolable. Therefore, it also follows that if we ever do succeed in stopping inflation we shall have held our aggregate money income gains to the pace of real output gains. Because the monetary and fiscal policies now extant have not been successful in reconciling full employment and stable prices, and because these policies have the inflationary side effects developed above, economists have been driven to develop incomes policy proposals.

Mark-Up Over Net Wages and "Labour" Income

It is possible to use the data developed in the above section to recast the Wage Cost MarkUp Equation of the Price Level in terms of disposable, rather than pre-tax income. As Appendix Table 5.4. indicates, Disposable Contractual Wage and Salary income was a virtually constant 45% of GNP in Canada from 1946 through 1970, thus when its reciprocal is used as a mark-up factor to explain the price level the fit is very good indeed. Appendix Table 5.11. considers two

---

[3] For a different approach to the same conclusions see Thomas Wilson's estimate that about one half of the inflation in Canada from 1964 through 1971 was directly attributable to tax increases. T.A. Wilson, "Taxes and Inflation," Canadian Tax Foundation, *1972 Conference Report,* Proceedings of the Twenty-Fourth Tax Conference (1973), pp. 174-84.

alternative mark-up equations over net labour income and they are graphed in Figure 5.5. The first equation is $P = k_5R_5$ where $k_5 =$ GNP/W_n and $R_5 = W_n/Q$. W_n is the index of Disposable Wages, Salaries and Supplementary Labour Income. As is evident in Figure 5.5. there is a virtually perfect correspondence between the P index and the "unit net wage cost" index R_5 and this because k_5 is constant.

When the equation is modified to include imputed net Farm and Unincorporated Enterprise Labour Income the fit is not so good. Thus $P = k_6R_6$ where k_6 equals GNP/L_n and L_n equals $W_n + .81$ (Disposable Farm Income) + .68 (Disposable Unincorporated Enterprise Income). Since k_6 increased from an index of 100 to 118 over the period, P rose more than did the "unit net labour cost" index R_6.

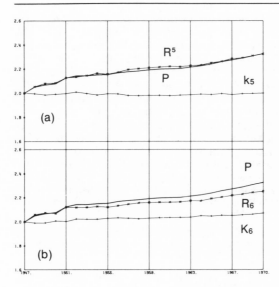

Figure 5.5 *Alternative Mark-Up over Net Incomes in Canada 1947-1970*
a) $P = k_5R_5$ where $k_5 = $ GNP/W_n; $R_5 = W_n/Q$
b) $P = k_6R_6$ where $k_6 = $ GNP/L_n ; $R_6 = L_n/Q$
     $W_n = $ Disposable Contractual Wages, Salaries and Supplementary Labour Income
     $L_n = W_n + .81$ (Disposable Farm Income) +
                .68 (Disposable Unincorp. Enterprise Income)

We saw in Chapter Two that the "fit" of the WCM explanation of inflation improved when we expanded the definition of labour income to include a portion of farm and enterprise "mixed" income. Now we see that in terms of net incomes the situation is reversed. The behavioural inference tendered in the "mark-up" theory is that k is constant because businesses in the various industries of the economy arrive at their selling prices by applying a mark-up to their wage costs. It is somewhat more difficult to come up with a plausible behavioural inference to account for the observed fixity of the *net* wage share, for certainly firms do not set their mark-ups relative to their employees' "take-home" pay. We might posit, "Workers demand that their take-home pay not fall below 45% of GNP and government and business see to it that it doesn't rise above 45% either," but who has observed any of these protagonists to do any of these things? We must therefore conclude that it just happened that way and that as long as k_5 is constant P and R_5 will move together and if in the future k_5 fluctuates P and R_5 will diverge. Much the same unsatisfactory situation plagues the "Phillips Curve" theory of inflation to which we turn.

Taxes and The Phillips Curve

Although much attacked, the Phillips Curve is still the reigning paradigm of "bastard-Keynesian" inflation theory. As we saw in Chapter One, the root concept of the "Phillips" curve; that the rate of change of wages is inversely correlated with the level of unemployment, can be found in *The General Theory,* indeed, it also can be traced back to *Das Capital*.[4] It remained for A. W. Phillips, however, to give his name to the relationship by claiming that the rate of change of money wages in the U.K. for the past one hundred years could be accounted for solely by changes in unemployment and in import prices.[5] Samuelson and Solow[6] soon made the Phillips or "trade-off" curve between unemployment and wages, and thus, minus productivity gains, prices, official on this side of the Atlantic and opened the floodgates of re-estimations, theoretical justifications, attacks and added explanatory variables which continues to the present. The Niagara of books, monographs, articles, and studies on the Phillips curve over the past decade and a half are both a tribute to the power of the basic concept and a sign of failure. For a "trade-off" curve which is both simple and stable has proved to be a chimera. Eckstein and Wilson[7] early found that the addition of a profit variable to the unemployment rate considerably improved the explanation of post WW II

---

[4] See Chapter One, footnote 46. It is interesting to speculate how far the trade-off concept would have gotten if it had been dubbed the "Marx Curve," and to what extent recent history would have been changed thereby.

[5] A.W. Phillips, "The Relationship Between Unemployment and the Rate of Change in Money Wages in the United Kingdom, 1861-1957, *"Economica,* November 1958, pp. 283-99.

[6] P.A. Samuelson and R. Solow, "Analytical Aspects of Anti-Inflation Policy," *American Economic Review,* May 1960, pp. 177-94.

[7] O. Eckstein and T. Wilson, "Determination of Money Wages in American Industry," *Quarterly Journal of Economics,* August 1962, pp. 379-414.

wages in U.S. manufacturing. Bowan and Berry[8] found the rate of change of unemployment as well as the level to be significant. Other Phillips Curve fitters added a domestic price change variable to unemployment, the rate of change of the money supply was likewise tested and trade union "pushfullness' was reduced to an index and found significant by Sylos-Labini[9]. It was inevitable that in all this elaboration of "explanatory" variables that the original unemployment, wage, price "nexus" would be much obscured and even erased. Thus we have had Hines'[10] finding that the level of unemployment explains virtually none of the change of wages in the U.K. since the turn of the century, R. J. Gordon's[11] showing that the short run Phillips Curve is horizontal, and Phelps[12] – and his fellow "natural raters' " argument that the long-run Phillips Curve is vertical. What emerges from much thought, experimentation and printer's ink is that the trade-off curve refuses to hold still and an unpredictable relationship is of little value to the policy maker. Let John Sheahan's conclusion summarize the whole effort, "More complex analysis using several variables is necessary to get good explanations of wage changes for any given period, and when a good regression relationship is established for any one set of years it nearly always turns out that the coefficients change significantly in the next period."[13]

Taxation and the Wage Equation

In view of the above, what is here offered is not another attempt to define "the" determinate, definitive, and invariant trade-off curve, but rather to explore the degree to which our taxation and interest level inferences may or may not account for the shifts which have so frustrated economists and policy makers alike. Our point of departure is the well known study for the Economic Council of Canada of Bodkin, Bond, Reuber and Robinson (BBRR henceforth).[14]

---

[8] W.G. Bowen and R.A. Berry, "Unemployment and Movements of the Money Wage Level," *Review of Economics and Statistics,* May 1963, pp. 163-72.

[9] P. Sylos-Labini "Oligopoly, Unions and Inflation," in N. Swan & D. Wilton eds. *Inflation and the Canadian Experience* (Kingston, Queens University Press, 1971) pp. 51-79.

[10] A.G. Hines, "Unemployment and the Rate of Change of Money Wage Rates in the United Kingdom 1862-1963. A Reappraisal," *Review of Economics and Statistics,* February 1968, pp. 60-7.

[11] R.J. Gordon, "Prices in 1970: The Horizontal Phillips Curve?" *Brookings Papers on Economic Activity* (Washington, Brookings, 1970) pp. 369-410.

[12] E.S. Phelps, "Money Wage Dynamics and Labor Market Equilibrium," in E.S. Phelps, ed., *Microeconomic Foundations of Employment and Inflation Theory,* (New York, Norton, 1970), pp. 124-66.

[13] John Sheahan, *The Wage-Price Guideposts* (Washington, Brookings, 1967), p. 10, For a more recent review of the literature coming to much the same conclusion see S. F. Kaliski, "Is the Phillips Curve Still With Us?," in N. Swan and D. Wilton, eds., *Inflation and the Canadian Experience* (Kingston, Queen's University Press, 1971), pp. 9-18.

[14] R.G. Bodkin, E.P. Bond, G.L. Reuber, T.R. Robinson, *Price Stability and High Employment: The Options for Canadian Economic Policy: An Econometric Study* (Ottawa, Economic Council of Canada CAL, E.C. S5, 1966).

In Chapter Three we made use of the most extreme wage change-unemployment curve derived by BBRR to demonstrate that a forward shifted indirect tax hike would result in a fall in aggregate demand and a rise in aggregate supply cost such that output, employment, and the rate of increase of wages would fall, but that the price level would increase. Here we re-estimate and expand BBRR's "favorite" equation to explain the rate of change of wages in Canada[15].

$$\mathring{W}_t = a + b \mathring{P}_t^* + c \left(\frac{Z}{Q}\right)_{t-2}^* + d \mathring{W}_{US_t}^* + e (U_t^*)^{-2} + f \mathring{W}_{t-4}$$

where

$\mathring{W}_t$ = Rate of change of wages,

$\mathring{P}_t^*$ = Rate of change of prices,

$\left(\frac{Z}{Q}\right)^*$ = Rate of profits

$\mathring{W}_{US_t}^*$ = Rate of change of wages in the U.S.,

U_t^* = Unemployment level

$\mathring{W}_{t-4}$ = Rate of change of wages four quarters previously. The symbol(*) refers to a distributed lag with fixed weights, while the coefficients a, b, c, d, e, and f were estimated by multiple regression over the period from the first quarter of 1953 to the second quarter of 1965. The following coefficients and significance test results were obtained:

Table 5.4. *BBRR "Favorite" Wage Equation Estimates*

Coefficients	t test[16]
a − 4.32	
b 0.487	6.42
c 0.0618	3.16
d 0.291	2.51
e 18.4	2.96
f − 0.116	3.02

$R^2 = 0.847$
F test − 2.42 (indicates shift at .05 level)
Durbin-Watson − 1.62

[15] BBRR pp. 121-2.

[16] t test; indicates the degree of significance to be associated with any particular coefficient. For approximately 45^0 of freedom and a confidence level of 95% the critical value is 2.02. R^2; The multiple coefficient of determination indicates the percentage variation of the dependent variable "explained" by variation in the independent variables. *F test;* General test of goodness of fit of the computed regression to actual data (95% confidence level used here) *Durbin-Watson;* tests for auto-correlation between independent variables.

In 1969 the Dominion Bureau of Statistics undertook a comprehensive revision of the National Accounts series used by BBRR. In order to assess the degree to which this revision affects the regression coefficients, we recalculated BBRR's equation for the period 1955-1970 with the new data.[17] The coefficients and test results obtained are given in Table 5.5

Table 5.5. *BBRR Wage Equation Re-estimated*

Coefficients		t test
a	2.360	
b	0.810	6.82
c	- 0.947	1.75
d	0.541	3.53
e	32.900	4.55
f	- 0.184	2.15

$R^2 = 0.773$
F test $= 33.27$
D.W. $= 1.68$

In our recalculation the profits variable fails the t test. Extensive testing with several time periods showed that the profit variable consistently fails and therefore we have deleted it from the subsequent regression equations of this study.

Two approaches were tried in assessing the impact of taxation on the rate of change of wages. The first approach was to strip off the variables added in "expanding" the Phillips curve and to regress first $\mathring{W}_t = a + b\ (U_t{}^*)^{-2}$ then add the tax variable and re-estimate the equation. The equations were estimated for the entire period 1955 through 1970 and for the sub-periods 1955 through 1966 and 1959 through 1970. Table 5.6. presents the results of this exercise.

---

[17] Thus our time period omits the first two years covered by BBRR and adds four years of observations beyond their time period. We started in 1955 to avoid the lagged effects of the Korean War. The fact that our coefficient estimates for the constant term, a, and for the profits term, c, are quite different from BBRR's is suggestive of shifts in the relationships studied.

Table 5.6. *Taxation and the Basic Phillips Curve in Canada*

Equations						
Period	(1) $\mathring{W}_t = a + b\,(U_t^*)^{-2}$			(2) $\mathring{W}_t = a + b\,(U_t^*)^{-2} + c\,(T_t^*/GNP_t)$		
	Coeff.	B Coeff.	t test	Coeff.	B Coeff.	t test
1955-1970	a 28.86 b 46.03	0.432	3.77	a −96.76 b 36.53 c 5.08	0.343 0.706	4.67 9.61
	$R^2 = .187$ F test = 15.68 D.W. = .45#			$R^2 = .677$ adds 60.3%[1] F test = 63.81 D.W. = .50#		
1955-1966	a 21.06 b 43.53	0.655	5.88	a 19.67 b 43.45 c 0.0006	0.654 0.006	5.66 0.05*
	$R^2 = .429$ F test = 36.66 D.W. = 1.45			$R^2 = .429$ adds 0% F test = 16.89 D.W. = .30#		
1959-1970	a 25.45 b 63.15	0.520	4.13	a −122.58 b 26.89 c 6.14	0.221 0.777	2.96 10.37
	$R^2 = .270$ F test = 16.32 D.W. = .22#			$R^2 = .785$ adds 70.6% F test = 81.97 D.W. = .45#		

* Insignificant at .95 # indicates positive serial correlation
New Variables Equation (2) T*/GNP = Distributed lag of Total Tax Receipts/Gross National Product

1) Percentage calculated as follows:

% added $\dfrac{R^2(2) - R^2(1)}{1.000 - R^2(1)}$

As Table 5.6 indicates, the addition of taxation per unit of output greatly increases the "explanatory" power of the basic Phillips curve. Over the entire period the basic equation's R^2 was only .187. Addition of taxation in the form of taxation as a percentage of GNP raised R^2 to .677. Thus taxation "explained" 60.3% of the variation in wages not explained by unemployment. In later work it would be interesting to test direct and indirect taxes separately, and together, or to test direct taxes in the wage equation and indirect taxes in the price equation. Here we are looking merely for the "brute" impact of the rise of taxation as a percentage of GNP. Both the size of B[18] coefficients and t tests of equation 2 confirm that taxation was more important than unemployment in explaining the rate of change of wages over the entire period.

Table 5.6. also indicates that the explanatory power of taxes increased greatly over the period. In the earlier 11 years, 1955-66, taxation accounts for little or none of the variation in wages, while in the latter period, 1959-1970, taxation per unit of output was highly significant. Thus T_t^*/GNP_t failed to pass the t test and added nothing to R^2 over the period 1955-66, but had a highly significant t value of 10.37 and explained 70.6% of the unexplained variation in 1959-70. Quite clearly, "tax push" becomes an important phenomenon in Canada in the 1960's, as the Economic Council alertly stated.

Table 5.7. examines the explanatory power of taxation when it is "tacked on" to an expanded Phillips curve of the type used by BBRR.

---

[18] B coefficients are estimated coefficients of the *standardized* independent variables. They give an indication of the relative importance of the independent variables in the estimation of the dependent variable.

The most statistically secure regression equation using BBRRs' variables for the entire period 1955-70 takes the form:

$$\mathring{W}_t = a + b\,\mathring{P}_t^* + c\,\mathring{W}^*_{USt} + d\,(U_t^*)^{-2}$$

(Table 5.7. equation 1)

This equation attains a very respectable R^2 of .835, with most of the explanatory power provided by the price and U.S. wage variable rather than unemployment. Equation 2 is formed by adding tax as a percentage of GNP to Equation 1, raising R^2 to .850. Thus taxes add 9.1% to the explanatory power of the expanded Phillips curve. Examination of the B coefficients and t tests indicate that the equation is correctly specified, in that taxes are, now narrowly, the least important of the four explanatory variables.

The most powerful equation we found for the 1955-66 period using BBRR variables took the form:

$$\mathring{W}_t = a + b\,\mathring{P}_t^* + c\,\mathring{W}^*_{USt} + d\,\mathring{W}_{t-4} + e\,(U_t^*)^{-2}$$

(Table 5.7. equation 3)

Table 5.7 *Taxation and the Expanded Phillips Curve in Canada*

Equations

(1) $W_t = a + b\mathring{P}_t^* + cW^*_{USt} + d(U_t^*)^{-2}$ (2) $\mathring{W}_t = (1) + e(T_t^*/GNP_t)$

Period	Coeff.		B Coeff	t test	Coeff.		B Coeff.	t test
1955-1970	a	-0.814			a	-3.743		
	b	0.876	0.539	8.75	b	0.668	0.411	5.22
	c	0.698	0.421	6.35	c	0.613	0.369	5.52
	d	21.118	0.198	3.48	d	22.334	0.210	3.82
					e	0.144	0.201	2.45

$R^2 = .835$ $R^2 = .850$ adds 9.1%[1]
F test 101.61   F test 84.08
D.W. = 1.23#   D.W. = 1.24#

(3) $\mathring{W}_t = a + b\mathring{P}_t^* + c\mathring{W}^*_{USt} + d\mathring{W}_{t-4} + e(U_t^*)^{-2}$ (4) $\mathring{W}_t = (3) + f(T_t^*/GNP_t)$

Period	Coeff.		B Coeff	t test	Coeff.		B Coeff.	t test
1955-1966	a	0.748			a	4.590		
	b	0.814	0.549	6.77	b	0.887	0.598	6.67
	c	0.430	0.292	2.97	c	0.285	0.194	1.59
	d	-0.250	-0.242	3.00	d	-0.289	-0.280	3.31
	e	29.385	0.442	4.47	e	35.417	0.533	4.48
					f	-0.002	-0.145	1.35

$R^2 = 0.745$ $R^2 = 0.755$ adds 3.9%
F test 31.26   F test 21.03
D.W. = 1.97   D.W. = 1.76

(5) $\mathring{W}_t = a + bW^*_{USt} + c\mathring{W}_{t-4} + d(U_t^*)^{-2}$ (6) $\mathring{W}_t = (5) + (T_t^*/GNP_t)$

Period	Coeff.		B Coeff	t test	Coeff.		B Coeff.	t test
1959-1970	a	-2.184			a	-6.692		
	b	1.442	0.842	8.99	b	1.207	0.705	7.45
	c	-0.056	-0.051	0.53[2]	c	-0.180	-0.167	1.77[3]
	d	46.202	0.380	7.21	d	39.374	0.324	6.39
					e	0.238	0.301	3.28

$R^2 = .899$ $R^2 = .912$ adds 20.7%
F test 118.79   F test 111.47
D.W. = 1.99   D.W. = 1.79

1) Percentage calculated as follows:

$$\frac{R^2(BBRR + Tax) - R^2(BBRR)}{1.000 - R^2(BBRR)}$$

2) This variable's t test improves when tax is added
3) This coefficient tested at 90% confidence passes.
   # Indicates Positive Serial Correlation.

Equation 3 attains an R^2 of .745, with most of the explanatory power provided by prices and unemployment. Addition of taxation adds virtually nothing to the explanatory power of the equation (equation 4) and the tax variable fails the t test.

For the 1959-1970 period the best equation found was:

$$\mathring{W}_t = a + b\mathring{W}^*_{USt} + c\mathring{W}^*_{t-4} + d(U_t^*)^{-2} \qquad \text{(Table 5.7 equation 5)}$$

This equation attains the high R^2 of .889. One of the variables, wages lagged 4 quarters, failed the t test, but it was retained because it added to R^2 and because it gained significance when taxes were added. In this equation most of the explanatory power is provided by wages in the U.S. with employment second. When taxes are added, they are highly significant, raising R^2 to .912, thus explaining 20.7% of the unexplained variation in wages. This again confirms that taxation was a significant factor in explaining the pace of wage changes in the 1960s.

The increasing power of taxation as an explanatory variable for wage changes is explored further in Table 5.8. Here simple correlation coefficients (R)s are calculated between our explanatory variables and the rate of change of Canadian wages for selected time periods. Over the entire period, the highest correlation is between prices and wages, followed closely by U.S. wages, and taxes. The second block of figures explores the changing correlations by overlapping 12 year intervals. The steady increase in the power of the tax variable is most evident. The third block of figures explore 5-year time periods without over-lap and the final two periods are of two 10-year over-lapping intervals, 1955-64 and 1961-70. All of the variants confirm that taxation has gained greatly as an explanatory variable of wage change over time.[19]

---

[19]See also C.J. Bruce, "The Wage-Tax Spiral: Canada 1953-1970," *Economic Journal,* 85, June 1975, pp. 372-6. Bruce hypothesized that Canadian wage changes in this period were a function of the rate of change of personal taxes, level of profits, rate of increase of sales, level of unemployment and rate of increase of consumer prices. He concludes " ... the data ... provides a significant degree of empirical support for the hypothesis that the rate of change of Canadian money wage rates have been positively correlated with the change in the average rate of tax incidence. Given that a policy of increasing taxes is conventionally viewed as anti-inflationary, the ramifications of these findings for fiscal policy are potentally very great, and would certainly appear to justify further more detailed research." pp. 375-6.

Table 5.8 *Simple correlation coefficients for all variables with rate of change of Canadian wages for selected time periods.*

Period	$\mathring{P}_t{}^*$	$(U_t{}^*)^{-2}$	$(Z/_Q)t^*_{-2}$	$\mathring{W}^*_{USt}$	$\mathring{W}^*_{t-4}$	$T_t{}^*/GNP_t$
1955-70	.785	.432	.167	.778	.580	.749
1955-66	.512	.655	.461	.552	.051	.151
1956-67	.607	.702	.099	.532	.180	.376
1957-68	.743	.658	.146	.698	.393	.593
1958-69	.856	.590	.080	.828	.611	.774
1959-70	.867	.520	.135	.869	.772	.862
1955-59	.432	.389	.444	.573	.390	.388
1960-65	.473	.839	.048	.387	.563	.710
1966-70	.484	.718	.157	.810	.641	.758
1955-64	.352	.550	.464	.657	.164	.213
1961-70	.929	.465	.196	.906	.912	.924

Interest and the "Trade-Off" Curve

In "Phillips Curve" studies the calculation of the wage change-unemployment curve is a prelude to calculation of a price change curve, by simple or complex transformation. The most simple transformation employs the fact of share stability to convert the wage change curve directly into a price change curve by writing $\mathring{P}_t = \mathring{W}_t - \mathring{A}_t$, where A_t is an index of output per employee. Thus if wages are increasing 9 per cent per annum, and productivity is increasing at 3 per cent, the forecast is for 6 per cent inflation. Many studies, however, calculate the price change curve separately, employing the rate of change of wages as one of a number of explanatory variables. Such a tack was taken by BBRR. Their "favorite" price equation for the period 1953 through 1965 was in the form:[20]

$$\mathring{P}_t = a + b \, \mathring{W}_t + c \, \mathring{F}_t + d \, \mathring{P}_{t-1}$$

where
$\mathring{P}_t$ = Rate of change of prices in Canada
$\mathring{W}_t$ = Rate of change of wages in Canada
$\mathring{F}_t$ = Rate of change of the implicit deflator of imports of goods and services.
The following coefficients and test results were obtained.

Coefficients	t test
a -0.622	
b 0.199	3.53
c 0.0998	2.97
d 0.817	15.6

$R^2 = 0.865$
F test = 0.86   (critical value at 5% = 2.59)
D.W. = 2.04

[20] BBRR p. 146 equation 5.36.

In this section we repeat the experiment of adding a new variable both to a "stripped down" and more complete regression equation to assess the power of the new variable to add to the explanatory power of the equation. The new variable is "the" level of interest rates. That rising rates of price increase and rising interest rates go together is known to every economics student; the experience of inflation, and the anticipation of further inflation causes lenders to demand, and would-be borrowers to be willing to pay, higher interest rates. Furthermore, the "lean against the wind" philosophy of the central bank causes it to slow down the growth of the money supply, further boosting interest rates, as a means of cutting "excess" demand. However, as developed in prior and subsequent chapters, interest is an important cost to business firms which they must recover in selling prices. Thus, like taxes, interest rates affect both aggregate supply and aggregate demand, so that the price level impact of an interest rate hike is ambiguous.

Here we set theoretical questions to one side and merely treat the interest rate as an explanatory variable which helps account for changes in the general price level. The alternative interest rate series used are:

R3   = Interest rate on government securities of 3 month maturity
R10 = Interest rate on 10 industrial bonds[21]

Table 5.9 presents a summary of the result of regressing the rate of change of the Canadian consumer price level first on the rate of change of wages alone and then adding the rate of interest in its "short-term" (R3) and "long-term" (R10) variants. Over the entire period 1955 to 1970 the addition of short-term interest to the rate of change of wages increased R^2 from .446 to .543, thus adding 17.5% to the power of the simple "trade-off" curve to "explain" the rate of change of prices. Turning to sub-periods, it is clear that the importance of interest as an explanatory factor in price movements is an increasing one, as shown both in the more marked rise in R^2 in the 1959-70 sub-period than in the 1955-66 sub-period and in the higher "t" values for R3 in the later period.

Similarly, when "long-term" interest is added to wages for the period 1956-69, R^2 increases only 11.6%. However, when just the sub-period 1961-69 is examined the improvement in R^2 is 22.7%.

---

[21] Data from McLeod, Young, Weir & Co. Ltd., *The Trend of Interest Rates*, January, 1971.

Table 5.9 *Interest and the Simple Trade-Off Curve in Canada*

Equations

	(1) $\mathring{P}_t = a + b\mathring{W}_t$			(2) $\mathring{P}_t = (1) + cR3$		
Period	Coeff.	B Coeff.	t test	Coeff.	B Coeff.	t test
1955-70	a -0.0826			a -0.710		
	b 0.487	0.668	7.07	b 0.224	0.307	2.31
				c 0.468	0.476	3.58
	R^2 = .446 F = 17.41 D.W. = 1.66			R^2 = .543 adds 17.5% F = 16.41 D.W. = 1.97		
1955-66	a 0.033			a -0.913		
	b 0.450	0.482	3.69	b 0.296	0.319	2.24
				c 0.447	0.343	2.41
	R^2 = .232 F = 10.71 D.W. = 1.68			R^2 = .333 adds 13.1% F = 10.06 D.W. = 1.84		
1959-70	a 0.229			a 0.825		
	b 0.476	0.781	8.47	b 0.171	0.281	1.94
				c 0.567	0.598	4.14
	R^2 = .610 F = 20.68 D.W. = 1.78			R^2 = .717 adds 27.4% F = 10.16 D.W. = 1.12#		

	(1) $\mathring{P}_t = a + b\mathring{W}_t$			(3) $\mathring{P}_t = (1) + cR10$		
1956-69	a 0.178			a -1.697		
	b 0.470	0.665	6.48	b 0.296	0.418	3.08
				c 0.452	0.354	2.61
	R^2 = .442 F = 41.99 D.W. = 2.09			R^2 = .507 adds 11.6% F = 26.70 D.W. = 1.62		
1961-69	a 0.123			a 1.543		
	b 0.555	0.910	12.80	b 0.379	0.622	4.20
				c 0.360	0.325	2.25
	R^2 = .828 F = 163.87 D.W. = 1.60			R^2 = .867 adds 22.7% F = 69.88 D.W. = .614#		

# Indicates Positive Serial Correlation

Interest and the "Expanded" Trade-Off Curve in Canada

The most statistically secure regression equation using BBRR's variables for the period 1955-1969 takes the form:[22]

$$\mathring{P}_t = a + b\mathring{W}_t + c\mathring{P}_{t-1}$$

Table 5.10 summarizes the results of adding to this equation our alternative measures of "the" rate of interest. As the table indicates, in either form the rate of interest proved a significant explanatory variable. When the short rate, R3, was used it added 6.7 per cent to "explained" variation of the consumer price level, and when R10 was used it added 8.1 per cent to R^2. Several shorter time periods and patterns of time lags were tried. However, the data available for shorter periods proved insufficient for strong statistical statements, and contemporaneous, rather than lagged interest rate relationships proved best.

Table 5.10 *Interest and the Expanded Trade-Off Curve in Canada 1955-69*

Equations

(1) $\mathring{P}_t = a + b\mathring{W}_t + c\mathring{P}_{t-1}$		(2) $\mathring{P}_t = (1) + cR3$		(3) $\mathring{P}_t = (1) + cR10$	
Coeff.	t test	Coeff.	t test	Coeff.	t test
a -0.306		a -0.741		a -1.914	
b 0.385	4.65	b 0.268	2.70	b 0.331	3.95
c 0.344	3.16	c 0.232	1.94	c 0.220	1.85
		d 0.309	2.03	d 0.385	2.22
R^2 0.552		$R^2 = .582$ adds 6.7%		$R^2 = 0.588$ adds 8.1%	
F = 14.51		F = 14.22		F = 16.10	
D.W. = 2.38		D.W. = 2.02		D.W. = 1.95	

Note

Since the above estimations of the Phillips Curve plus taxes and interest were made, all such estimates have come under attack by J. C. R. Rowley and D. A. Wilton as containing serious autocorrelation.[23] Rowley and Wilton dismiss as "pseudo-results" all t, F and D.W. results, such as ours above, which involve overlapping quarterly moving averages of the dependent and independent variables whether the computation method involves ordinary least squares (as above) or the SCAN method. Recalculating the BBRR study we have used together with the Bank of Canada's RDXI wage equation[24] and Perry's study of the U.S. wage-unemployment relationship,[25] by the unbiased Generalized Least Squares Method, (GLS), Rowley and Wilton find

[22] Ft proved to be insignificant as an independent variable in this and other periods tested.

[23] J.C.R. Rowley and D.A. Wilton, "Quarterly Models of Wage Determination: Some New Efficient Estimates," *American Economic Review*, 63, June 1973, pp. 380-9.

[24] Helliwell *et al* "*The Structure of RDXI,* Bank of Canada Staff Research Studies, No. 3, 1969.

[25] G.L. Perry *Unemployment, Money Wage Rates, and Inflation,* Cambridge, MIT Press, 1966.

that most of the independent variables used to "explain" wages in the three studies fail the t test, while F test values (of the significance of the variables jointly in explaining the dependent variable) are much reduced, and the Durban-Watson statistics are considerably increased. They conclude:

"A comparison of Student's t statistics based on correct formulae with the pseudo-results suggest that the latter must be reduced by at least fifty per cent in most cases. The inferential consequences of these reductions are severe and cannot be neglected. The roles of certain variables, which are usually considered to be of major importance in the determination of wage levels, are in doubt. For example, in the eight equations for which GLS estimates are calculated, unemployment is significant at the .05 level twice and not seven times as indicated by the results for the conventional OLS procedure. Similarly, the change in prices is significant twice at this critical level although the OLS results indicate eight times."[26]

In Table 5.11 is summarized the result of applying Rowley and Wilton's suggested "quick test" of the significance of the "pseudo-results" of our OLS wage and price equations. The quick test consists of dividing the Student's t statistics of our equations by 2 and only accepting the result as "significant" if $t/2 > 2$.

Thus, where formerly we would have accepted the rate of change of prices, $(\overset{\circ}{P}_t)$ and level of unemployment (U_t^{-2}) as significant in all wage equations containing taxes listed in this chapter, we see that while $\overset{\circ}{P}_t$ is still always significant, U_t^{-2} is so only in 4 out of 6 equations. The level of taxation (T_t/GNP_t) which by our early standards we accepted as significant in 4 out of 6 regressions, Rowley and Wilton would accept as "significant" only in 2 out of 6 regressions (the "basic" Phillips equations from 1955-70 and 1959-70 where $t/2$ are an impressive 4.81 and 5.18 respectively).

Similarly, the Price equations containing interest are of reduced significance: the rate of change of wages $(\overset{\circ}{W}_t)$ falls from being a "significant" explanatory variable in 6 out of 7 cases to at most 2 out of 7 and our R3 and R10 interest rate variables which were collectively significant in 7 out of 7 "appearances" are now only so in 1 case, that case being the sub-period 1959-70 where $t/2 > 2.07$.

Where this leaves the "Phillips Curve" in general, and our tax and interest rate argument in particular, is left to time and the reader to decide. If, as many now maintain, the Phillips curve either (a) does not exist or (b) is now obsolete, a lot of paper and computer time have gone for nothing. Far worse, while many econometricians at least had their unemployment disguised, millions of less fortunate souls lost their employment, and society lost billions of dollars worth of output because policy makers believed that they could "trade off" men's jobs for inflation abatement.

The above discussion does, at the very least, demonstrate the simple level of taxation and interest rate variables behave "no worse" than the variables commonly employed in "trade-off" and other regression analyses. Since our purpose here is merely to demonstrate this, we leave the next round to future work. GLS program containing estimates of rate of change of direct and indirect taxes, anyone?

[26] Rowley & Wilton, "Quarterly Models of Wage Determination," p. 386.

Table 5.11 *Quick Test of t Values of Independent Variables*

Quick Test: t/2 > 2.00 = "significant"

Wage equations containing taxes (Independent Variables) t/2

Period	$\overset{\circ}{P}_t$	$\overset{\circ}{W}_{USt}$	U_t^{-2}	W_{t-4}	T_t/GNP_t
1955-70	2.61	2.76	1.91		1.23
1955-66	3.34	0.80	2.24	1.66	0.68
1959-70	3.78		3.20	0.89	1.64
1955-70			2.34		4.81
1955-66			2.83		.03
1959-70			1.48		5.18

Price equations containing interest (Independent Variables) t/2

Period	$\overset{\circ}{W}_t$	P_{t-1}	R3	R10
1955-70	1.16		1.78	
1955-66	1.12		1.21	
1959-70	0.97		2.07	
1956-69	1.54			1.31
1955-69	1.35	0.97	1.02	
1955-69	1.98	0.93		1.11

Appendix Table 5.1.
Taxes Payable by Occupation as a Percentage of Total Taxes Payable – Canada 1947-1970

Year	Employees	Farmers & Fishermen	Pensioners	All Others
1947	64.7	2.5	.2	32.6
1948	67.2	3.2	.2	29.4
1949	62.0	3.8	.2	34.0
1950	64.3	2.5	.2	33.0
1951	67.0	2.8	.2	30.0
1952	70.3	2.8	.2	26.7
1953	73.1	2.3	.2	24.4
1954	74.5	1.2	.2	24.1
1955	73.8	1.5	.2	25.2
1956	75.1	1.2	.2	23.5
1957	76.8	1.1	.2	21.9
1958	74.7	1.5	.3	23.5
1959	76.0	1.4	.3	22.3
1960	77.0	1.3	.3	21.5
1961	77.0	1.5	.4	21.1
1962	77.7	1.8	.5	20.0
1963	78.0	1.8	.5	19.6
1964	78.1	2.1	.6	19.3
1965	78.5	2.2	.7	18.6
1966	80.6	2.3	.9	16.2
1967	81.4	2.3	1.0	15.3
1968	82.0	1.7	1.1	15.1
1969*	82.6	1.4	1.2	14.8
1970*	83.0	1.4	1.3	14.3

*Our estimates

Source: Based on *Canada Year Book 1970-71*, table 15, p. 1154 and corresponding table in earlier issues.

Appendix Table 5.2.
Direct Taxes of Persons plus other Current Transfers from Persons paid by Occupation – Canada 1947-1970 (millions of dollars)

Year	Direct taxes: Persons – other current transfers from people	Employees	Farmers	Pensioners	All Others
1947	962	622.4	24.1	1.9	313.6
1948	1033	694.2	33.0	2.1	303.7
1949	1013	628.1	38.5	2.0	344.4
1950	977	628.2	24.4	2.0	322.4
1951	1356	908.5	38.0	2.7	406.8
1952	1670	1174.0	46.8	3.3	445.9
1953	1832	1339.2	42.1	3.7	447.0
1954	1849	1377.5	22.2	3.7	445.6
1955	1934	1427.3	15.5	3.9	487.4
1956	2224	1670.2	26.7	4.4	522.6
1957	2456	1886.2	27.0	4.9	537.9
1958	2338	1746.5	35.1	7.0	549.4
1959	2668	2027.7	37.4	8.0	595.0
1960	3028	2331.6	36.3	9.1	651.0
1961	3200	2464.0	48.8	12.8	675.2
1962	3448	2679.1	62.1	17.2	689.6
1963	3661	2855.6	65.9	18.3	721.2
1964	4233	3306.0	88.9	25.4	812.7
1965	4804	3771.2	105.7	33.6	893.5
1966	6203	4999.6	142.7	55.8	1004.9
1967	7416	6036.6	170.6	74.2	1134.6
1968	8786	7213.3	149.4	96.6	1326.7
1969	10841	8954.7	151.8	130.1	1604.5
1970	12505	10379.2	175.1	162.6	1788.2

Appendix Table 5.3.
Employee Taxes and Other Current Transfers from Persons as a Percentage of Wages, Salaries and other Supplementary Income – Canada 1947-1970 (millions of dollars)

Year	Wages, Salaries & Supplementary Income	Employee taxes & other transfers	Taxes/ Wages x 100
1947	$6,482	$ 622.4	9.60%
1948	7,496	694.2	9.26
1949	8,115	628.1	7.74
1950	8,766	628.2	7.17
1951	10,340	908.5	8.79
1952	11,633	1,174.0	10.09
1953	12,671	1,339.2	10.57
1954	13,009	1,377.5	10.59
1955	13,967	1,427.3	10.22
1956	15,815	1,670.2	10.56
1957	17,191	1,886.2	10.97
1958	17,660	1,746.5	9.89
1959	18,862	2,027.7	10.75
1960	19,862	2,331.6	11.74
1961	20,746	2,464.0	11.88
1962	22,249	2,679.1	12.04
1963	23,727	2,855.6	12.03
1964	25,886	3,306.0	12.77
1965	28,858	3,771.2	13.07
1966	32,658	4,999.6	15.31
1967	36,114	6,036.6	16.72
1968	39,353	7,213.3	18.33
1969	44,101	8,954.7	20.31
1970	47,949	10,379.2	21.65

Code for Appendix Tables 5.4. to 5.11.

GNP	*Gross National Product*
P	*Implicit G.N.P. Deflator*
WAG	*Disposable Wages, Salaries and Supplementary Labour Income including Military Pay and Allowances*
FRM	*Disposable Farm Income*
UNC	*Disposable Income of Nonfarm Unicorp. business including Rents*
LAB	*Disposable Labour Income*
INT	*Disposable Interest, Dividends and misc. investment income*
CTR	*Disposable Current Transfers (Excluding Interest on the Public Debt)*
DPY	*Disposable Personal Income (sum of WAG + FRM + UNC + INT + CTR)*
RET	*Earnings Not Paid Out to Persons*
CCA	*Capital Consumption Allowances and Miscellaneous Valuation Adjustments*
OTH	*Other Business equals Dividends pd. to non-residents + current transfers from Corp. – Capital assistance – Inventory value adjustments*
DBY	*Disposable Business Income equals RET + capital assistance + CCA + Inventory value adjustment – Current transfer from Corporations + Dividends paid to non-residents*
CATR	*Capital Transfers equals Govt. Transfers to Persons + transfers from non-residents + transfers to non-residents*
SUB	*Subsidies + capital assistance*
DBT	*Interest on the Public Debt*
DGY	*Disposable Government Income equals Total Govt. Revenue + Capital Consumption Allowance – Govt. transfers from non-residents – capital assistance – Current transfers from non-residents – DBT – SUB – Current transfers from other levels of govt. – current transfers to non-residents*
RES	*Residual Error of Estimate*
CAPXY	*Disposable "Capital" Income of Farm and Non-Farm Enterprise CAPXY = .19 FRM + .32 UNC*
Q	*Real Gross National Product equals GNP/P*
W_n	*Index of WAG, 1947 = 100*
L_n	*Index of LAB, 1947 = 100*
R_5	*Index of W_n/Q*
R_6	*Index of L_n/Q*
k_5	*Index GNP/Index W_n*
k_6	*Index GNP/Index L_n*

Table 5.4
Gross National Product as Gross Disposable Income

Year	P	GNP	WAG	FRM	UNC	INT	CTR	DPY
1947	100.0	13169	5859.6	1046.9	1219.1	619.3	876.1	9621
1948	112.2	15127	6801.8	1433.0	1322.0	666.3	904.9	11128
1949	116.8	16300	7486.9	1287.5	1420.3	699.3	995.0	11889
1950	119.5	17955	8137.8	1146.6	1493.3	848.3	1078.0	12704
1951	133.4	21060	9431.5	1835.0	1548.9	903.3	1084.3	14803
1952	139.1	24042	10459.0	1786.2	1647.6	927.5	1409.7	16230
1953	139.1	25327	11331.8	1451.9	1863.3	933.7	1519.3	17100
1954	141.4	25233	11631.5	913.9	1951.8	964.5	1695.3	17157
1955	142.3	27895	12539.7	1054.5	2151.9	1093.7	1799.2	18639
1956	147.2	31374	14144.8	1228.3	2161.0	1212.4	1846.5	20593
1957	150.2	32907	15304.8	890.0	2281.0	1406.1	2162.1	22044
1958	152.3	34094	15913.5	1086.9	2368.6	1473.0	2713.0	23555
1959	155.6	36266	16834.3	982.6	2462.0	1640.0	2838.1	24757
1960	157.5	37775	17530.4	981.7	2420.1	1759.9	3200.9	25893
1961	158.5	39080	18282.0	764.0	2432.2	1920.6	2821.6	26211
1962	159.1	42353	19569.9	1276.9	2430.3	2214.1	3026.8	28518
1963	163.7	45465	20871.4	1337.1	2695.1	2444.7	3099.7	30448
1964	167.7	49783	22580.0	1079.1	2795.6	2619.7	3310.6	32385
1965	173.5	54897	25086.8	1329.3	2968.3	2858.2	3544.4	35787
1966	181.4	61421	27568.4	1651.3	3150.6	3195.5	3843.2	39499
1967	187.6	65722	30077.4	1208.4	3363.2	3409.2	4733.8	42792
1968	194.1	71388	32139.7	1540.6	3566.6	3702.7	5477.4	46427
1969	203.3	78560	35146.3	1492.2	3654.3	4112.2	6152.0	50557
1970	211.7	84468	37569.8	986.9	3733.8	4429.0	6875.5	53595

Year	RET	CCA	OTH	DBY	CATR	SUB	DBT	DGY
1947	618	1157	840	935	897	183	559	2322
1948	780	1333	778	1336	907	85	558	2550
1949	617	1554	454	1707	974	90	572	2531
1950	786	1759	810	1735	1052	74	544	2964
1951	755	2052	1054	1753	1063	142	609	4239
1952	730	2272	260	2742	1391	116	651	4504
1953	897	2564	361	3100	1508	127	620	4640
1954	781	2853	286	3348	1671	102	650	4396
1955	1266	3207	630	3843	1779	94	664	4921
1956	1452	3655	747	4360	1814	154	718	5810
1957	1215	4002	613	4604	2130	149	774	5834
1958	1321	3977	602	4696	2698	168	826	5176
1959	1525	4289	707	5107	2836	272	1023	5915
1960	1415	4571	592	5394	3194	331	1093	6092
1961	1425	4651	730	5346	2819	342	1169	7035
1962	1730	5020	794	5956	3005	402	1300	7784
1963	1950	5319	876	6393	3103	478	1413	8314
1964	2553	5652	958	7247	3306	528	1527	9632
1965	2854	6032	1169	7717	3562	549	1642	11004
1966	2780	6550	1235	8095	3955	698	1811	13136
1967	2658	6956	1228	8386	4899	730	1974	14224
1968	2961	7423	1191	9193	5611	729	2268	16081
1969	3099	7983	1391	9691	6335	782	2621	18855
1970	2744	8708	1090	10362	7145	848	3030	20222

Year	RES
1947	291
1948	113
1949	173
1950	552
1951	265
1952	566
1953	487
1954	332
1955	492
1956	611
1957	425
1958	667
1959	487
1960	396
1961	488
1962	95
1963	310
1964	519
1965	389
1966	691
1967	320
1968	313
1969	543
1970	289

Table 5.5.
Distribution of Gross Disposable Product: Canada

Year	GNP	Wn	.81 FRM	.68 UNC	CAPXY	INT	CTR	DPY
1947	100	44.5	6.4	6.3	4.5	4.7	6.7	73.1
1948	100	45.0	7.7	5.9	4.6	4.4	6.0	73.6
1949	100	45.9	6.4	5.9	4.3	4.3	6.1	72.9
1950	100	45.3	5.2	5.7	3.9	4 7	6.0	70.8
1951	100	44.8	7.1	5.0	4.0	4.3	5.1	70.3
1952	100	43.5	6.0	4.7	3.6	3.9	5.9	67.5
1953	100	44.7	4.6	5.0	3.4	3.7	6.0	67.5
1954	100	46.1	2.9	5.3	3.2	3.8	6.7	68.0
1955	100	45.0	3.1	5.2	3.2	3.9	6.4	66.8
1956	100	45.1	3.2	4.7	2.9	3.9	5.9	65.6
1957	100	46.5	2.2	4.7	2.7	4.3	6.6	67.0
1958	100	46.7	2.6	4.7	2.8	4.3	8.0	69.1
1959	100	46.4	2.2	4.6	2.7	4.5	7.8	68.3
1960	100	46.4	2.1	4.4	2.5	4.7	8.5	68.5
1961	100	46.8	1.6	4.2	2.4	4.9	7.2	67.1
1962	100	46.2	2.4	3.9	2.4	5.2	7.1	67.3
1963	100	45.9	2.4	4.0	2.5	5.4	6.8	67.0
1964	100	45.4	1.8	3.8	2.2	5.3	6.7	65.1
1965	100	45.7	2.0	3.7	2.2	5.2	6.5	65.2
1966	100	44.9	2.2	3.5	2.2	5.2	6.3	64.3
1967	100	45.8	1.5	3.5	2.0	5.2	7.2	65.1
1968	100	45.0	1.7	3.4	2.0	5.2	7.7	65.0
1969	100	44.7	1.5	3.2	1.8	5.2	7.8	64.4
1970	100	44.5	0.9	3.0	1.6	5.2	8.1	63.5

Year	RET	CCA	OTH	DBY	CATR	SUB	DBT	DGY
1947	4.7	8.8	6.4	7.1	6.8	1.3	4.2	17.6
1948	5.2	8.8	5.1	8.8	6.0	0.6	3.7	16.9
1949	3.8	9.5	2.8	10.5	6.0	0.6	3.5	15.5
1950	4.4	9.8	4.5	9.7	5.9	0.4	3.0	16.5
1951	3.6	9.7	5.0	8.3	5.0	0.7	2.9	20.1
1952	3.0	9.5	1.1	11.4	5.8	0.5	2.7	18.7
1953	3.5	10.1	1.4	12.2	6.0	0.5	2.4	18.3
1954	3.1	11.3	1.1	13.3	6.6	0.4	2.6	17.4
1955	4.5	11.5	2.3	13.8	6.4	0.3	2.4	17.6
1956	4.6	11.6	2.4	13.9	5.8	0.5	2.3	18.5
1957	3.7	12.2	1.9	14.0	6.5	0.5	2.4	17.7
1958	3.9	11.7	1.8	13.8	7.9	0.5	2.4	15.2
1959	4.2	11.8	1.9	14.1	7.8	0.8	2.8	16.3
1960	3.7	12.1	1.6	14.3	8.5	0.9	2.9	16.1
1961	3.6	11.9	1.9	13.7	7.2	0.9	3.0	18.0
1962	4.1	11.9	1.9	14.1	7.1	0.9	3.1	18.4
1963	4.3	11.7	1.9	14.1	6.8	1.1	3.1	18.3
1964	5.1	11.4	1.9	14.6	6.6	1.1	3.1	19.3
1965	5.2	11.0	2.1	14.1	6.5	1.0	3.0	20.0
1966	4.5	10.7	2.0	13.2	6.4	1.1	2.9	21.4
1967	4.0	10.6	1.9	12.8	7.5	1.1	3.0	21.6
1968	4.1	10.4	1.7	12.9	7.9	1.0	3.2	22.5
1969	3.9	10.2	1.8	12.3	8.1	1.0	3.3	24.0
1970	3.2	10.3	1.3	12.3	8.5	1.0	3.6	23.9

Year	RES
1947	2.2
1948	0.7
1949	1.1
1950	3.1
1951	1.3
1952	2.4
1953	1.9
1954	1.3
1955	1.8
1956	1.9
1957	1.3
1958	2.0
1959	1.3
1960	1.0
1961	1.2
1962	0.2
1963	0.7
1964	1.0
1965	0.7
1966	1.1
1967	0.5
1968	0.4
1969	0.7
1970	0.3

Table 5.6.
Shares of Inflation: Assumption 1

Year	P	WAG	FRM	UNC	INT	CTR	DPY	RET
1947	100.0	100.0	100.0	100.0	100.0	100.0	100.0	100.0
1948	112.2	105.5	101.2	101.1	100.5	100.7	109.0	100.6
1949	116.8	107.7	101.3	101.5	100.7	101.0	112.3	100.6
1950	119.5	108.8	101.2	101.6	100.9	101.2	113.8	100.9
1951	133.4	115.0	102.9	102.5	101.4	101.7	123.5	101.2
1952	139.1	117.0	102.9	102.7	101.5	102.3	126.4	101.2
1953	139.1	117.5	102.2	102.9	101.4	102.3	126.4	101.4
1954	141.4	119.1	101.5	103.2	101.6	102.8	128.1	101.3
1955	142.3	119.0	101.6	103.3	101.7	102.7	128.3	101.9
1956	147.2	121.3	101.8	103.3	101.8	102.8	131.0	102.2
1957	150.2	123.3	101.4	103.5	102.1	103.3	133.6	101.9
1958	152.3	124.4	101.7	103.6	102.3	104.2	136.1	102.0
1959	155.6	125.8	101.5	103.8	102.5	104.4	138.0	102.3
1960	157.5	126.7	101.5	103.7	102.7	104.9	139.4	102.2
1961	158.5	127.4	101.1	103.6	102.9	104.2	139.2	102.1
1962	159.1	127.3	101.8	103.4	103.1	104.2	139.8	102.4
1963	163.7	129.2	101.9	103.8	103.4	104.3	142.7	102.7
1964	167.7	130.7	101.5	103.8	103.6	104.5	144.0	103.5
1965	173.5	133.6	101.8	104.0	103.8	104.7	147.9	103.8
1966	181.4	136.5	102.2	104.2	104.2	105.1	152.3	103.7
1967	187.6	140.1	101.6	104.5	104.5	106.3	157.0	103.5
1968	194.1	142.4	102.0	104.7	104.9	107.2	161.2	103.9
1969	203.3	146.2	102.0	104.8	105.4	108.1	166.5	104.1
1970	211.7	149.7	101.3	104.9	105.9	109.1	170.9	103.6

Year	CCA	OTH	DBY	CATR	SUB	DBT	DGY	RES
1947	100.0	100.0	100.0	100.0	100.0	100.0	100.0	100.0
1948	101.1	100.6	101.1	100.7	100.1	100.5	102.1	100.1
1949	101.6	100.5	101.8	101.0	100.1	100.6	102.6	100.2
1950	101.9	100.9	101.9	101.1	100.1	100.6	103.2	100.6
1951	103.3	101.7	102.8	101.7	100.2	101.0	106.7	100.4
1952	103.7	100.4	104.5	102.3	100.2	101.1	107.3	100.9
1953	104.0	100.6	104.8	102.3	100.2	101.0	107.2	100.8
1954	104.7	100.5	105.5	102.7	100.2	101.1	107.2	100.5
1955	104.9	101.0	105.8	102.7	100.1	101.0	107.5	100.7
1956	105.5	101.1	106.6	102.7	100.2	101.1	108.7	100.9
1957	106.1	100.9	107.0	103.2	100.2	101.2	108.9	100.6
1958	106.1	100.9	107.2	104.1	100.3	101.3	107.9	101.0
1959	106.6	101.1	107.8	104.3	100.4	101.6	109.1	100.7
1960	107.0	100.9	108.2	104.9	100.5	101.7	109.3	100.6
1961	107.0	101.1	108.0	104.2	100.5	101.7	110.5	100.7
1962	107.0	101.1	108.3	104.2	100.6	101.8	110.9	100.1
1963	107.5	101.2	109.0	104.3	100.7	102.0	111.6	100.4
1964	107.7	101.3	109.9	104.5	100.7	102.1	113.1	100.7
1965	108.1	101.6	110.3	104.8	100.7	102.2	114.7	100.5
1966	108.7	101.6	110.7	105.2	100.9	102.4	117.4	100.9
1967	109.3	101.6	111.2	106.5	101.0	102.6	119.0	100.4
1968	109.8	101.6	112.1	107.4	101.0	103.0	121.2	100.4
1969	110.5	101.8	112.7	108.3	101.0	103.4	124.8	100.7
1970	111.5	101.4	113.7	109.4	101.1	104.0	126.7	100.4

Table 5.7.
Real G.N.P. in Canada by Net Income Category   D.Y. (1947) x Real GNP Index

Year	P	GNP	WAG	FRM	UNC	INT	CTR	DPY
1947	100.0	13169.	5859.6	1046.9	1219.1	619.3	876.1	9621.0
1948	112.2	13482.	5998.9	1071.8	1248.1	634.0	896.9	9849.8
1949	116.8	13955.	6209.5	1109.4	1291.9	656.3	928.4	10195.6
1950	119.5	15025.	6685.5	1194.5	1390.9	706.6	999.6	10977.0
1951	133.4	15787.	7024.5	1255.0	1461.5	742.4	1050.3	11533.7
1952	139.1	17284.	7690.6	1374.0	1600.0	812.8	1149.9	12627.3
1953	139.1	18208.	8101.6	1447.5	1685.6	856.3	1211.3	13302.2
1954	141.4	17845.	7940.3	1418.6	1652.0	839.2	1187.2	13037.3
1955	142.3	19603.	8722.4	1558.4	1814.7	921.9	1304.1	14321.5
1956	147.2	21314.	9483.7	1694.4	1973.1	1002.3	1418.0	15571.5
1957	150.2	21909.	9748.4	1741.7	2028.2	1030.3	1457.5	16006.1
1958	152.3	22386.	9960.8	1779.6	2072.4	1052.8	1489.3	16354.8
1959	155.6	23307.	10370.6	1852.9	2157.6	1096.1	1550.6	17027.8
1960	157.5	23984.	10671.8	1906.7	2220.3	1127.9	1595.6	17522.3
1961	158.5	24656.	10970.9	1960.1	2282.5	1159.5	1640.3	18013.3
1962	159.1	26620.	11844.8	2116.2	2464.3	1251.9	1771.0	19448.3
1963	163.7	27773.	12357.9	2207.9	2571.1	1306.1	1847.7	20290.6
1964	167.7	29686.	13208.8	2359.9	2748.1	1396.0	1974.9	21687.8
1965	173.5	31641.	14078.8	2515.4	2929.1	1488.0	2105.0	23116.2
1966	181.4	33859.	15065.9	2691.7	3134.5	1592.3	2252.6	24737.0
1967	187.6	35033.	15588.1	2785.0	3243.1	1647.5	2330.7	25594.4
1968	194.1	36779.	16364.9	2923.8	3404.8	1729.6	2446.8	26869.9
1969	203.3	38642.	17194.1	3072.0	3577.3	1817.2	2570.8	28231.3
1970	211.7	39900.	17753.6	3171.9	3693.7	1876.4	2654.4	29150.0

Year	RET	CCA	OTH	DBY	CATR	SUB	DBT	DGY
1947	618.0	1157.0	840.0	935.0	897.0	183.0	559.0	2322.0
1948	632.7	1184.5	860.0	957.2	918.3	187.4	572.3	2377.2
1949	654.9	1226.1	890.2	990.8	950.6	193.9	592.4	2460.7
1950	705.1	1320.1	958.4	1066.8	1023.4	208.8	637.8	2649.3
1951	740.9	1387.0	1007.0	1120.9	1075.3	219.4	670.1	2783.6
1952	811.1	1518.5	1102.5	1227.2	1177.3	240.2	733.7	3047.6
1953	854.5	1599.7	1161.4	1292.8	1240.2	253.0	772.9	3210.4
1954	837.4	1567.8	1138.3	1267.0	1215.5	248.0	757.5	3146.5
1955	919.9	1722.3	1250.4	1391.8	1335.2	272.4	832.1	3456.5
1956	1000.2	1872.6	1359.5	1513.3	1451.8	296.2	904.7	3758.1
1957	1028.1	1924.9	1397.5	1555.5	1492.3	304.5	930.0	3863.0
1958	1050.5	1966.8	1427.9	1589.4	1524.8	311.1	950.2	3947.2
1959	1093.8	2047.7	1486.7	1654.8	1587.6	323.9	989.3	4109.6
1960	1125.5	2107.2	1529.9	1702.9	1633.7	333.3	1018.1	4229.0
1961	1157.1	2166.2	1572.7	1750.6	1679.4	342.6	1046.6	4347.4
1962	1249.3	2338.8	1698.0	1890.0	1813.2	369.9	1130.0	4693.8
1963	1303.4	2440.1	1771.6	1971.9	1891.8	385.9	1178.9	4897.1
1964	1393.1	2608.1	1893.5	2107.7	2022.0	412.5	1260.1	5234.3
1965	1484.9	2779.9	2018.3	2246.5	2155.2	439.7	1343.1	5579.0
1966	1589.0	2974.8	2159.8	2404.0	2306.3	470.5	1437.3	5970.2
1967	1644.0	3077.9	2234.6	2487.3	2386.3	486.8	1487.1	6177.1
1968	1726.0	3231.3	2346.0	2611.3	2505.2	511.1	1561.2	6485.0
1969	1813.4	3395.0	2464.8	2743.6	2632.1	537.0	1640.3	6813.5
1970	1872.4	3505.5	2545.1	2832.9	2717.8	554.5	1693.7	7035.3

Year	RES
1947	291.0
1948	297.9
1949	308.4
1950	332.0
1951	348.9
1952	381.9
1953	402.3
1954	394.3
1955	433.2
1956	471.0
1957	484.1
1958	494.7
1959	515.0
1960	530.0
1961	544.8
1962	588.2
1963	613.7
1964	656.0
1965	699.2
1966	748.2
1967	774.1
1968	812.7
1969	853.9
1970	881.7

Table 5.8.
Excess G.N.P.: Assumption 2 – Canada

Year	P	GNP	WAG	FRM	UNC	INT	CTR	DPY
1947	100.0	0.	0.0	0.0	0.0	0.0	0.0	0.0
1948	112.2	1645.	802.9	361.2	73.9	32.3	8.0	1278.2
1949	116.8	2345.	1277.4	178.1	128.4	43.0	66.6	1693.4
1950	119.5	2930.	1452.3	-47.9	102.4	141.7	78.4	1727.0
1951	133.4	5273.	2407.0	580.0	87.4	160.9	34.0	3269.3
1952	139.1	6758.	2768.4	412.2	47.6	114.7	259.8	3602.7
1953	139.1	7119.	3230.2	4.4	177.7	77.4	308.0	3797.8
1954	141.4	7388.	3691.2	-504.7	299.8	125.3	508.1	4119.7
1955	142.3	8292.	3817.3	-503.9	337.2	171.8	495.1	4317.5
1956	147.2	10060.	4661.1	-466.1	187.9	210.1	428.5	5021.5
1957	150.2	10998.	5556.4	-851.7	252.8	375.8	704.6	6037.9
1958	152.3	11708.	5952.7	-692.7	296.2	420.2	1223.7	7200.2
1959	155.6	12959.	6463.7	-870.3	304.4	543.9	1287.5	7729.2
1960	157.5	13791.	6858.6	-925.0	199.8	632.0	1605.3	8370.7
1961	158.5	14424.	7311.1	-1196.1	149.7	761.1	1181.3	8197.7
1962	159.1	15733.	7725.1	-839.3	-34.0	962.2	1255.8	9069.7
1963	163.7	17692.	8513.5	-870.8	124.0	1138.6	1252.0	10157.4
1964	167.7	20097.	9371.2	-1280.8	47.5	1223.7	1335.7	10697.2
1965	173.5	23256.	11008.0	-1186.1	39.2	1370.2	1439.4	12670.8
1966	181.4	27562.	12502.5	-1040.4	16.1	1603.2	1590.6	14762.0
1967	187.6	30689.	14489.3	-1576.6	120.1	1761.7	2403.1	17197.6
1968	194.1	34609.	15774.8	-1383.2	161.8	1973.1	3030.6	19557.1
1969	203.3	39918.	17952.2	-1579.8	77.0	2295.0	3581.2	22325.7
1970	211.7	44568.	19816.2	-2185.0	40.1	2552.6	4221.1	24445.0

Year	RET	CCA	OTH	DBY	CATR	SUB	DBT	DGY
1947	0.0	0.0	0.0	0.0	0.0	0.0	0.0	0.0
1948	147.3	148.5	-82.0	378.8	-11.3	-102.4	-14.3	172.8
1949	-37.9	317.9	-436.2	716.2	23.4	-103.9	-20.4	70.3
1950	80.9	438.9	-148.4	668.2	28.6	-134.8	-93.8	314.7
1951	14.1	665.0	47.0	632.1	-12.3	-77.4	-61.1	1455.4
1952	-81.1	753.5	-842.5	1514.8	213.7	-124.2	-82.7	1456.4
1953	42.5	964.3	-800.4	1807.2	267.8	-126.0	-152.9	1429.6
1954	-56.4	1285.2	-852.3	2081.0	455.5	-146.0	-107.5	1249.5
1955	346.1	1484.7	-620.4	2451.2	443.8	-178.4	-168.1	1464.5
1956	451.8	1782.4	-612.5	2846.7	362.2	-142.2	-186.7	2051.9
1957	186.9	2077.1	-784.5	3048.5	637.7	-155.5	-156.0	1971.0
1958	270.5	2010.2	-825.9	3106.6	1173.2	-143.1	-124.2	1228.8
1959	431.2	2241.3	-779.7	3452.2	1248.4	-51.9	33.7	1805.4
1960	289.5	2463.8	-937.9	3691.1	1560.3	-2.3	74.9	1863.0
1961	267.9	2484.8	-842.7	3595.4	1139.6	-0.6	122.4	2687.6
1962	480.7	2681.2	-904.0	4066.0	1191.8	32.1	170.0	3090.2
1963	646.6	2878.9	-895.6	4421.1	1211.2	92.1	234.1	3416.9
1964	1159.9	3043.9	-935.5	5139.3	1284.0	115.5	266.9	4397.7
1965	1369.1	3252.1	-849.3	5470.5	1406.8	109.3	298.9	5425.0
1966	1191.0	3575.2	-924.8	5691.0	1648.7	227.5	373.7	7165.8
1967	1014.0	3878.1	-1006.6	5898.7	2512.7	243.2	486.9	8046.9
1968	1235.0	4191.7	-1155.0	6581.7	3105.8	217.9	706.8	9596.0
1969	1285.6	4588.0	-1073.8	6947.4	3702.9	245.0	980.7	12041.5
1970	871.6	5202.5	-1455.1	7529.1	4427.2	293.5	1336.3	13186.7

Year	RES
1947	0.0
1948	-184.9
1949	-135.4
1950	220.0
1951	-83.9
1952	184.1
1953	84.7
1954	-62.3
1955	58.8
1956	140.0
1957	-59.1
1958	172.3
1959	-28.0
1960	-134.0
1961	-56.8
1962	-493.2
1963	-303.7
1964	-137.0
1965	-310.2
1966	-57.2
1967	-454.1
1968	499.7
1969	-310.9
1970	-592.7

Table 5.9.
Excess Disposable Income as a % of Excess GNP: Assumption 2 – Canada

Year	GNP	WAG	FRM	UNC	INT	CTR	DPY	RET
1948	100.0	43.3	19.5	4.0	1.7	0.4	69.0	7.9
1949	100.0	51.3	7.2	5.2	1.7	2.7	68.1	-1.5
1950	100.0	53.3	-1.8	3.8	5.2	2.9	63.4	3.0
1951	100.0	44.9	10.8	1.6	3.0	0.6	61.0	0.3
1952	100.0	42.1	6.3	0.7	1.7	3.9	54.8	-1.2
1953	100.0	45.9	0.1	2.5	1.1	4.4	54.0	0.6
1954	100.0	49.5	-6.8	4.0	1.7	6.8	55.3	-0.8
1955	100.0	46.4	-6.1	4.1	2.1	6.0	52.4	4.2
1956	100.0	47.0	-4.7	1.9	2.1	4.3	50.6	4.6
1957	100.0	50.2	-7.7	2.3	3.4	6.4	54.6	1.7
1958	100.0	51.6	-6.0	2.6	3.6	10.6	62.4	2.3
1959	100.0	49.8	-6.7	2.3	4.2	9.9	59.5	3.3
1960	100.0	49.2	-6.6	1.4	4.5	11.5	60.1	2.1
1961	100.0	50.5	-8.3	1.0	5.3	8.2	56.6	1.9
1962	100.0	47.6	-5.2	-0.2	5.9	7.7	55.8	3.0
1963	100.0	47.3	-4.8	0.7	6.3	7.0	56.4	3.6
1964	100.0	46.3	-6.3	0.2	6.0	6.6	52.9	5.7
1965	100.0	46.7	-5.0	0.2	5.8	6.1	53.8	5.8
1966	100.0	45.3	-3.8	0.1	5.8	5.8	53.4	4.3
1967	100.0	46.5	-5.1	0.4	5.7	7.7	55.2	3.3
1968	100.0	44.9	-3.9	0.5	5.6	8.6	55.7	3.5
1969	100.0	44.6	-3.9	0.2	5.7	8.9	55.5	3.2
1970	100.0	43.9	-4.8	0.1	5.7	9.3	54.1	1.9

Year	CCA	OTH	DBY	CATR	SUB	DBT	DGY	RES
1948	8.0	-4.4	20.4	-0.6	-5.5	-0.8	9.3	1.3
1949	12.8	-17.5	28.8	0.9	-4.2	-0.8	2.8	0.3
1950	16.1	-5.4	24.5	1.0	-4.9	-3.4	11.5	0.6
1951	12.4	0.9	11.8	-0.2	-1.4	-1.1	27.2	0.0
1952	11.5	-12.8	23.0	3.2	-1.9	-1.3	22.1	0.1
1953	13.7	-11.4	25.7	3.8	-1.8	-2.2	20.3	0.0
1954	17.2	-11.4	27.9	6.1	-2.0	-1.4	16.8	0.0
1955	18.0	-7.5	29.8	5.4	-2.2	-2.0	17.8	0.0
1956	18.0	-6.2	28.7	3.7	-1.4	-1.9	20.7	0.0
1957	18.8	-7.1	27.6	5.8	-1.4	-1.4	17.8	0.0
1958	17.4	-7.2	26.9	10.2	-1.2	-1.1	10.7	0.0
1959	17.3	-6.0	26.6	9.6	-0.4	0.3	13.9	0.0
1960	17.7	-6.7	26.5	11.2	-0.0	0.5	13.4	0.0
1961	17.2	-5.8	24.8	7.9	-0.0	0.8	18.6	0.0
1962	16.5	-5.6	25.0	7.3	0.2	1.0	19.0	0.1
1963	16.0	-5.0	24.6	6.7	0.5	1.3	19.0	0.0
1964	15.0	-4.6	25.4	6.3	0.6	1.3	21.7	0.0
1965	13.8	-3.6	23.2	6.0	0.5	1.3	23.0	0.0
1966	12.9	-3.3	20.6	6.0	0.8	1.4	25.9	0.0
1967	12.4	-3.2	18.9	8.1	0.8	1.6	25.8	0.0
1968	11.9	-3.3	18.7	8.8	0.6	2.0	27.3	0.0
1969	11.4	-2.7	17.3	9.2	0.6	2.4	29.9	0.0
1970	11.5	-3.2	16.7	9.8	0.6	3.0	29.2	0.0

Table 5.10.
Shares of Inflation: Assumption 2 – Canada

Year	P	WAG	FRM	UNC	INT	CTR	DPY	RET
1947	100.0	100.0	100.0	100.0	100.0	100.0	100.0	100.0
1948	112.2	105.	102.4	100.5	100.2	100.1	108.4	101.0
1949	116.8	108.6	101.2	100.9	100.3	100.4	111.4	99.7
1950	119.5	110.4	99.7	100.7	101.0	100.6	112.4	100.6
1951	133.4	115.0	103.6	100.5	101.0	100.2	120.4	100.1
1952	139.1	116.5	102.4	100.3	100.7	101.5	121.4	99.5
1953	139.1	118.0	100.0	101.0	100.4	101.7	121.1	100.2
1954	141.4	120.5	97.2	101.7	100.7	102.8	122.9	99.7
1955	152.3	119.6	97.4	101.7	100.9	102.5	122.2	101.8
1956	147.2	122.2	97.8	100.9	101.0	102.0	123.9	102.1
1957	150.2	125.2	96.1	101.1	101.7	103.2	127.4	100.8
1958	152.3	127.0	96.9	101.3	101.9	105.5	132.6	101.2
1959	155.6	127.7	96.3	101.3	102.3	105.5	133.1	101.8
1960	157.5	128.3	96.2	100.8	102.6	106.6	134.6	101.2
1961	158.5	129.5	95.2	100.6	103.1	104.8	133.1	101.1
1962	159.1	128.1	96.9	99.9	103.5	104.6	133.0	101.7
1963	163.7	130.1	96.9	100.4	104.0	104.4	135.9	102.3
1964	167.7	131.4	95.7	100.2	104.1	104.5	135.8	103.9
1965	173.5	134.3	96.3	100.1	104.3	104.5	139.5	104.3
1966	181.4	136.8	96.9	100.0	104.7	104.7	143.5	103.5
1967	187.6	140.7	95.6	100.3	105.0	106.8	148.4	102.9
1968	194.1	142.3	96.3	100.4	105.3	108.1	152.4	103.3
1969	203.3	146.1	95.9	100.2	105.9	109.2	157.3	103.3
1970	211.7	149.0	94.6	100.1	106.3	110.4	160.5	102.2

Year	CCA	OTH	DBY	CATR	SUB	DBT	DGY	RES
1947	100.0	100.0	100.0	100.0	100.0	100.0	100.0	100.0
1948	101.0	99.5	102.5	99.9	99.3	99.9	101.1	100.2
1949	102.1	97.1	104.8	100.2	99.3	99.9	100.5	100.1
1950	103.1	98.9	104.8	100.2	99.0	99.3	102.3	100.1
1951	104.1	100.3	103.9	99.9	99.5	99.6	109.1	100.0
1952	104.5	95.0	109.0	101.3	99.3	99.5	108.7	100.0
1953	105.4	95.6	110.0	101.5	99.3	99.2	107.9	100.0
1954	107.1	95.3	111.6	102.5	99.2	99.4	106.9	100.0
1955	107.6	96.8	112.6	102.3	99.1	99.1	107.5	100.0
1956	108.5	97.1	113.5	101.7	99.3	99.1	109.8	100.0
1957	109.4	96.4	113.8	102.9	99.3	99.3	108.9	100.0
1958	109.1	96.3	114.1	105.3	99.4	99.4	105.6	100.0
1959	109.6	96.7	114.8	105.3	99.8	100.1	107.7	100.0
1960	110.2	96.1	115.2	106.4	100.0	100.3	107.7	100.0
1961	110.0	96.6	114.5	104.6	100.0	100.5	110.9	100.0
1962	109.8	96.7	114.8	104.3	100.1	100.6	111.2	100.1
1963	110.2	96.8	115.6	104.3	100.3	100.8	112.1	100.0
1964	110.2	96.9	117.2	104.3	100.4	100.9	114.7	100.0
1965	110.1	97.4	117.1	104.4	100.3	100.9	116.9	100.0
1966	110.5	97.3	116.8	104.9	100.7	101.1	121.1	100.0
1967	110.9	97.2	116.6	107.1	100.7	101.4	122.6	100.0
1968	111.2	96.9	117.6	108.3	100.6	101.9	125.7	100.0
1969	111.8	97.2	117.8	109.5	100.6	102.5	130.9	100.0
1970	112.9	96.4	118.6	110.9	100.7	103.3	132.6	100.0

Table 5.11.
Alternative Net Mark-up Ratios: Canada

Year	GNP	Q	Wn	Ln	R5	R6	k5	k6
1947	100.0	100.0	100.0	100.0	100.0	100.0	100.0	100.0
1948	114.9	102.4	116.1	117.6	113.4	114.8	99.0	97.7
1949	123.8	106.0	127.8	126.0	120.6	118.9	96.9	98.2
1950	136.3	114.1	138.9	133.8	121.7	117.2	98.2	101.9
1951	159.9	119.9	161.0	158.8	134.3	132.5	99.4	100.7
1952	182.6	131.2	178.5	172.8	136.0	131.7	102.3	105.6
1953	192.3	138.3	193.4	182.8	139.9	132.2	99.4	105.2
1954	191.6	135.5	198.5	181.8	146.5	134.1	96.5	105.4
1955	211.8	148.9	214.0	197.1	143.8	132.4	99.0	107.5
1956	238.2	161.8	241.4	220.4	149.1	136.2	98.7	108.1
1957	249.9	166.4	261.2	233.2	157.0	140.2	95.7	107.1
1958	258.9	170.0	271.6	244.2	159.8	143.7	95.3	106.0
1959	275.4	177.0	287.3	256.1	162.3	144.7	95.9	107.5
1960	286.8	182.1	299.2	265.0	164.3	145.5	95.9	108.2
1961	296.8	187.2	312.0	272.7	166.6	145.7	95.1	108.8
1962	321.6	202.1	334.0	295.3	165.2	146.1	96.3	108.9
1963	345.2	210.9	356.2	315.6	168.9	149.7	96.9	109.4
1964	378.0	225.4	385.4	336.4	170.9	149.2	98.1	112.4
1965	416.9	240.3	428.1	373.9	178.2	155.6	97.4	111.5
1966	466.4	257.1	470.5	412.0	183.0	160.2	99.1	113.2
1967	499.1	266.0	513.3	442.4	193.0	166.3	97.2	112.8
1968	542.1	279.3	548.5	475.2	196.4	170.1	98.8	114.1
1969	596.6	293.4	599.8	515.4	204.4	175.6	99.5	115.8
1970	641.4	303.0	641.2	542.8	211.6	179.2	100.0	118.2

6 Harrod's dichotomy and the price level

with Hamid Habibagahi

The purpose of this chapter is to explore "Harrod's dichotomy" in a comparative statics model.[1] According to Harrod there are two reasons why demand restriction may have a perverse effect upon the price level. First, if firms encounter "short run increasing returns to scale," their costs rise as the output level falls, a situation which may lead them to raise rather than lower their prices. Second, the interest and tax hikes used to "stop inflation" raise variable costs and thus tend to raise the price level at an employment level.

In the following analysis it is assumed that direct taxes do not affect the cost level and therefore affect the price level only through their effects upon aggregate demand and output while indirect taxes are shifted "forward" in higher prices.[2]

The model

Consider the following model:

Excess demand for real output $\equiv E_x$

$$= C\ (X\ (N),\ r,\ T) + I\ (X\ (N),\ r,\ T) + G - X\ (N) \tag{1}$$

Excess demand for real balances $\equiv E_m$

$$= L\ (X\ (N),\ r) - M/P \tag{2}$$

---

[1] Roy Harrod writes: "The 'dichotomy' is as follows. If aggregate demand is running ahead of supply potential, this will tend to pull prices up. In these circumstances deflationary policies, designed to reduce aggregate demand, will have the effect of reducing, or, in the absence of wage-push trouble, eliminating, any price increases . . . But, if initially aggregate demand is not above supply potential, it is no longer clear that deflationary policies, so called, will have the effect of reducing or eliminating any price inflation that is occurring. It may even be the other way round"[13, p. 624].

[2] The very considerable literature concerning the shiftability and "direction" of shifting of direct and indirect taxes has been virtually ignored by inflation theorists. It is easy to show that in a purely competitive market "maximizers," whether workers or businessmen, are unable to shift the burden of direct, or "income" taxes in the "short run," although they have more scope in the "long run" [16, 18]. It is also shown in this literature that in virtually all cases indirect taxes, that is, sales, value added, and excise taxes, are fully or partially shifted in the short run and thus affect relative prices. Most theorists have seen indirect taxes as raising the price level [7, 15, 16] and empirical studies have given much support to this view [3, 4, 9, 23]. Rolph, however, has maintained that excise taxes are shifted "backward" in lower factor incomes and thus tend to lower the price level [19]. Empirical studies also tend to demonstrate that the corporate profits tax is also shifted in the short run [11, 14, 21]. Furthermore, it is often argued that labor unions increasingly bargain in terms of net or "take-home" pay. If they are able to shift the income tax "forward" in higher gross pay, the strictures developed here against the indirect tax as an anti-inflation measure would apply, perhaps in lesser measure, to direct taxes as well.

Price level equation $\equiv E_p$

$= MC \ (w, \ r, \ T, \ X \ (N)) - P$ where $MC \geq AC$ (3a)

$= AC \ (w, \ r, \ T, \ X \ (N)) - P$ where $MC < AC$ (3b)

Tax receipts equation $\equiv E_t$ (4)

$= t \ (X \ (N)) - T$

Where
X = real output
I = real investment expenditures
C = real consumption expenditures
G = real government expenditures
L = demand for real money balances
M = supply of nominal money balances
w = money wage rate
P = price level
N = level of employment
r = interest rate
MC = marginal cost
AC = average cost
T = real tax receipts
t = marginal rate of taxation

The above system has four endogenous variables N, r, P, T, and four exogenous variables G, M, w, t. Equations (1), (2), and (4) require little comment. Equations (3), the price-level equations, are central to the analysis of Harrod's dichotomy.

It is specified that when marginal cost is greater than, or equal to, average cost, the equilibrium price level is equal to marginal cost, as in conventional analysis. It was also specified that in a situation of general excess capacity, where $MC < AC$ that the equilibrium price level is equal to average cost, because a price lower than this entails losses to the firms. The ability of firms to so price their output involves some degree of imperfect competition which raises several issues not further explored here. The assumption further means that as output expands toward capacity average cost, price falls as long as $MC < AC$ whether

$$\frac{\partial MC}{\partial X} \gtrless 0.[3]$$

We do not assume that when the economy is in equilibrium $(E_x = 0, E_m = 0, E_p = 0, E_t = 0)$ that there is full employment of the labor force because the exogenously determined money wage may not result in a real wage (w/P) compatible with full employment.

Using the comparative static analysis [20], one can find the directional changes of P, r, N, and T for changes in G, M, w, and t. Differentiating the equilibrium positions of equations (1), (2), (3a) and (4) with respect to all variables we obtain

---

[3] Gustav Cassel long ago argued that $P = MC$ under conditions of increasing cost and $P = AC$ under conditions of decreasing cost. See his "Supplementary Principles of Pricing" discussion [5, pp. 99-105].

$$
\begin{bmatrix}
a_{11} & a_{12} & a_{13} & a_{14} \\
a_{21} & a_{22} & a_{23} & a_{24} \\
a_{31} & a_{32} & a_{33} & a_{34} \\
a_{41} & a_{42} & a_{43} & a_{44}
\end{bmatrix}
\begin{bmatrix}
dN' \\
dr' \\
dP' \\
dT'
\end{bmatrix}
=
\begin{bmatrix}
-dG \\
\dfrac{1}{P}dM \\
-\dfrac{MC}{\partial w}dw \\
-X(N)dt
\end{bmatrix}
\quad (1)
$$

Where dN', dr', dP' and dT' are changes in the equilibrium values of N, r, P, and T. The elements a_{ij} are:

$$a_{11} = \left(\frac{\partial C}{\partial X} + \frac{\partial I}{\partial X} - 1\right)\frac{\partial X}{\partial N} \qquad a_{12} = \frac{\partial C}{\partial r} + \frac{\partial I}{\partial r}$$

$$a_{21} = \left(\frac{\partial L}{\partial X}\right)\left(\frac{\partial X}{\partial N}\right) \qquad a_{22} = \frac{\partial L}{r}$$

$$a_{31} = \left(\frac{\partial MC}{\partial X}\right)\left(\frac{\partial X}{\partial N}\right) \qquad a_{32} = \frac{\partial MC}{\partial r}$$

$$a_{41} = t\left(\frac{\partial X}{\partial N}\right) \qquad a_{42} = 0$$

$$a_{13} = 0 \qquad a_{14} = \frac{\partial C}{\partial T} + \frac{\partial I}{\partial T}$$

$$a_{23} = \frac{M}{P^2} \qquad a_{24} = 0$$

$$a_{33} = -1 \qquad a_{34} = \frac{\partial MC}{\partial T}$$

$$a_{43} = 0 \qquad a_{44} = -1$$

The traditional case $MC \geq AC$, direct taxes

Let us make the standard qualitative assumptions concerning the elements of the matrix A, when equation (3a) applies; that is, $MC \geq AC$, government is financed by direct taxes (so that $\partial MC/\partial T = 0$), and the cost effect of interest rate changes are assumed to be "of order zero."

$$\frac{\partial C}{\partial X} > 0; \quad \frac{\partial I}{\partial X} > 0; \quad \frac{\partial X}{\partial N} > 0; \quad \frac{\partial I}{\partial r} < 0; \quad \frac{\partial C}{\partial r} < 0$$

$$\frac{\partial L}{\partial X} > 0; \quad \frac{\partial L}{\partial r} < 0; \quad \frac{\partial MC}{\partial X} > 0; \quad \frac{\partial MC}{\partial r} = 0; \quad \frac{\partial C}{\partial T} < 0$$

$$\frac{\partial I}{\partial T} < 0; \quad \frac{\partial MC}{\partial T} = 0$$

The coefficient matrix A would have the following sign pattern.

$$
\begin{bmatrix}
- & - & 0 & - \\
+ & - & + & 0 \\
+ & 0 & - & 0 \\
+ & 0 & 0 & -
\end{bmatrix}
\quad (2)
$$

$|A|$ is positive for all the values of a_{ij}, given the above sign pattern.

Premultiplying the vector (dN', dr', dP', dT') by the inverse of the matrix A, we get

$$
\begin{bmatrix} dN' \\ dr' \\ dP' \\ dT' \end{bmatrix}
=
\begin{bmatrix} - & + & + & + \\ - & - & - & + \\ - & + & - & + \\ - & + & + & - \end{bmatrix}
\begin{bmatrix} -dG \\ \dfrac{1}{P}dM \\ -\dfrac{\partial MC}{\partial w}dw \\ -X(N)dt \end{bmatrix}
$$

Allowing variables to change one at a time the following comparative static results emerge:

$$\frac{dN'}{dG} > 0 \qquad \frac{dr'}{dG} > 0 \qquad \frac{dP'}{dG} > 0 \qquad \frac{dT'}{dG} > 0$$

$$\frac{dN'}{\frac{1}{P}dM} > 0 \qquad \frac{dr'}{\frac{1}{P}dM} < 0 \qquad \frac{dP'}{\frac{1}{P}dM} > 0 \qquad \frac{dT'}{\frac{1}{P}dM} > 0$$

$$\frac{dN'}{dw} < 0 \qquad \frac{dr'}{dw} > 0 \qquad \frac{dP'}{dw} > 0 \qquad \frac{dT'}{dw} \quad ?$$

$$\frac{dN'}{dt} < 0 \qquad \frac{dr'}{dt} < 0 \qquad \frac{dP'}{dt} < 0 \qquad \frac{dT'}{dt} > 0$$

The above results are consistent with the usual or traditional directional changes in economic variables. That is, regarding anti-inflationary policy, a decrease in government spending, or in the money supply, or an increase in taxes unambiguously lowers the equilibrium price level $dP'/dG > 0$, $dP'/dM > 0$, $dP'/dt < 0$.

Case 2: $MC \geq AC$, indirect taxes

All the assumptions are the same as in the previous section (traditional case), except $\partial MC/\partial T > 0$.

In this case the sign pattern of the coefficient matrix A is

$$
\begin{bmatrix} - & - & 0 & - \\ + & - & + & 0 \\ + & 0 & - & + \\ + & 0 & 0 & - \end{bmatrix} \tag{3}
$$

since $|A| > 0$ we obtain

$$
\begin{bmatrix} dN' \\ dr' \\ dP' \\ dT' \end{bmatrix}
=
\begin{bmatrix} - & + & + & + \\ - & - & - & ? \\ - & + & - & ? \\ - & + & + & - \end{bmatrix}
\begin{bmatrix} -dG \\ \dfrac{1}{P}dM \\ -\dfrac{\partial MC}{\partial w}dw \\ -X(N)dt \end{bmatrix}
$$

Changing one variable at a time the following comparative static results emerge:

$$\frac{dN'}{dG} > 0 \qquad \frac{dr'}{dG} > 0 \qquad \frac{dP'}{dG} > 0 \qquad \frac{dT'}{dG} > 0$$

$$\frac{dN'}{\frac{1}{P}dM} > 0 \qquad \frac{dr'}{\frac{1}{P}dM} < 0 \qquad \frac{dP'}{\frac{1}{P}dM} > 0 \qquad \frac{dT'}{\frac{1}{P}dM} > 0$$

$$\frac{dN'}{dw} < 0 \qquad \frac{dr'}{dw} > 0 \qquad \frac{dP'}{dw} > 0 \qquad \frac{dT'}{dw} \ ?$$

$$\frac{dN'}{dt} < 0 \qquad \frac{dr'}{dt} \ ? \qquad \frac{dP'}{dt} \ ? \qquad \frac{dT'}{dt} > 0$$

The sign of $\frac{dr'}{dt}$ and $\frac{dP'}{dt}$ is ambiguous as expected, since sign $\frac{dr'}{dt}$

= sign

$$\left[\left(\frac{\partial C}{\partial T} + \frac{\partial I}{\partial T} \right) \frac{\partial L}{\partial X} + \frac{\partial L}{\partial r} \left(\frac{\partial MC}{\partial X} \frac{\partial X}{\partial N} \right) - \left(\frac{\partial C}{\partial X} + \frac{\partial I}{\partial X} - 1 \right) \frac{M}{P^2} \frac{\partial MC}{\partial T} \right]$$

Assuming $\frac{\partial L}{\partial r}$ is very small

$$=> \text{sign} \frac{dr'}{dt} = \text{sign} \left[\left(\frac{\partial C}{\partial T} + \frac{\partial I}{\partial T} \right) \frac{\partial L}{\partial X} - \left(\frac{\partial C}{\partial X} + \frac{\partial I}{\partial X} - 1 \right) \frac{M}{P^2} \frac{\partial MC}{\partial T} \right]$$

Note that the determinant of A is positive for all values given by the sign pattern (3).

$\frac{\partial P'}{\partial t}$ is also ambiguous since

$$\text{sign} \frac{dP'}{dt} = \text{sign} \left[\left(\frac{\partial C}{\partial X} + \frac{\partial I}{\partial X} - 1 \right) \frac{\partial MC}{\partial T} \frac{\partial L}{\partial r} \right.$$

$$\left. - \left(\frac{\partial C}{\partial r} + \frac{\partial I}{\partial r} \right) \frac{\partial L}{\partial X} \frac{\partial MC}{\partial T} - \left(\frac{\partial C}{\partial T} + \frac{\partial I}{\partial T} \right) \left(\frac{\partial MC}{\partial X} \frac{\partial L}{\partial r} \right) \right]$$

thus raising the level of indirect taxes might lower, or raise, the equilibrium price level.

Case 3: (Harrod's dichotomy) $MC \geq AC$, $\partial MC / \partial t > 0$, $\partial MC / \partial r > 0$

All the assumptions are the same as in the above section except $\partial MC / \partial r > 0$. This realistically allows the interest rate to enter as a cost as well as a demand suppressant.

The sign pattern of A in this case is

$$\begin{bmatrix} - & - & 0 & - \\ + & - & + & 0 \\ + & + & - & + \\ + & 0 & 0 & - \end{bmatrix} \qquad (4)$$

In order to have the determinant of A signed (unambiguously), we assume that: $\partial MC/\partial r < -\partial L/\partial r$, thus $|A| > 0$ for all the values of a_{ij}, given the sign pattern (4). Using the same procedure as in Case 2, the following comparative static results are obtained:

$$\frac{dN'}{dG} > 0 \qquad \frac{dr'}{dG} > 0 \qquad \frac{dP'}{dG} > 0 \qquad \frac{dT'}{dG} > 0$$

$$\frac{dN'}{\frac{1}{P}dM} > 0 \qquad \frac{dr'}{\frac{1}{P}dM} < 0 \qquad \frac{dP'}{\frac{1}{P}dM} \; ? \qquad \frac{dT'}{\frac{1}{P}dM} > 0$$

$$\frac{dN'}{dw} < 0 \qquad \frac{dr'}{dw} > 0 \qquad \frac{dP'}{dw} > 0 \qquad \frac{dT'}{dw} \; ?$$

$$\frac{dN'}{dt} < 0 \qquad \frac{dr'}{dt} \; ? \qquad \frac{dP'}{dt} \; ? \qquad \frac{dT'}{dt} > 0$$

The above results are the same as in Case 2, except that the sign of $\dfrac{dP'}{\frac{1}{P}dM}$ is also ambiguous in this case, since sign dP'/dM = sign

$$\left[-\frac{\partial MC}{\partial r}\left(\frac{\partial C}{\partial T} + \frac{\partial I}{\partial T} \right) - \left(\frac{\partial C}{\partial r} + \frac{\partial I}{\partial r} \right)\frac{\partial MC}{\partial T} \right]$$

Thus the variation in price level due to money is dependent upon the effect of r and T on cost of production and on total demand. The sign of dr'/dt and dP'/dt are ambiguous due to the same reasons that were mentioned in Case 2, except that in case of dP'/dt, there will be a new term added to the terms we had in the previous section, namely

$$\left(\frac{\partial C}{\partial T} + \frac{\partial I}{\partial T} \right) \left(\frac{\partial L}{\partial X}\frac{\partial X}{\partial N} \right) \; \frac{\partial MC}{\partial r} \text{ while before } \partial MC/\partial r \text{ was zero.}$$

Case 4: Harrod's dichotomy $MC < AC$, $\partial AC/\partial t > 0$, $\partial AC/\partial r > 0$

We now turn to analyzing an economy in which the equilibrium level of output is sufficiently below the full employment level so that average cost is greater than marginal cost. In such a case, average cost declines as output expands toward the minimum cost level where $MC = AC$. We assume that in such circumstances $P = AC$, thus equation (3b) expresses the price level. Elements of the matrix A containing the marginal cost term must be modified appropriately, thus:

$$a_{31} = \left(\frac{\partial AC}{\partial X} \right)\left(\frac{\partial X}{\partial N} \right) \qquad a_{32} = \frac{\partial AC}{\partial r} \qquad a_{34} = \frac{\partial AC}{\partial T}$$

In this case the coefficient matrix A has the following sign pattern.

$$\begin{bmatrix} - & - & 0 & - \\ + & - & + & 0 \\ - & + & - & + \\ + & 0 & 0 & - \end{bmatrix} \qquad (5)$$

Assuming $\partial AC/\partial r < -\partial L/\partial r$ and $\partial L/\partial X > -\partial AC/\partial X$, then $|A| > 0$ for all the values of a_{ij}, given the above sign pattern for A.

Using the same procedure as is indicated in the previous section, the following comparative static results are obtained, when $\partial AC/\partial w > 0$ and $\partial AC/\partial r > 0$.

$$\frac{dN'}{dG} > 0 \qquad \frac{dr'}{dG} > 0 \qquad \frac{dP'}{dG} \quad ? \qquad \frac{dT'}{dG} > 0$$

$$\frac{dN'}{\frac{1}{P}dM} > 0 \qquad \frac{dr'}{\frac{1}{P}dM} < 0 \qquad \frac{dP'}{\frac{1}{P}dM} \quad ? \qquad \frac{dT'}{\frac{1}{P}dM} > 0$$

$$\frac{dN'}{dw} < 0 \qquad \frac{dr'}{dw} > 0 \qquad \frac{dP'}{dw} > 0 \qquad \frac{dT'}{dw} \quad ?$$

$$\frac{dN'}{dt} < 0 \qquad \frac{dr'}{dt} \quad ? \qquad \frac{dP'}{dt} \quad ? \qquad \frac{dT'}{dt} > 0$$

Examining these results we see that all the price-level impacts of policy assumed by the "conventional wisdom" have become ambiguous. Thus an increase (decrease) in government expenditures might raise, or lower, the price level, and the same applies to an increase (decrease) in the money supply or a decrease (increase) in taxes. In addition, the impact of a change in taxes on the interest rate is ambiguous, as in Case 2 above.

Analyzing the sign of dP'/dM further we have: sign $dP'/dM = $ sign

$$\left[\left(\frac{\partial C}{\partial X} + \frac{\partial I}{\partial X} - 1\right)\left(\frac{\partial X}{\partial N}\frac{\partial AC}{\partial r}\right)\right]$$

$$-\left[\left(\frac{\partial C}{\partial r} + \frac{\partial I}{\partial r}\right)\left(\frac{\partial AC}{\partial X}\frac{\partial X}{\partial N}\right)\right] + t\left[\left(\frac{\partial C}{\partial T} + \frac{\partial I}{\partial T}\right)\right.$$

$$\left.\left(\frac{\partial X}{\partial N}\frac{\partial AC}{\partial r}\right)\right] - t\left[\left(\frac{\partial C}{\partial r} + \frac{\partial I}{\partial r}\right)\left(\frac{\partial X}{\partial N}\frac{\partial AC}{\partial T}\right)\right]$$

We may assume that $\partial AC/\partial T \lesssim 0$ except when t, the marginal rate of taxation, is changed. This amounts to the assumption that indirect taxes are a flat percentage of final sales price. Under this assumption the sign of dP'/dM becomes negative.

Thus in such an economy, "tight money" would have the perverse effect of raising the price level, while an expansion of the money supply would increase output and lower the price level, as long as $AC > MC$.

Turning to the question of the sign of dr'/dt we find the following: sign $dr'/dt = $ sign

$$\frac{M}{P^2}\left[\left(\frac{\partial Ac}{\partial X}\right)\left(\frac{\partial C}{\partial T} + \frac{\partial I}{\partial T}\right) \quad -\frac{\partial AC}{\partial T}\right.$$

$$\left(\frac{\partial C}{\partial X} + \frac{\partial I}{\partial X} - 1\right)\right] + \left[\left(\frac{\partial C}{\partial T} + \frac{\partial I}{\partial T}\right)\frac{\partial L}{\partial X}\right]$$

The terms in first bracket indicate $dr'/dt > 0$ while the term in the second bracket implies $dr'/dt < 0$. If $\partial AC/\partial T \lesssim 0$, then $dr'/dt < 0$ since by our assumption $\partial L/\partial X > -\partial AC/\partial X$ and $M/P^2 < 1$. However, if $\partial AC/\partial T > 0$, as we assume when t is changed, then dr'/dt has an ambiguous sign.

Further analyzing the ambiguity of dP'/dt we have:

$$\text{sign } dP'/dt = \text{sign}$$

$$\frac{\partial AC}{\partial T}\left[\frac{\partial L}{\partial r}\left(\frac{\partial C}{\partial X}+\frac{\partial I}{\partial X}-1\right)\right.$$

$$\left.-\frac{\partial L}{\partial X}\left(\frac{\partial C}{\partial r}+\frac{\partial I}{\partial r}\right)\right]+\left(\frac{\partial C}{\partial T}+\frac{\partial I}{\partial T}\right)\left[\frac{\partial AC}{\partial r}\frac{\partial L}{\partial X}\right.$$

$$\left.-\frac{\partial AC}{\partial X}\frac{\partial L}{\partial r}\right]$$

The terms in the first bracket indicate $dP'/dt > 0$ while the terms in the second bracket show ambiguity. Thus $dP'/dt > 0$ if

$$\frac{\partial AC}{\partial X}\frac{\partial L}{\partial r} > \frac{\partial AC}{\partial r}\frac{\partial L}{\partial X}$$

If $\partial AC/\partial T \approx 0$ and the above inequality are reversed, we can have $dP'/dt < 0$; however, we rule out $\partial AC/\partial T \approx 0$ when the level of indirect taxes is changed, leaving $dP'/dt > 0$ as the more likely, albeit heretical case.

The ambiguous sign of dP'/dG may be similarly analyzed but it would be insignificant and thus it is not discussed.

The stability of the model

The comparative static analysis is meaningful if the system is a stable one. The following definitions and propositions were used in the foregoing analysis:

Definition 1 [1]. If $A = (a_{ij})_1{}^n$, when sign $A = [\text{sign } a_{ij}]_1{}^n$ and $Q_A = \{B|\text{ sign } B = \text{sign } A\}$ then Q_A is an equivalence class of matrices that we refer to as a qualitative matrix.

Definition 2 [1]. A is said to be:

i) a stable matrix if the real part of the eigenvalue of A is negative

ii) a sign stable matrix if $B \epsilon Q_A$ implies B is stable; and

iii) potentially stable if there exist $B \epsilon Q_A$ such that B is a stable matrix.

Proposition 1 [10]. If a matrix A has a nested sequence of principal minors, the ith of which has sign $(-1)^i$ $i = 1, \ldots, n$, then there exists a positive diagonal matrix D such that DA is stable.

Proposition 2 [10]. A is a Hicksian stable if and only if every principal minor of A of even order is positive and every principal minor of A of odd order is negative.

Lemma 1: If the qualitative matrix A has the same sign pattern as of (2), (3), (4), or (5), then A is potentially stable.

Proof:

For matrices (2) and (3) the following conditions hold

i) $a_{11} < 0$

ii) $(a_{11}a_{22} - a_{12}a_{21}) > 0$

iii) $A_{44} < 0$ (The cofactor of a_{44})

iv) $|A| > 0$

Thus by proposition 1, there exists a positive diagonal matrix D ($d_{ij} = 0, i \neq j$) such that $DA = B$ is stable. But B has the same sign pattern as A, hence $B \epsilon Q_A$ and by definition 2(iii), A is potentially stable.

In case of matrices (4) and (5) the above conditions hold by imposing the following quantitative restrictions.

$-a_{22} > +a_{32}$ for the matrix   (4)

$a_{21} > -a_{31}$ and $-a_{22} > a_{32}$ for the matrix   (5)

Under above restrictions and conditions (i), (ii), (iii) and (iv) are satisfied and hence the matrices (4) and (5) are potentially stable. Note however that these quantitative restrictions have already been considered in Cases 3 and 4 with $MC \gtreqless AC$. With the above quantitative restrictions for matrices (4) and (5), every principal minor of the coefficient matrix A, of even order is positive and every principal minor of A, of odd order is negative, thus by proposition 2, A is a Hicksian stable matrix.

Conclusions

The foregoing analysis indicates that, given an economy which is potentially stable, the usual monetary and fiscal policies would work appropriately if the economy is near full employment and the cost effects of interest and tax boosts are "of order zero." This is demonstrated in the traditional case.

However, as soon as the assumption of the cost neutrality of tax increases is relaxed, the price and interest rate impact of tax increases become ambiguous (that is, a tax increase might raise the price level rather than lower it and it might raise the rate of interest rather than lower it). This is shown in Case 2.

Case 3 demonstrates that if we couple the assumption that increased indirect taxes raise costs to the assumption that increased interest rates raise costs, the price-level impact of tax hikes remains ambiguous and, in addition, monetary policy becomes ambiguous. That is, a decrease in the money supply might raise the price level rather than lower it.

In Case 4 where $MC < AC$, an economy was examined where the equilibrium level of aggregate demand was sufficiently below full employment. It is assumed that under these conditions the price level equals average cost and we may enquire again concerning the "sign" of fiscal and monetary policy moves. Taken one at a time, their impacts on the price level are all ambiguous. That means that an increase in government spending may raise, or lower, the price level; an increase in indirect taxes may raise, or lower, the price level; and an increase in the money supply may raise, or lower the price level. Also, an increase in taxes may raise, or lower, the rate of interest.

Analyzing the price-level impact of changes in the money supply, it is found that it becomes unambiguously perverse (a decrease in M raises P) if one assumes flat rate indirect taxes such that $\partial AC/\partial T \leq 0$ except when the marginal rate of taxation, t, is changed. The assumption that $\partial AC/\partial T > 0$ when t is changed causes tax increases to have a perverse price-increasing effect.

Finally, the stability of the comparative static model was examined and it is shown that all the matrices used to study the traditional and Harrod cases are potentially stable matrices, given reasonable quantitative restrictions in the case of matrices (4) and (5).

Application of the model – some possible objections

Since the above analysis demonstrates that Harrod's dichotomy obtains within a potentially stable qualitative model, it demonstrates that this is a possible case. That is, it is possible for the economy to enter and remain in a situation where monetary, tax, and government expenditure impacts upon the price level are the reverse of those confidently expected and intended.

But is Harrod's dichotomy a real world case, and if so, is it the present case in, say, the United States and Canada? Harrod is reluctant to affirm the conclusion that "deflationary" measures usually have inflationary effects. Instead, he adopts the attitude of a "strict agnostic." (Things may go one way or they may go the other) [13, p. 624]. We would likewise conclude that a perverse impact of recent policies is "quite possible."

There is considerable evidence of supernormal productivity gains as slack is taken up in an economic recovery. As Bodkin found, "classical diminishing returns is probably confined in its operation to a range very close to full utilization of the labour (and capital) factors of production" [2, p. 372]. Wilson and Eckstein theorized that firms in a depressed period do not minimize their short-run costs; instead, they are driven onto a "short-run maladjustment curve" [24]. Because of such labour hoarding, a 1 percent increase in output can be achieved in such a slack period with much less than a 1 percent increase in employment. "Okun's Law," that a 3 percent increase in real GNP will decrease unemployment by only 1 percent, points to the same conclusion (while also reflecting greater labour-force participation as jobs become more plentiful) [17]. Thus, the assumption that $AC > MC$ and would decline with an increase in output (with given factor prices) is relevant to our economy in 1976.

It appears equally conclusive that indirect taxes are shifted forward in higher prices and thus, as Evans and Klein put it, are "of dubious anti-inflationary benefit" [9, p. 68]. Nor is the effect one way, for reductions in excise taxes will reduce the price level. Brownlee and Perry's study of the effects of the 1965 Federal Excise Tax reduction found: "On all commodities where retail excise taxes were eliminated . . . retail prices fell approximately the full amount of the tax . . . with no apparent time lag" [4, p. 235].

The implicit assumption made by macro theorists that the cost effect of interest hikes is "of order zero" is also unjustified. At present levels of corporate debt, a 1 percent boost in the average rate of interest increases the costs of corporations in the short run by $2 to 3 billion and in the long run by $7 billion.[4] The short-run cost impact is of the same order of magnitude as the United States profits surcharge of 1968, which was expected to have major impacts upon investment, output, and the price level.[5] Furthermore, a tax increase in theory, at least, does not lead to increased government expenditure, while higher interest rates lead directly to higher incomes of creditors, both individual and institutional, and thus to higher expenditures by them.

---

[4] Net public and private debt in the United States in 1969 totaled $1,700 billion. Net corporate debt was $692 billion, which included current liabilities of $238 billion [6, pp. 248, 287].

[5] Impacts which were slow in materializing, if indeed they did materialize at all, or had the intended "sign." For arguments regarding the possibly positive sign of $\partial I/\partial t$ and small size of $\partial C/\partial t$ see Eisner [8].

This moderates the fall in aggregate consumption and possibly reverses the sign of $\partial C/\partial r$.[6] If conventional theory is rejected here also, the perverse side of Harrod's dichotomy would predominate all the more.

However objections may be made against our assumptions: (1) that wages are exogenous; (2) that when average cost exceeds marginal cost, price will equal average cost. Let us conclude with a brief defense of these assumptions and exploration of alternatives.

In an economic world where "everything depends on everything else," it is not possible to isolate a wholly exogenous variable. Nevertheless, the case for treating the money wage as exogenous to a small, short-run model such as discussed above, is stronger than the case for its endogeneity. In the short run, wages are largely predetermined by their previous value and by long-term contracts. Over time, they are also responsive to pressure from public authorities, as the "open mouth" operations of the guideposts interval indicate, and to institutional changes. Furthermore, the Phillips curve inspired search for a simple tradeoff between the level of unemployment and the rate of change of wages and/or prices appears thwarted.

Harrod has argued elsewhere that under conditions of monopolistic competition, price will approximate average cost in the short run as well as in the long run, and we followed him here by using average cost as the best available proxy of the equilibrium price level in an underemployed economy [12]. Average cost pricing, or average cost plus a fixed mark-up, is a widespread, if to the economist deplorable, business policy.

Alternatively, we might have related price to marginal cost by arguing that the degree of monopoly power is an institutional datum and that it is constant over the business cycle, enabling us to use profit-maximizing pricing: thus $P > MR = MC$. Since MC will be falling as output expands over a wide range where $AC > MC$, demand repression will tend to raise MC and thus P. The alternative used was chosen largely for simplicity.

Harrod's dichotomy may well be part of the explanation of our continuing inflation with administered depression. If so, this dark cloud may have a silver lining, for the dichotomy would also indicate that the rapid expansion envisioned by current "game plans" should involve less than "expected" inflation. This effect would seem to be particularly strong if the expansionary medicine is administered in the form of reductions of indirect taxes and interest rates rather than in expenditure boosts. If such a program could be combined with a workable restraint on the pace of wage increases, an economy may yet achieve the heretofore unattainable goal of full employment with stable prices.

---

[6] See Weber for an argument leading to the conclusion that consumers "increase current consumption in response to interest rate increase" [22, 23].

References

[1] L. Bassett, J. Maybee and J. Quirk, "Qualitative Economics and the Scope of the Correspondence Principle," *Econometrica* 36:544-63 (July-October 1968).

[2] Ronald C. Bodkin, "Real Wages and Cyclical Variations in Employment: A Re-examination of the Evidence," *Canadian Journal of Economics* 2:353-74 (August 1969).

[3] C. Brennan and D.A.L. Auld, "The Tax Cut as an Anti-Inflationary Measure," *Economic Record* 44:520-25 (December 1968).

[4] O. Brownlee and G.L. Perry, "The Effects of the 1965 Federal Excise Tax Reduction on Prices," *National Tax Journal* 20:235-49 (September 1967).

[5] Gustav Cassel, *The Theory of Social Economy,* New York, A.M. Kelley, 1967.

[6] Council of Economic Advisors, *Economic Report of the President, Washington, D.C., February 1971.*

[7] P. Davidson, "Rolph on the Aggregate Effects of a General Excise Tax," *Southern Economic Journal* 27:37-42 (July 1960).

[8] R. Eisner, "Fiscal and Monetary Policy Reconsidered," *American Economic Review* 59:897-905 (December 1969).

[9] M.K. Evans and L.R. Klein, *The Wharton Econometric Forecasting Model,* Philadelphia, Pa., University of Pennsylvania, 1967.

[10] M.E. Fisher and A.T. Fuller, "On the Stability of Matrices and the Convergence of Linear Iterative Processes," *Proceedings of the Cambridge Philosophical Society* 54:417-25, 1958.

[11] R.J. Gordon, "The Incidence of the Corporation Income Tax in U.S. Manufacturing, 1925-62," *American Economic Review* 57:731-58 (September 1967).

[12] Sir Roy Harrod, "Increasing Returns," in R.E. Kuenne (ed.), *Monopolistic Competition Theory, Essays in Honor of Edward H. Chamberlin,* New York, Wiley, 1967, pp. 63-76.

[13] _____,"Reassessment of Keynes' Views of Money," *Journal of Political Economy* 78:617-25 (July-August 1970).

[14] M. Krzyaniak and R.A. Musgrave, *The Shifting of the Corporation Income Tax,* Baltimore, Johns Hopkins Press, 1963.

[15] R.A. Musgrave, "General Equilibrium Aspects of Incidence Theory," *American Economic Review, Proceedings* 43:504-17 (May 1953).

[16] _____, *The Theory of Public Finance,* New York, McGraw Hill, 1959.

[17] Arthur M. Okun, "Potential GNP: Its Measurement and Signifi-cance," *1962 Proceedings Business and Economic Statistics Section, American Statistical Association* (reprinted as Cowles Foundation Paper 190) New Haven, Conn., Yale University, 1963.

[18] James Quirk, "The Correspondence Principle: A Macro-economic Application," *International Economic Review* 9:294-306 (1968).

[19] E.R. Rolph, *The Theory of Fiscal Economics,* Berkeley, Calif., University of California Press, 1954.

[20] Paul A. Samuelson, *Foundations of Economic Analysis,* Cambridge, Harvard University Press, 1955.

[21] B. Spencer, "The Shifting of the Corporation Income Tax in Canada 1926-65," *Canadian Journal of Economics* 3:21-34 (February 1969).

[22] W.E. Weber, "The Effect of Interest Rates on Aggregate Consumption," *American Economic Review* 60:591-600 (September 1970).

[23] _____,"Interest Rates, Inflation and Consumer Expenditures, *"American Economic Review,* 65:843-58 (December 1975)

[24] R.A. Wilson and O. Eckstein, "Short-Run Productivity Behavior in U.S. Manufacturing," *Review of Economics and Statistics* 46:41-59 (February 1964).

7 Some Dynamics of Harrod's and Galbraith's Dichotomies

with George Lermer and Hamid Habibagahi

Introduction: The Collapse of the "Neoclassical Synthesis"

The comfortably comprehensible world view provided to a generation of students, professors and policy makers by the "neoclassical synthesis" of "Keynesian" macroeconomics and "neoclassical" microeconomics has been increasingly disturbed in recent years by the rude irruption of unruly reality. Scarce a decade ago mainstream economists were supremely confident that the simple fiscal and monetary prescriptions of Paul Samuelson's textbook were sufficient, if competently carried out by government, to guarantee countries such as the United States entry into an abiding place in the promised land of full employment, stable prices, balanced international payments, and sustained growth. The sole important dissent from this complacent view came in the even more comforting doctrines of monetarism, tirelessly preached by Milton Friedman and his disciples, which held that all four desiderata can be obtained merely by keeping the money supply growing at an optimal low rate.

Now, after the fiscal and monetary failures of the Vietnam War inflationary period, the stagflationary recessions, recurring international payment crises, and the ever more virulent inflation triggered by the oil, food and raw material crises, the simple Samuelson prescriptions: to fight inflation raise taxes and interest rates while cutting government spending, to fight recession do just the opposite, are seen to be inadequate by an increasing number of economists and policy makers.

To whom then shall we go? To the simplistic certainties of Chicago's "moneytheistic" approach? To the equal, but opposite certainties of neo-Marxist radical economics? Or to the uncomfortable complexities and uncertainties of what has been dubbed, "ultra-Keynesianism"? (see Knapp 1973) This chapter is an exploration of some of the complexities and uncertainties implicit in the work of two of the most important theorists of the ultra-Keynesian school, Sir Roy Harrod and John Kenneth Galbraith. If their "dichotomy" insights are essentially correct they go far to explain recent policy failures and, more hopefully, provide important aid toward the design of more successful policies. However, as we shall see, they picture the path of the macro policy maker as thorny indeed.

The Harrod, Galbraith Dichotomy

Sir Roy Harrod (1970) has suggested that an important "dichotomy" flaws and perhaps negates the "anti" inflationary effect of restrictive monetary and fiscal policy; while J.K. Galbraith (1973: 1,2) maintains that the economy is itself dichotomized between the "market system"

– composed of some twelve million small firms in the United States
and producing about one-half of private GNP – and the "planning
system" of about one thousand great corporations providing the
remainder.

In two earlier papers Hotson and Habibagahi (1972) analyzed
Harrod's dichotomy in a comparative statics framework. They concluded their finding that Harrod's dichotomy obtains in potentially
stable models, (as soon as the implicit assumption of the "conventional wisdom" that interest and taxes do not affect variable costs are
relaxed) supports the idea that the dichotomy obtains in the real world
also. In this chapter we extend the analysis by considering two
dynamic models which incorporate the varying price-output behaviour of Galbraith's market system "price takers" and planning
system "price makers".[1] Thus, we consider the implications of
"Harrod's dichotomy" for officials charged with making macro policy
for a "Galbraith's dichotomy" world.

The essence of Galbraith's insight is that while the neoclassical
micro model approximates the behaviour of the "market" half of the
modern economy (the main failure of neoclassical description being
the lack of attention paid to the influences of the state and the "planning" sector upon the "market" sector), it does not describe the
planning sector. The large corporation is "not passive in response to
the market or the state" (Galbraith, 1973: 1, p. 44).

*"In the market system consumer behavior, costs, the response of
suppliers, the behavior of the state, are all beyond the reach of the
individual firm. In the planning system the firm seeks and wins power
or influence over all of these things. It follows that prices are no longer
of unique importance in telling how resources are distributed. What
counts is the whole deployment of power – over prices, costs, consumers, suppliers, the government." (p. 111)*

Galbraith maintains that prices in the planning system are set according to the protective purposes (survival of control by maintaining
sufficient revenues) and affirmative purposes (sustained growth of
sales and profits) of the "technostructure". Prices are not set to
maximize profits over either the short or the long run, as is assumed
by the neoclassical economist.

*"The prices that are so set – that reflect the affirmative purposes of the
technostructure – will almost always be lower, and on occasion much
lower, than those that would maximize profits over some period
relevant to managerial calculations." (p. 116)*

The strong committment of the technostructure to growth rather than
profit maximization, Galbraith sees as a consequence of a) the impossibility of anyone determining whether or not profits are indeed being
maximized, b) the ease with which the growth of sales and profits can
be determined, c) the fact that the rewards of the technostructure;
salaries, bonuses, lissome secretaries, and keys to the executive toilet
are tied to b) not to a).

In addition to extending the study of Harrod's dichotomy from
statics to some dynamics of Galbraith's two systems, this chapter
makes a methodological contribution. This consists of the classifica-
tion of variables into three categories for analysis according to their
speeds of adjustment. Rapidly adjusting variables we analyze by

[1] The terms price "maker" and "taker" have a fairly established usage, tracing
back at least to P.J.D. Wiles, *Price, Cost, and Output* (Oxford, 1956)

comparative static relations, more slowly adjusting variables we analyze by dynamics, and variables which are very slow to adjust we treat as exogenous parameters. We believe this technique may prove to be a useful tool in the simplification of complex dynamic models.

The Models

The comparative static model investigated by Hotson and Habibagahi may be represented by the following equations:

1) $P = C(X,r)$

2) $X = I(X,r,T) + G$

3) $L(X,r) = \dfrac{M}{P+T}$

Where P = the price level net of indirect taxes[2]
C = marginal (and where noted, average) cost[3]
X = real output
r = nominal interest rate
I = aggregate demand function
T = rate of taxation
G = government expenditure
L = demand for real balances
M = nominal money balances

Which of the variables of the model should be taken as rapidly adjusting, which slowly adjusting – and which as very slowly adjusting? We assume that output (X) and interest rate (r) adjust instantly to restore real and money market equilibrium (equations 2 and 3) while price adjusts according to our alternative dynamic adjustment equations. Thus, our analysis is for an economy of continuous production, one of

---

[2] P is defined net of indirect taxes so that P can be handled as a continuous variable, that is $\dot{P}$ is defined everywhere. This is convenient and there is no loss in generalization. Our models assume an exogenous increase in indirect taxes to be immediately added to the current price. Markets then adjust as demand and real balances fall ($\partial I/\partial T < 0$). On the other hand, an increase in direct taxes is assumed to have no immediate effect on the price level, its eventual effects coming from changed demand and supply conditions.

[3] Over a wide range of below capacity operations MC is less than AC, and firms would operate at a loss if they equate P and MC. Several alternative hypotheses regarding firm behaviour in this circumstance are available. Thus we might follow Gustav Cassel (1932, pp. 99-105) and argue that $P=MC \geq AC$ and $P=AC \geq MC$. Sir Roy Harrod (1967) has argued that under conditions of monopolistic competition $P=AC=MC$. Alternatively one might argue that the degree of monopoly power is constant over the business cycle and that $P=kMC$, or $P=k'AC$. Here we have adopted the conservative course of adhering closely to the $P=MC$ tradition, even though alternative specifications are more conducive to the prevalence of the perverse side of Harrod's dichotomy. In any case, a constant degree of mark-up (k) over cost does not effect our analysis of the rate of change of P, MC and AC.

manufactures and services, rather than agriculture.[4] Real life, of course, is further "dichotomized" by the fact that both continuous and batch production techniques are important.

The alternative behaviour assumptions and dynamic models are:

Model A: Price "Maker" or "Planning" Model
Firms adjust output in response to excess demand while adjusting price at a rate proportional to the difference between marginal cost and price.

4) $\overset{\circ}{P} = (S_A P_0) (C(X,r) - P_0)$

5) $X = I(X,r,T) + G$

6) $L(X,r) = \dfrac{M}{P + T}$

Here $\overset{\circ}{P}$ refers to the rate of change of price while P_0 is the initial equilibrium price and S_A is the speed of adjustment. All other variables were defined previously.

Model B: Price "Taker" or "Market" Model
Firms take the price as given by the market and adjust output in proportion to the difference between marginal cost and price.

7) $\overset{\circ}{P} = (S_B P_0) (I(X,r,T) + G - X)$

8) $P_0 = C(X,r)$

9) $L(X,r) = \dfrac{M}{P + T}$

All variables are as defined above. Although the dynamics of Models A and B are quite different, they reduce to our initial static model (equations 1 – 3) if equilibrium is assumed. Models A and B are locally stable for most reasonable specifications of the signs of the appropriate partial derivatives (see Appendix p. 187) Model A is, however, more likely to be unstable if

$C_x < 0 \ (C_x = \dfrac{\partial C}{\partial X})$,

---

[4] Axel Leijonhufvud (1966: 21, 24-54) maintained that the essential differences between Marshall and Keynes involved alternative assumptions concerning the relative speeds of adjustment of prices and qualities. Marshall assumed that price adjusts quickly to equilibrium while output adjusts slowly. He saw Keynes as assuming that output adjusts rapidly, and price adjustments are slow enough to allow the dynamic "multiplier" to work its mischief.

Leijonhufvud has recently recanted this position as follows:

"It is *not* correct to attribute to Keynes a general revision of the Marshallian ranking of relative price and quantity adjustment velocities. In the 'shortest run' for which system behavior can be defined in Keynes' model, output-prices *must* be treated as perfectly flexible." (A. Leijonhufvud: 1974: 169).

We do not know whether Leijonhufvud now wishes to disown the following passage in which he sees Keynes as assuming with most economists that, "Adjustment in 'securities' markets . . . proceeds faster than in other markets . . . stock market prices adjust on the 'market day' . . . effective excess demands in commodities markets become zero only in the 'short run'. There is ample evidence for the assumption of this ranking of the relative adjustment speeds in Keynes' work." (1966: 329).

Whether or not it is correct to attribute the assumption of rapid quantity adjustment, and slow price adjustment to Keynes, the assumption is, we believe, a useful one, particularly in analyzing Galbraith's "planning sector". For an interesting analysis of price and output adjustment in terms of "spot" and "forward" markets see Paul Davidson (1974).

thus if marginal costs are falling. Model B is locally stable for quite a range of values of the partial derivatives even if $C_x < 0$.[5]

Throughout our analysis of Models A and B we shall consider wages as exogenously given and constant – perhaps held fixed by formal wage contracts with a longer period of calendar time to run than the period here analyzed, or merely fixed by our assumption that wages are a "very slowly" adjusting price. For a fully developed model of Harrod's Dichotomy such a treatment is not satisfactory, as, clearly, the rate of change of wages is the "prime mover" in any realistic cost function. Our present analysis is, therefore, limited to the *initial* direction of change of prices to a change in macroeconomic policy. Given, however, the rapid changes in policy engineered by policy makers as they attempt to "fine tune" the economy, these *initial* changes may be the ones that matter – much as the bulk of the "action" of the "period multiplier" occurs in the first few periods.

Response to Policy Changes

The initial response of the rate of change of prices charged by price "makers" to changes in the policy variables; Government Spending (G), Money Supply (M), and Taxation (T), is explored in equation 10. Here E refers to any exogenous variable (G, M, or T), and the initial condition is assumed to be one of equilibrium. Differentiating equation 4 with respect to E we have:

10) $d\dot{P} = S_1 P_0 (C_x X_E + C_r r_E) dE$

since $P_E = 0$.[6] Subscripted variables are partial derivatives, i.e.

$$C_x = \frac{\partial C}{\partial X}, \; X_E = \frac{\partial X}{\partial E}.$$

(This notation will be used throughout the chapter.)

X_E and r_E are evaluated from equations 5 and 6 as follows:

In the neighborhood of equilibrium I and L are assumed to be linear functions. We have

11) $I = I_x X + I_r r + I_T T$

where $1 > I_x \gtrless 0$, $I_r \leq 0$, $I_T \leq 0$

12) $L = L_x X + L_r r$

where $L_x \geq 0$ and $L_r \leq 0$.

Substituting (11) and (12) in equations 5 and 6, and solving for r and X we have:

13) $r = \frac{1}{\xi_A} \left[\frac{Ms}{(P+T)} - (G+I_T T)L_x \right]$

14) $X = \frac{1}{\xi_A} \left[\frac{MI_r}{(P+T)} + (G+I_T T)L_r \right]$

---

[5] Model B is not independent of the units of measurement of price and output. However, for local stability analysis this does not pose a problem.

[6] $(\frac{\partial P}{\partial E})$

is zero by the assumption that P is slow to adjust relative to r and X. Therefore, from the point of view of the analysis which is concerned with the initial rate of change of P only, P is exogenous and X, r and $\dot{P}$ are the endogenous variables.

where

15) $\xi_A = sL_r + L_x \, I_r$

and where

$s = 1 - I_x > 0$

Except where a change in T is being analyzed, T will be set equal to zero. Note also that $\xi_A \leq 0$.

Similarly, for Model B the initial price adjustment to a change in an exogenous variable is given by differentiating equation 7 with respect to E:

16) $d\dot{P} = (S_B P_0) \, (X_E(-s) + I_r \, r_E + I_T \, T_E) \, dE$

where

$s = 1 - I_x$

and X_E, r_E and T_E are evaluated from equations 8 and 9 as follows:

Substituting equations (11) and (12) in (8) and (9) we have:

17) $r = \dfrac{1}{\xi_B} \left(PL_x - \dfrac{M}{P+T} \, C_x \right)$

18) $X = \dfrac{1}{\xi_B} \left(P \, |L_r| + \dfrac{M}{P+T} \, C_r \right)$

where

19) $\xi_B = C_r \, L_x - C_x \, L_r$

Note that $\xi_B > 0$ whenever C_r and C_x are both positive, and that ξ_B may be < 0, when $C_r > 0$ and $C_x < 0$.

Equations 10 and 16 give the initial change in the rate of change of the price level after the interest rate and output have moved to establish equilibrium in the real and money markets.[7] X_E, r_E and T_E are partial derivatives, derived from the comparative static analysis of the fast-adjusting variables. These in turn are used to investigate the dynamics of the slow-adjusting variable. In this chapter, price is the slow-adjusting variable.

Case (1) Response to an increase in government expenditure (or decrease in direct taxes).[8]

Model A – "Price Makers"

20) $d\dot{P} = S_A \, (C_x \, |L_r| - C_r L_x) \, \dfrac{dG}{|\xi_A|}$

where $|\,\,|$ stands for the absolute value. The direction of change of the price level in equation 20 depends upon the sign of C_x and C_r. When the economy is very close to capacity $C_x > 0$, otherwise $C_x < 0$ appears to be the rule, despite economists' stress on the "law of

---

[7] The notation $d\dot{P}$ is the total derivative of $\dot{P}$. However, since $\dot{P}$ is zero in the original equilibrium $d\dot{P}$ is the same as $\dot{P}$, the initial rate of change of the price level.

[8] We assume that direct taxes affect prices solely through their effect upon aggregate demand. Indirect taxes are assumed to be added on to supply price and thus affect both aggregate demand and supply.

diminishing returns"[9] Economists have generally ignored interest cost in macro theory, implying that the first derivative of total cost with respect to interest is "of order zero". Hotson (1967, 1971) has argued that this is a mistake as the interest costs of short-run business borrowing are not negligible. Here we stipulate that throughout $C_r > 0$.

Price makers are seen as responding to increased government spending by running down inventory and increasing output at initially constant prices. If expanded sales raise their costs (as interest rates rise and/or $C_x > 0$), they subsequently raise their prices. If, on the other hand, increased output lowers their costs, they lower their prices.[10]

Model B – "Price Takers"
In Model B government expenditures appear only in the price change equation. Therefore, a raise in G leads to increased supply by causing a divergence between P and Marginal cost leading to:

21) $\dfrac{d\dot{P}}{dG} = (S_BP_o) > 0$

the conventional conclusion that higher government spending leads to higher prices. That this is the only possible outcome is a shortcoming of our model. For Galbraith's "market system" price takers include all perfect and imperfect competitors, even pure monopolists, who attempt to maximize short or long run profits. Under pure competition a divergence between P and MC could only occur where MC is increasing. Given imperfect competition, however, it is possible for increased government spending to cause a divergence between P (or rather marginal revenue) and MC where MC is falling, thus leading to falling prices and the "perverse" side of Harrod's dichotomy.

---

[9] That costs tend to rise as output falls, and the contrary, at least as long as wages are constant, has been widely observed and documented. This appears to be largely because labour is much more of a fixed cost to firms than our instantaneously cost minimizing models of the firm allow for. Thus T.A. Wilson and O. Eckstein, (1964) argue that a fall in demand pushes firms onto a "short run maladjustment curve", with too much labour relative to capital and output. They estimate that as of 1960 a rise of 1 per cent in output required only a 0.52 per cent rise in man hours (*Ibid.*, p. 52). For similar conclusions in a Canadian setting see George Lermer, (1971). As A.M. Okun (1962) puts the matter, "The record clearly shows that manhour productivity is depressed by low levels of utilization, and that periods of movement toward full employment yield considerably above average productivity gains". Arthur M. Okun, "Potential GNP: Its Measure and Significance", *Proceedings of the Business and Economic Statistics Section of the American Statistical Association,* 1962. Reprinted in Readings in *Money, National Income, and Stabilization Policy,* Revised Ed., W.L. Smith and R.L. Teigen eds. (Homewood, 1970), pp. 313-322. Thus "effective" marginal cost curves slope downward until near full employment so that, with constant factor prices, increased output would mean lower prices.

It is interesting that the Government of Canada's "Candide" econometric model conforms to these insights. The result is that an increase in government expenditures cause an initial fall in the rate of price change, and only in later quarters in this reversed, via wage hikes. One looks forward with interest to further simulations employing various tax, monetary, and interest rate changes.

[10] To say merely "they raise their prices" or "they lower their prices" as we do here is to miss the discretionary nature of price changes in the "planning" sector. Thus, in pursuit of growth, firms may not raise prices when costs increase, at least over a certain range. Similarly, if profits are viewed as inadequate they may not lower prices merely because costs have fallen. Thus, as is usually the case, even our dichotomy models overstate the determinateness of the situation.

Case (2) Response to an increase in the Money Supply

Model A – "Price Makers"
The effect of an increase in the money supply on the direction of change of the price level is ambiguous since

$$\frac{\partial r}{\partial M} < 0$$

and it is possible that $C_x < 0$ obtains over the relevant range.

22) $d\mathring{P} = \frac{S_A}{|\xi_A|} (C_x | I_r | - C_r s) \, dM$

where $\xi_A = sL_r + I_r L_x \leq 0$

    Thus, an increased money supply leads to increased demand which price makers satisfy at initially constant prices. If $(C_x | I_r | - C_r s) > 0$ increasing output raises their costs and they then (tend) to raise their prices. However, it is shown in the appendix that it is possible for $(C_x | I_r | - C_r s) < 0$ and for Model A to be stable.[11]

Model B – "Price Takers"

23) $d\mathring{P} = S_B [-\frac{1}{\xi_B} (C_x | I_r | - C_r s)] \, dM$

where $\xi_B = C_r L_x + C_x | L_r | \gtrless 0$.

    In Model B the perverse side of Harrod's dichotomy may occur because $(C_x | I_r | - C_r s)$ may be less than zero and Model B remain stable. In addition, if C_x is negative then ξ_B may change sign, so that Model B monetary expansion may be anti-inflationary even when $(C_x | I_r | - C_r s)$ is positive.
    In model B an increase in the money supply drives nominal interest rates down, so that aggregate supply increases. But aggregate demand also increases. If supply increases more than aggregate demand, then prices will fall. Similarly, a fall in the money supply could raise the price level in Model B.
    Furthermore, if $C_x < 0$ and $C_r > 0$ then the sign of ξ_B depends upon

$$|C_x| \gtrless \frac{C_r L_x}{L_r}.$$

The sign of the numerator is certainly negative. Therefore, monetary expansion will be anti-inflationary if

$C_x < 0, C_r > 0$ and $|C_x| < \frac{C_r L_x}{|L_r|}$.

    L_r is the response of demand for money to a change in the interest rate. This is high in a depressed economy by the familiar "liquidity trap" argument. As

$$L_r \to \infty, \frac{C_r L_x}{L_r} \to 0$$

---

[11] The necessary condition for stability is that

$$(C_r s - C_x I_r) < \frac{|\xi_A| P^2}{M},$$

therefore, $C_r s - C_x I_r$ may be positive and the system stable, giving rise to a perverse result, that is, monetary expansion is initially "deflationary".

so that $|C_x|$ necessarily becomes greater than

$$\frac{C_r L_x}{L_r} \, .$$

Therefore, at the limit, monetary expansion becomes powerless even to lower the price level!

Case (3) Response to a change in Indirect Taxes

Model A

24) $d\overset{\circ}{P} = S_A P_o \, [\frac{M}{|\xi_A|(P+T)^2} (C_r s - C_x |I_r|) - \left|\frac{I_T}{\xi_A}\right| (L_x C_r + C_x |L_r|)] \, dT$

An increase in indirect taxes per unit of output is likely to reduce the price net of tax while raising price gross of tax, since $(C_r s - C_x |I_r|)$ is negative by virtue of the stability condition (see Appendix). Nevertheless, a net-of-tax price increase can occur in Model A, if C_r is "small" and C_x is negative.

Model B
In Model B the channel of adjustment is different.

25) $d\overset{\circ}{P} = (S_B P_o) \, [\frac{M}{\xi_B \, (P+T)^2} (C_r s - C_x \lceil I_r \rceil) + I_T] \, dT$

The indirect tax increase reduces demand directly by raising price gross of tax. It causes the interest rate to rise because of the fall in real balances which reduces demand still further. However, the increased indirect tax induced interest rate hike also raises costs. If the latter force causes output to fall more than aggregate demand has fallen then prices net of tax may indeed rise. If marginal costs *rise* rapidly as output falls ($C_x < 0$) this reinforces the reduction in output and adds to the likelihood of a net price increase. Alternatively, a reduction in indirect taxes may result in a price decline net, as well as gross, of tax.

The response of the price level to a per unit indirect tax increase is similar to the response due to a monetary expansion. For Model A we have that

26) $\dfrac{d\overset{\circ}{P}}{dT} = -S_A P_o \, [\dfrac{M}{(P+T)} (\dfrac{d\overset{\circ}{P}}{dM})_A + \left|\dfrac{I_T}{\xi_A}\right| [(L_x C_r + C_x |L_r|)]]$

for Model B we have

27) $\dfrac{d\overset{\circ}{P}}{dT} = -S_B P_o \, [\dfrac{M}{(P+T)} (\dfrac{d\overset{\circ}{P}}{dM})_B + |I_T|]$

In Model A, when monetary expansion is inflationary then a tax decrease will likely be inflationary. On the other hand, if monetary expansion is non-inflationary, the tax reduction may still be inflationary.

$C_x < 0$, $C_r \approx 0$ are conditions that are conducive to the possibility that tax reduction not be inflationary.

For Model B we can be more certain: if monetary expansion is inflationary then so will be indirect tax reduction. On the other hand, if monetary expansion is anti-inflationary we are still uncertain whether indirect tax reduction will be anti-inflationary or not – this latter requires that

$$\left|I_T\right| < \frac{M}{(P+T)} \left|(\frac{d\overset{\circ}{P}}{dM})_B\right| \, .$$

Summary

The introduction of interest rates into the cost function permits one to distinguish inflationary policies from expansionary ones. The possibility that marginal (or average) costs decline below capacity increases the likelihood that expansionary policies will be anti-inflationary. The major difficulty is that initial price effects of policies are very sensitive to the specification of the dynamic model, a subject on which the economic literature is particularly quiet.

If Model A, the "planning" or "price maker" model, best describes the world, then a fiscal policy of reducing direct taxes or increasing government expenditures is the policy of the three considered that is most likely to have initially anti-inflationary effects under less than capacity conditions. If Model B holds, this fiscal policy is the *least* likely to be anti-inflationary. For Model A, indirect tax reductions are second best, and monetary expansion is the worst, given that our criterion is expansion without inflation.

For Model B, an increase in government expenditure is the worst policy, indirect tax reductions are second best, and monetary expansion appears most likely to be initially anti-inflationary.

Galbraith's argument that the economy of a modern nation is about one-half planning, Model A, price "making", and one-half Model B, price "taking", thus presents an additional dilemma to the policy maker, (and to the policy taker).[12] What is anti-inflationary policy for one-half the economy may be causing inflation in the other half with the net outcome uncertain indeed!

On balance, the reduction of indirect taxes appears to be the policy most likely to be successful in expanding output while simultaneously limiting price inflation. The policy turned up as possibly anti-inflationary for both Models A and B, whereas monetary expansion may be anti-inflationary as far as the effects captured by our model are concerned, but the inflationary effect of a fall in foreign exchange rates in response to a decline in nominal interest rates; and the inflationary expectations that may be generated if households all behave as quantity theorists, would likely result in a net inflationary impact. Neither of these factors appear to negate our conclusions regarding indirect tax reductions.

Conclusion

Much more attention must be paid by economists to the possibly perverse effects of current "anti"-inflationary policies. Not only do they cause not inconsiderable loss of output and employment, they may be "counter-productive" as well in all but "fully employed" economies.

---

[12] For recent evidence regarding the prevalence of "administered" prices see Gardiner C. Means, (1972). Means finds a "new dimension" in the administered price thesis in that "industrial prices in recent years has disclosed many cyclical cases in which price behaviour has been the *reverse* of that to be expected from classical theory, the price raising with recession and falling with recovery". *Ibid.*, 297. Means concludes that fifty administered price commodity indexes behaved "in a contracyclical manner in 87 of the 200 possible movements or 43.5 per cent of the opportunities", *Ibid.*, 298. He offers no explanation of this phenomena, but as we have seen, Harrod does. See also John M. Blair, (1974) and Alfred S. Eichner, (1973).

Appendix

Our methodology calls for investigating the direction of change of the price variable after an exogenous policy variable is shifted. The change is measured from an equilibrium position.

Model A – "Price Maker"
Local stability of Model A can be investigated from the following equation:

$$\frac{\mathring{P}}{P_0} = S_A \left(\frac{\partial C(X(P), r(P))}{\partial P} - 1\right)(P - P_0)$$

where $\dfrac{\partial C}{\partial P}$

is evaluated at P_0, and P_0 is the equilibrium value of P.
In the neighbourhood of equilibrium we write:

$$I = I_x X + I_r r \qquad I_x \geq 0, \; I_r \leq 0$$

$$L = L_x X + L_r r \qquad L_x \geq 0, \; L_r \leq 0$$

so that

$$r(P) = \frac{P}{M} \frac{s}{\xi_A} - \frac{GL_x}{\xi_A}$$

$$X(P) = \frac{M}{P} \frac{I_r}{\xi_A} + \frac{GL_r}{\xi_A}$$

where $s = 1 - I_x$
and $\xi_A = sL_r + I_r L_x$.
Note that $\bar{\xi}_A \leq 0$ and $s \geq 0$.

We have:

$$\mathring{P} = S_A \left[\frac{M}{|\xi_A| P^2} \left[(C_r s - C_x |I_r|)\right] - 1\right](P - P_0)$$

$(C_r s - C_x |I_r|) < 0$ is a sufficient condition though not necessary condition for stability. Since this term appears frequently in the text, and since stability is a valuable property for this analysis, it seems appropriate to err on the side of security and impose this condition, when using Model A.
The necessary condition is

$$(C_r s - C_x I_r) \frac{|\xi_A| P^2}{M}.$$

It appears safe to say that stability is unlikely if $C_x < 0$, given that C_r is always assumed to be positive.

Model B
Stability can be inferred from:

$$\frac{\mathring{P}}{P_0} = S_B \left[\frac{\partial I(X(P), r(P))}{\partial P} - \frac{\partial X(P)}{\partial P}\right](P - P_0)$$

where $\dfrac{\partial I(P)}{\partial P}$

and $\dfrac{\partial X(P)}{\partial P}$ are evaluated at equilibrium.

We have:

$$r(P) = \frac{1}{\xi_B} (PL_x - \frac{M}{P} C_x)$$

$$X(P) = \frac{1}{\xi_B} (PL_r + \frac{M}{P} C_r)$$

where $\xi_B = C_r L_x + C_x |L_r|$.

Note that $\xi_B > 0$ as $C_r > 0$ if $C_x > 0$.

We have:

$$\overset{\circ}{P} = -[\frac{s}{\xi_B} (|L_r| - \frac{C_r M}{P^2}) + \frac{|I_r|}{\xi_B} (L_x + \frac{C_x M}{P^2})] (P - P_0).$$

Therefore the system is stable unless C_x is negative and

$$\frac{sC_r M}{P^2} < s|L_r| + |I_r| (L_x + \frac{C_x M}{P^2}).$$

Even if $C_x < 0$, the system is likely to be stable. For instance $|C_x| <$ $L_x P^2$ is a sufficient (still not necessary) condition, and this appears to be a rather weak requirement. Not surprisingly, the price taker's model appears to be stable for a wider range of parameter values than a price maker model, even though X and r both adjust to equilibrium in zero time. If $C_r \simeq 0$ and $C_x > 0$ the system is certainly stable.

To economists steeped in "diminishing returns" it seems perverse to assume $C_x < 0$. However, there is no difference in the analysis of this paper if $C(X,r)$ is assumed to be an average cost curve and firms follow an average cost pricing principle. In this case it is natural to write $C_x < 0$ during a period of excess capacity, and Model B would appear to be preferable for our analysis to A since it is more likely to be stable. Under these conditions, monetary expansion and indirect tax reduction both appear to be anti-inflationary policies. It is interesting that according to Harrod and Galbraith, the conventional economics misunderstands even the "market" half of the economy.

Stability of Models A & B in Response to Alternative Policy Moves

A comparative qualitative analysis of Models A & B may be made with the aid of the following diagrams.

Response to a change in Government Expenditures, G, (or Direct taxes)

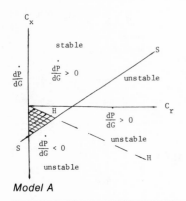

No dichotomy. As shown in the text, p. 183, an increase in G necessarily entails an increase in P_0, a shortcoming of our model.

Model A   *Model B*

The rising solid line (S) divides the field between pairs of values of C_x and C_r for which Model A is stable (above S), and unstable (below S). The falling dotted line (H) divides the field between pairs of values of C_x and C_r for which the conventional $(\partial P/\partial G > 0)$ and the "perverse" $(\partial P/\partial G < 0)$ sides of Harrod's dichotomy will obtain. The small cross-hatched region represents the $C_x \leq 0$, $C_r \geq 0$ area in which a locally stable "perverse" Harrod's dichotomy result would be realized. Thus, the more likely result of an increase of government spending in a Model A economy is an increase in P from $C_x > 0$, $C_r > 0$. Note, however, that without quantitative data we cannot specify the slope or critical values of lines S and H.

Response to an Increase in the Money Supply

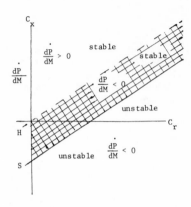

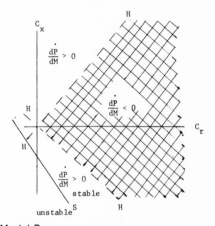

Model A
Here we see there is quite an area of $C_x \gtrless 0$ paired with $C_r \geq 0$ for which monetary policy might have "perverse" $(d\dot{P}/dM < 0)$ rather than conventional results in a Model A economy.

Model B
As is evident there is a broad area of combinations of $C_x \gtrless 0$, $C_r > 0$ for which the perverse side of Harrod's dichotomy obtains. i.e. where a rise in M causes a fall in interest rates leading to a larger increase in supply than in demand and, therefore, a fall in P. On either side of this area are stable conventional wisdom "outcomes" where

$$\frac{d\dot{P}}{dM} > 0.$$

Response to an Increase in Indirect Taxes

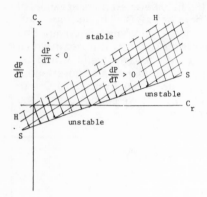

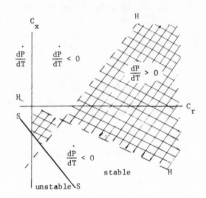

Model A
Again, a fairly large stable area of $C_x \gtreqqless 0$ and $C_r \geq 0$ pairs yielding a "perverse"

$$\frac{d\mathring{P}}{dT} > 0$$

result is evident in Model A. In this area prices net of taxes rise when indirect taxes increase.

Model B
Model B is almost certainly stable with $C_r > 0$, and there is a broad area yielding the perverse rather than conventional response of prices to higher indirect taxes.

Stability Analysis of the More General Model

In the text we analyzed the rate of change of prices dynamically, while assuming that output and interest rates adjust immediately, when disturbed, to equilibrium. Without attempting a full analysis involving three dynamic equations, we offer here merely a stability analysis of the model first with three and then with two dynamic equations.

Model A1 – Price Maker Model with Three Dynamic Equations

Model A1

$$\mathring{P} = S_{Ar}(C(X,r) - P)$$

$$\mathring{X} = S_{AX}(I(X,r) + G - X)$$

$$\mathring{L}(X,r) = S_{AL}\left(\frac{M}{P} - L(X,r)\right)$$

Local Stability:

$$\begin{vmatrix} -1 & C_x & 0 \\ -0 & -s & 0 \\ \frac{M}{P^2} & -L_x & -1 \end{vmatrix} \begin{vmatrix} P-\bar{P} \\ X-\bar{X} \\ L-\bar{L} \end{vmatrix} = 0$$

The roots of the matrix are given by the equation:

$$(1+\lambda)(s+\lambda)(1+\lambda) = 0.$$

There are no positive roots so that the system is stable provided only that $s \geq 0$, where s is the marginal propensity to save.

Model B1 – Price Taker Model with Three Dynamic Equations

Model B1

$\mathring{P} = S_{BP}(I(X,r) + G - X)$

$\mathring{X} = S_{BX}(P - C(X,r))$

$\mathring{L}(X,r) = S_{BM}(\frac{M}{P} - L(X,r))$

Local Stability:

$$\begin{vmatrix} 0 & -s & 0 \\ 1 & -C_x & 0 \\ -\frac{M}{P^2} & -L_x & -1 \end{vmatrix}$$

$(1+\lambda)(\lambda^2 + \lambda C_x + s) = 0$

$\lambda_1 = -1, \quad \lambda_2 = \frac{1}{2}C_x + \frac{1}{2}\sqrt{C_x 2 - 2s}, \quad _3 = -\frac{1}{2}C_x - \frac{1}{2}\sqrt{C_x 2 - 2s}.$

Therefore, if $2s < C_x^2$, then all roots are negative and the system is stable.

Model A2 – Price Maker Model with Two Dynamic Equations
Here it is assumed that the money market is always in equilibrium and that prices and quantities in the commodity market adjust dynamically toward equilibrium. Models A2 and B2 are stable if $C_x > 0$ and $C_r > 0$ and $C_r M / |L_r| P^2 < 1$. If C_x is negative stability is unlikely but possible, requiring that

$C_x + \frac{C_r L_x}{|L_r|} \geq 0.$

Model A2

$\mathring{P} = S_{AP}(C(X,r) - P)$

$\mathring{X} = S_{AX}(I(X,r) + G - X)$

$L(X,r) = \frac{M}{P}$

Local Stability:

$$\begin{array}{cc} -(1 - \frac{C_r M}{|L_r| P^2}) & (C_x + \frac{C_r L_x}{|L_r|}) \\ -\frac{|I_r| M}{|L_r| P^2} & -(s + \frac{|I_r| L_x}{L_r}) \end{array}$$

If C_r and C_x are both positive s and

$\frac{C_r M}{|L_r| P^2} < 1$

then the matrix has the following sign pattern $= \overset{+}{-}$

which is stable. See Chapter Six discussion or Lemma 5.1 in Maybee and Quirk, (1969, p.39).

Model B2 – Price Taker Model with Two Dynamic Equations

Model B2

$\overset{\circ}{P} = S_{BP}(I(X,r) + G - X)$

$\overset{\circ}{X} = S_{BX}(P - C(X,r))$

$L(X,r) = \dfrac{M}{P}$

From the last equation we have:

$r = \dfrac{M}{L_r P} - \dfrac{L_x X}{L_r}$

where L_r and L_x are evaluated at equilibrium.

Local Stability:

$$-\dfrac{|I_r| M}{|L_r| P^2} \qquad\qquad -(S + \dfrac{|I_r| L_x}{|L_r|})$$

$$1 - \dfrac{C_r M}{|L_r| P^2} \qquad\qquad -(C_x + \dfrac{C_r L_x}{|L_r|})$$

If $C_x > 0$, $C_r > 0$ then a sufficient condition for stability is that

$\dfrac{C_r M}{|L_r| P^2} < 1.$

References

Blair, John M., "Market Power and Inflation", *Journal of Economic Issues,* VIII, 2 June 1974, 453-78.

Blinder, A.S. and Solow, R.M., "Analytical Foundations of Fiscal Policy", in *The Economics of Public Finance* (Washington, Brookings 1974) 3-115.

Cassell, Gustav, *Theory of Social Economy,* 5th ed., 1932, (New York, 1967).

Davidson, Paul, "Disequilibrium Market Adjustment: Marshall Revisited," *Economic Inquiry,* June 1974, 146-58.

Eichner, A.S., "A Theory of the Determination of the Mark-Up Under Oligopoly," *Economic Journal,* 83, December 1973, 1184-1200.

Eisner, Robert, "What Went Wrong?", *Journal of Political Economy,* 79, (May/June 1971), 629-41).

Galbraith, J.K., *Economics and the Public Purpose,* (Boston, 1973).

————, "Power and the Useful Economist", *American Economic Review,* 63, (March 1973), 1-11.

Harrod, R., "Increasing Returns", *Monopolistic Competition Theory, Essays in Honor of Edward H. Chamberlin,* R.E. Kuenne ed., (New York, 1967), 63-76.

————, "Reassessment of Keynes' Views on Money", *Journal of Political Economy,* 78, (July/August 1970), 63-76.

Hotson, J.H. and Habibagahi, H., "Comparative Static Analysis of Harrod's Dichotomy", *Kyklos,* 25, (1972), 154-66.

Knapp, John, "Economics or Political Economy?", *Lloyd's Bank Review,* 110, January 1973, 19-43.

Leijonhufvud, A., *On Keynesian Economics and the Economics of Keynes,* (Oxford, New York, 1966).

————, "Keynes Employment Function: Comment", *History of Political Economy,* Summer 1974, 164-70.

Lermer, George. "Some Lessons From and Observations About the Current Cyclical Experience of the Canadian Economy", *Waterloo Economic Series,* No. 40, (April 1971).

Maybee, J. and Quirk, J., "Quantitative Problems in Matrix Theory", *Siam Review,* 11, (January 1969).

Means, G.C., "The Administered-Price Thesis Reconfirmed", *American Economic Review,* 62, (June 1972), 292-306.

Okun, A.M., "Potential GNP: Its Measure and Significance", *Proceedings of the Business and Economic Statistics Section of the American Statistical Association,* 1972; reprinted in *Readings in Money, National Income, and Stabilization Policy,* Revised ed., W.L. Smith and R.L. Teigen eds., (Homewood, 1970), 313-22.

Wiles, P.J., *Price, Cost and Output,* (Oxford, 1956).

Wilson, T.A. and Eckstein, O., "Short-Run Productivity Behavior in U.S. Manufacturing", *Review of Economics and Statistics,* 46, (Feb. 1964), 41-59.

8 Incomes Policies and the Current Inflation

Introduction: Present Incomes Policies or Confusion Twice Confounded

This chapter seeks to explain why economists and governments must take incomes policy very seriously, it deals with the most familiar objections to these policies, and it outlines a few alternative approaches.

My choice of the European term "incomes policies" rather than the more common North American terms "guideposts" or "wage and price controls" is deliberate. "Incomes policies" is a portmanteau term covering *all* varieties of specifics from complete laissez faire to wartime regulation of all prices and quantities. I define incomes policies as: *the net resultant of all government policies, direct and indirect, upon the distribution of, and the growth rate of, the incomes of individuals and groups.*

In the sense of this definition all countries have, and will continue to have, "incomes policies" just as they have "monetary policies," "fiscal policies," "crime control policies" or "foreign policies." Only a very foolish and naive person would argue that a country "should not have" a foreign policy, or a fiscal policy. All real questions regarding foreign, or fiscal, or monetary or incomes policies involve not "whether" but "what, which, and how?" What are the present incomes policies of Canada? To what ends are these policies directed? Are they well adapted to achieve these ends? If not, how might they be improved? Are the ends sought in fact attainable? Whose ends are abetted by these policies, whose ends are thwarted? These are real questions, but they are little asked and we do not begin to have the answers, because instead economists, columnists and political leaders have been diverted by the naive question, " Should Canada have an incomes policy?"

It is, of course, possible that the best policy *is* to do nothing – laissez faire – or to do nothing consciously new. Thus the policy of the Dominion of Canada toward the sun, moon, and tides is to let them alone, or to cooperate with their well understood activities as life has from time immemorial. However, the "solar policy" of the United States and Russia in recent decades has been to seek to harness the sun's power more fully to man's purposes through control of nuclear fusion and through solar furnaces. Their "lunar policy" has been to spend a non-trivial fraction of GNP to explore the moon and planets. Canada, likewise, has actively considered going beyond the mere attempt to predict the tides to projects to harness the tides of the Bay of Fundy for power. A similar movement from laissez faire to planned, sustained, purposeful action is, I believe, necessary in the realm of incomes policies.

For the central doctrine of classical and neo-classical economics
– that if things were left to run themselves everything would be fine – is
not so. In addition to all the "micro" problems centering around the
fact that profit maximizing behavior might well entail monopolization,
suppression of new methods, child or slave labour, and adulterated
products, we have the "macro" problem that Say's Law – or Walras'
Law – is false.

So government has had to expand its role to pursuing actively
"full employment" by changing its monetary policy from that of an
automatic gold standard, to a "lean against the wind" policy and its
fiscal policy from "balance the budget" to "balance the economy at
higher employment." Clear thinkers like Keynes and Robinson saw
from the beginning of the "Keynesian Revolution" that these important changes in monetary and fiscal policy necessitated some drastic
changes in incomes policies if we were to obtain the blessing of "full
employment" without the curse of continuous inflation. Unhappily,
less clear thinkers were in the overwhelming majority. Joan Robinson
puts it as follows:

*"The proposition that, in an industrial economy, the level of money-
wage rates governs the level of prices was an essential element in the
analysis of Keynes'* General Theory of Employment, Interest and
Money, *published in 1936. The part of his argument which concerned
the need for government policy to maintain 'a high and stable level of
employment' was accepted into the canon of received orthodoxy in
this country even before the end of the war in 1945 but the part which
concerned wages and prices was resisted much longer. It was easy to
predict that if we stumbled into near-full employment with institutions
and attitudes unchanged, the balance of power in wage-bargaining
would tip in favour of the workers, so that a vicious spiral of wages and
prices would become chronic. Yet it took about fifteen years of experience for the point to really sink home. Many professional
economists and most Chancellors of the Exchequer continued to
maintain that the movement of prices was something to do with the
management of the monetary system."*[1]

In the following passages Keynes sketches every aspect of a full
employment without inflation "incomes policy" save one – how to get
the people to comply:

*". . . I am now of the opinion that the maintenance of a stable general
level of money wages is, on the balance of considerations, the most
advisable policy for a closed system; whilst the same conclusion will
hold good for an open system provided that equilibrium with the rest
of the world can be secured by means of fluctuating exchanges. There
are advantages in some degree of flexibility in the wages of particular
industries so as to expedite transfers from those which are relatively
declining to those that are relatively expanding. But the money-wage
level as a whole should be maintained as stable as possible, at any rate
in the short period.*

*This policy will result in a fair degree of stability in the price level;
– greater stability, at least, than with a flexible wage policy. Apart from
'administered' or monopoly prices, the price level will only change in
the short period in response to the extent that changes in the volume
of employment affect marginal prime costs; whilst in the long period*

---

[1] Joan Robinson, *Economics, An Awkward Corner*, (New York: Pantheon 1967)
  p. 11.

they will only change in response to changes in the cost of production due to new technique and new or increased equipment.

It is true that, if there are, nevertheless, large fluctuations in employment, substantial fluctuations in the price level will accompany them . . . Thus with a rigid wage policy the stability of prices will be bound up in the short period with the avoidance of fluctuations in employment. In the long period . . . we are left with the choice between a policy of allowing prices to fall slowly with the progress of technique and equipment whilst keeping wages stable, or of allowing wages to rise slowly whilst keeping prices stable. On the whole my preference is for the latter alternative, on account of the fact that it is easier with an expectation of higher wages in the future to keep the actual level of employment within a given range of full employment than with an expectation of lower wages in future, and on account also of the social advantages of gradually diminishing the burden of debt, the greater ease of adjustment from decaying to growing industries, and the psychological encouragement likely to be felt from a moderate tendency for money wages to increase."[2]

As stressed in Chapter Three, Keynes' long run theory of the price level, like his short run theory, ran entirely in terms of wage and non-wage costs and productivity as in the following quotation:

". . . the long run stability or instablity of prices will depend on the strength of the upward trend of the wage unit (or, more precisely, of the cost unit) compared with the rate of increase in the efficiency of the production system."[3]

During the 19th century heyday of capitalism, unemployment in even the most rapidly advancing countries of Europe and North America averaged something close to 10 per cent, while the underdeveloping bulk of humanity languished in secular stagnation with much higher unemployment, open or disguised. It is the great accomplishment of Keynesian economics of the post World War II world to reduce drastically these wastes by adding a dash of planning in the form of active fiscal and monetary policies. With present incomes policies, however, economies attempting to run at full employment achieve accelerating inflation, so further planning is necessary.

Canada's "incomes policy" prior to Thanksgiving Day 1975, was an unintended net result of a series of federal, provincial, and municipal enactments seeking only particular ends rather than over-all coherence. It is difficult even to describe that policy, which, like Topsy, "just growed." "Laissez faire" is clearly dead as regards income distribution, if indeed it ever "lived", but we are still far from a rationally debated and chosen "incomes policy."

Prior to the incomes policy white paper *Attack on Inflation*, "policy" was that – subject only to legal sanctions against excessive force or fraud, and the vague, but potent force of public opinion, – any group which could gain power through the market, politics, or the ability collectively to withhold their needed services, could obtain more rapid increases in income than those who cannot wield power. Thus the stockholders and managements of corporations facing less than cutthroat competition – perhaps because of tariff, quota, or patent favours conferred by government – achieve incomes far above average. Employees of these "strong oligopolies" can wrest from

---

[2] *G.T.* pp. 270-1.

[3] *G.T.* p. 309.

these firms above average compensations, and their ability to do so is enhanced by present labour laws and payment of unemployment compensation to those on strike. Unions facing less strong corporations or individual proprietorships, such as abound in agriculture and services, are much less able to wring super-normal gains. Indeed, many of them are hard pressed to keep the real income of their memberships growing at all.

In many occupations the prospective gains through unionization appear so small, or the obstacles to organization to be overcome appear so daunting, that unionization makes little headway. Thus "white collar" workers and those employed by "small" firms are little unionized – however exceptions exist. Most construction firms are "small" to "medium" size and yet construction unions abound and are potent in gaining high incomes for their members.

Where once the pace of growth of the incomes of federal, provincial, and municipal workers was set by the compensation of "comparable" workers in the private sector, in recent years the public sector has more and more set the pace. The rapidly growing government sector has made increasingly more competitive bids for labour force entrants, and has proved less resistant to pressure for raises than private businesses. One of the most useful ways for Canadian governments to contribute to the reining in of inflation is to put their own houses in order – by refusing to grant 15%, 20%, or 30% raises that the policemen, firemen, teachers, and yes, university professors, are demanding. Additionally, government mediators must avoid setting off inflationary wage rounds like the disgraceful "Pearson Guidepost" (in 1966) of 30% increases for the Seaway workers. The government must remove this "beam" from its own eye, before it can have any success in removing the "specks" in the private sector.

It is a hopeful omen that Prime Minister Trudeau's Thanksgiving Day Address specifically recognizes this. But everything will depend on implementation, and at this writing the evidence is not yet in.

It is an overstatement to say that traditional Canadian incomes "policy" is "Them what has-gets. Them what has not-gets left." The market does work, after a fashion. When long established wage relativities are too much distorted by power wielding front runners, those with lesser power obtain raises too. This ameliorates the problem of perceived "social justice" between, say, the bricklayers and the department store clerks, but increases inflation. And where the market does little for "losers" such as farmers, or nothing, as in the case of pensioners, the government steps in with higher price supports and social insurance benefits, but usually only with a lag. Thus, we obtain relief from the unravelling of the social fabric that inflation would otherwise entail only at the cost of another round of inflation.

Notoriously, those with "fixed" interest bearing claims suffer losses of real income with inflation – while the debtors gain. As inflation continues and expectations adjust, however, interest rates rise, partly through the market and partly through central bank action to peg interest rates higher to "stop inflation." Whatever this does to the pace of inflation – and we have seen reasons above for being highly skeptical of the "conventional wisdom" here – it does check, remove, or reverse, the erosion of "rentier" income and that of the financial institutions which manage their funds.

Canada, like most other nations, has been on the secular inflation treadmill for some 35 years now. As long as the wage-price-profit-tax-interest income spiral turned slowly enough to result in inflation of only one to three per cent, the public, politicians, pundits and professors did little but grumble and make vague resolutions to "do something" next year. But these days are gone – 7% to 12% inflation per annum is not "tolerable" and it becomes a political necessity to "do something," but what? Fiscal and monetary restraint "work," if at all, only by causing considerable unemployment, thus *indirectly* forcing us collectively to cut back on our demands. But what an insane policy – because even our full employment national income is not sufficient to satisfy all the money income demands we collectively make on it, we cut our real national income rather than cutting our demands on it!

Thus monetary and fiscal policies are also *incomes* policies – but dreadfully indirect, inefficient and unjust incomes policies when they are used to "fight inflation" by creating unemployment. The decision to invoke "tight money" is a decision to impoverish, directly and surely, home builders and other contractors who depend for finance wholly on the availability of mortgage money, and those construction workers whom they lay off. Those not laid off suffer no loss in hourly earnings since pay rates are set by union contracts (though overtime becomes more scarce), so there is no *direct* effect on this main component of the cost of construction. A housing slump feeds back as a slump in demand for the products of the supplying industries with consequent fall in the profits and wage incomes in these industries. This distress *may* lead – in time – to some fall in the price of these materials, but at great cost to society in general and to these firms' owners and employees in particular. Furthermore, many of these supplying firms are strong enough to administer their prices – rather than allowing them to fluctuate according to short-run changes in demand – so price reductions will be small and slow in materializing.

As the incomes of those connected to the housing industry fall, they, in turn, comsume fewer of the products of other industries. Unemployment compensation provides for food and rent, but car sales suffer. As is well known, unemployment is particularly the lot of the less educated, less skilled, and of minority groups, so social injustice is added to economic injustice. One group particularly suffers – new entrants to the labour force having never been employed, are not entitled to unemployment compensation. Furthermore, tight money plays hob with the ability of the lower levels of government to finance needed schools, sewers and water treatment plants.

All these sacrifices are exacted for an *incomes* policy end – in the hope that if enough unemployment is created, if some contractors are driven into bankruptcy, if enough supplying firms are suffering reduced or negative profits, if GM sells fewer cars, that the *next* round of wage negotiations will be less inflationary!

While all these sacrifices are piling up, there is one group in society whose incomes and consequent expenditures – are being increased. Creditors' incomes rise, despite the slowdown in new loans, because of higher interest rates on new and refinanced debts. About one-quarter of government debt and one-third of corporate debt, together with much consumer debt, matures within one year, and increasingly even mortgages pay the current rather than the historical interest rate. As we saw in Chapter Two, total debt is one of the "biggest numbers" in economics so that the increase in the interest incomes is "non-trivial". Table 8.1 brings together some relevant figures regarding the Canadian economy in the past few years.

Table 8.1.
The Level of Unemployment and Some Rates of Change in Canada
1969 – 1974

Year	U	$\overset{\circ}{Q}$	$\overset{\circ}{r}_2$	$\overset{\circ}{R}$	$\overset{\circ}{P}$	$\overset{\circ}{T}$	$\overset{\circ}{i}$	$\overset{\circ}{Y}i$
1969	4.7%	6.8%	8.2%	4.5%	4.5%	6.1%	12.3%	17.5%
1970	5.9	2.7	8.0	5.5	4.6	2.2	4.4	11.2
1971	6.4	5.6	12.8	4.0	3.2	1.6	-12.1	11.1
1972	6.3	5.8	7.4	4.8	4.8	.8	4.0	14.7
1973	5.6	6.8	8.1	5.3	7.6	1.1	4.6	18.5
1974	5.4	3.7	16.9	12.4	13.1	4.9	17.7	40.6

Year	$\overset{\circ}{Y}i\text{-}\overset{\circ}{P}$	$\overset{\circ}{H}S$
1969	13.0%	6.9%
1970	6.6	-9.5
1971	7.9	22.6
1972	9.9	7.0
1973	10.9	7.4
1974	27.5	-17.3

Explanation of Symbols:

U = Level of unemployment
$\overset{\circ}{Q}$ = Rate of change of real output
$\overset{\circ}{r}_2$ = Rate of change of money to goods ratio
$\overset{\circ}{R}$ = Rate of change of unit wage costs
$\overset{\circ}{P}$ = Rate of change of price level
$\overset{\circ}{T}$ = Rate of change of total Gov't. revenue as % of GNP
$\overset{\circ}{i}$ = Rate of change of government bond yields
$\overset{\circ}{Y}i$ = Rate of change of interest and misc. investment income
$\overset{\circ}{Y}i\text{-}\overset{\circ}{P}$ = Rate of change of real interest income
$\overset{\circ}{H}S$ = Rate of change of housing starts

Source: Chapter 2, Appendix Table 2; Dept. Finance, *Economic Review April 1975;* IMF, *International Financial Statistics.*

Canada's economy was healthier in 1969 than it has been in any subsequent year to date, with unemployment a "mere" 4.7% and real output (Q) growing at 6.8%. The money supply was growing too fast so that the money to goods ratio (r_2) increased 8.2%. However, the price level increased 'only'' 4.5%, or exactly as much as unit wage cost (R) had increased – as the wage cost mark-up theory of inflation would lead one to expect. Taxes as a percentage of GNP (T) rose 6.1%(from 34.4% of GNP in 1968 to 36.5% in 1969) and interest rates, here taken as the interest rate on government bonds, rose 12.3% (from 6.75% to 7.58%). Interest and miscellaneous investment incomes (Yi), were up a heady 17.5% (from $2,023 millions in 1968 to $3,082 million in 1969) so real interest income was up 13% *after deduction of the price level change.* Thus real "rentier" income was increasing almost twice as fast as real output– a far cry from Keynes' proposed "euthanasia" through low interest rates, or from the textbook word pictures of lenders being destroyed by inflation. The final column of Table 8.1 for 1969 indicates that housing starts were up 6.9% from 1968, about the same percentage as real output as a whole.

Canada's subsequent stagflationary adventures leave varying tracks in the columns of the table. The increase of real output slumped badly in the recessions of 1970 and 1974, while in both of these misadventures unit wage costs rose at an increasing rate as wages continued to rise and productivity fell. Clearly unit wage costs do not wholly determine the price level, however. The divergences between $\overset{\circ}{R}$ and $\overset{\circ}{P}$ in 1970-71 and 1973-74 are to be largely explained by foreign developments: In 1970-71 the upward float of the Canadian dollar caused a reduction in the rate at which foreign inflation was transmitted to Canada so $\dot{P}$ rose less than $\dot{R}$, while in 1973-74 the devaluation of the U.S. and Canadian dollars relative to most of the world's currencies, and the food and fuel crises, caused $\dot{P}$ to rise more rapidly than $\dot{R}$. Also the fall of interest rates in 1971 and the steep rise of interest rates in 1974 helps to account for $\dot{P}$ rising less than $\dot{R}$ in 1971 and the reverse in 1974.

However, the relationship upon which the Wage Cost Mark-up (WCM) theory focuses remains strong even in these stormy times. Not so the quantity of money to goods relationship upon which the Equation of Exchange (EOE) theory focuses. Throughout, the money supply increases "too fast", but an 8% rise in r_2 corresponds to quite differing rates of inflation in 1969, 1970 and 1973, while the rapid rise of 12.8% in 1971 occurs with the least inflation of the period.

Note, however, the wild gyrations in the rate of change of housing starts (H$\dot{S}$). With an inadequate growth in real money, (M_2/P), in 1971 and 1974 in the face of rapid inflation – other sectors bid away mortgage funds and housing starts fell. With large increases of r_2 and fall of i in the "recovery" of 1971, housing boomed. Throughout the period "rentiers" did very well, their real incomes rising more rapidly than real output in every year, their most incredible gain being the most recent. In 1974 interest and misc. income increased a phenomenal 40.6% (from $5,180 million in 1973 to $7,281 millions in 1974) for a real income gain of 27.5%, while, in contrast housing starts fell 17.3%.

In the strange mental world of the bastard Keynesian, a rise in steel prices, steel wages, or physicians' fees are all possible inflation causes, but a rise in interest rates, and interest incomes are *deflationary*. This is because interest rates enter the analysis in a disembodied manner as neither a subsectoral price index representing "the price of money" nor a cost, but merely as a "demand suppressant." Having done their work of suppressing demand, interest payments are supposed to disappear into a magician's hat, never to reappear as income and hence consumption demand by rentiers. We have said quite a bit about this strange analysis above and need not repeat it here.

In the strange mental world of the monetarist, none of the above are inflation causes, but only consequences. The sole cause of inflation is too rapid an increase in the money supply. If the government would stop creating so much money, inflation would stop and so would the excessive growth of particular incomes. But if the monetarist is (usually) consistent – neither excessive increases in steel wages nor interest rates can cause inflation – the non-monetarist bastard Keynesian is not. Bastard Keynesians do give some support to incomes policies to hold down, say, construction workers wage hikes, *and* the monetary policies to dry up construction through tight money. Now it is doubtless true that the construction unions are as sinful as any in pushing up wages, and that the housing industry has been highly inflationary, especially in the past few years. But few would argue that rentiers are such noble specimens of humanity, so uniquely deserving, that their incomes should rise far more rapidly than the growth of real output as a whole in boom or semi bust, while those otherwise attached to the construction industry are such uniquely undeserving specimens that their incomes are to be sacrificed whenever we need to "disinflate" the economy. But just such an "incomes policy" had been the unintended result of our "conventional wisdom" monetary policies. Again – we already have "incomes policies" but not being well thought out, or even recognized as such, they do not make much sense. Surely we can do better.

There is, as Galbraith has observed, a certain difficulty in avoiding the inevitable. So, despite the chorus of carping critics chanting "Price and wage controls have never, can never and will never work!" Canada now has them – and will continue to have them, and so will other "mixed economies". How well they will work will depend on how well they are thought out, adapted to our actual situation, on the degree of consensus we can generate and maintain, on the quality and quantity of leadership and administration devoted to them – and luck.

The latest Canadian federal budget message listed the three anti-inflationary policy options open to the government as:
1) cause a deeper depression by tighter money and tax hikes;
2) depend upon voluntary restraints on wages and prices;
3) enact compulsory wage and price controls; and then rejected all three for a "policy" of muddling through in the hope that the economy would "turn up" somewhat in late 1975 or in 1976 and that inflation will taper off. Rumor has it that then Finance Minister John Turner argued hard for compulsory controls – given the failure of his attempt to get the Canadian Labour Conference to agree to voluntary "guideposts" – but failed to convince Prime Minister Trudeau to adopt Robert Stanfield's policy. Belatedly, the Liberals have been forced to enact, tardily, apologetically and lamely, the very controls they would have enacted boldly years ago had they not been misled by the wishful thinking of bastard Keynesianism.

To date there has been a pattern of "too little and too late" about the whole effort of inflation control through incomes policies in every country. Under favorable circumstances purely voluntary "guideposts" can improve matters – as the Kennedy -Johnson experience of 1962-66 will demonstrate to anyone willing to be convinced. Over time, however, consensus breaks down in charges of unfairness and some power of compulsion must be obtained or the policy will fail. In 1966 President Johnson had to choose between "leaning on" General Motors to lower the price of its cars and its profits – in order to maintain the commitment of the labour unions to exercise restraint in wage bargaining, or the enactment of compulsory controls, or to let the guideposts lapse. He chose the latter course and inflation accelerated.

In August 1971 the Nixon administration came to the reluctant conclusion that their "game plan" of mainly monetary management of the economy had failed (ie. excessive inflation, excessive unemployment and excessive balance of payments deficits) and that it would be unwise to face the electorate with the economy in such disarray. Thereupon President Nixon announced his "New Economic Policy," a considerable venture into economic planning involving, among other things a wage-price freeze ("Phase 1") and compulsory controls ("Phase 2") on wages and prices. With the brakes on inflation the money supply was allowed to grow more rapidly (M_1 rising 8.7% in 1972 VS 6.9% in 1971) to continue the growth in real output from the 1970 "administrated recession," (Q rose about 6% in both 1971 and 1972) – and get President Nixon re-elected.

Whether viewed econometrically[4] or politically Phases 1 and 2 were a considerable success – whereupon the administration abandoned them for Phase 3, a voluntary programme for which there were

---

[4] See William Poole, "Wage and Price Controls: Where Do We Go From Here?" *Brookings Papers on Economic Activity,* 1, 1973; pp. 285-99, and Robert J. Gordon, "The Response of Wages and Prices to the First Two Years of Controls," *Brookings Papers on Economic Activity,* 3, 1973, pp. 765-79.

few, if any, volunteers. As Galbraith has put it, "The notion that if a policy is working, it should be abandoned reflects a novel approach to public policy,"[5] but then Nixon's was a novel administration. As the Watergate revelations made evident, part of the controls' successes were tainted by corruption and their abandonment in January 1973 was part of the deal – "Milk producers, oil companies, you can raise your prices only after my re-election. Please leave your illegal campaign contributions in unmarked bills with my aides". The liberal hope is to use the power of government to achieve public benefits not otherwise attainable. Conservatives point out the flaw – government programmes will be corrupted to serve special, not general ends, and all too often prove that they are right by themselves corrupting the programmes! Galbraith said that, "Asking Nixon to administer a price control programme is like asking the Pope to administer a birth control programme." In view of the lawlessness revealed by Watergate it would be closer to say, "like asking the Mafia to suppress crime."

We see here one of the great dilemmas of modern times. We have reluctantly concluded we need "big" government to deal with the increasing complexities of 20th century life – yet it is not at all clear that we have solved the problem of keeping this vital institution reasonably honest, efficient and responsive over the long run. However, no retreat into laissez-faire is possible. Some pruning of luxuriant bureaucratic growth would doubtlessly be useful. Some instances of pure Parkinson's Law growth without function can be exposed and, hopefully, exorcised, but big government, for better or for worse, is here to stay. The task is to make it "for better."

Nor can the task of managing the economy stop at the level of the nation state. As the food and fuel crises of 1973 and 1974 demonstrate anew, the world is increasingly interdependent, and prone to disruption. Phase 1 and Phase 2 owed their successes, in part, to the fact that most of the cost factors pushing up the U.S. price level in 1971-72 were a) domestic, b) in the "planning" sector of big business and big labour, where prices are already administered. But in 1973 the inflationary impulses came from shortages in agriculture (in part the result of poor planning, in part the result of crop failures in the USSR and China), higher oil and metal prices and two devaluations of the U.S. dollar resulting in dramatic increases in import prices.[6] After six months of accelerating inflation, in July 1973 the Nixon administration attempted another freeze followed by "Phase 4" along "Phase 2" lines. It is generally conceded that "Phase 4" was a disaster. As Nordhaus and Shoven put it,

"The (1973) inflation was driven by basic commodities, and there is not a great deal of economic discretion, in these markets. When auto workers' wages or automobile prices are depressed a few per cent, there will be no wholesale defections from the auto industry. But when primary prices are artificially depressed, the slim margins turn to losses, and all sorts of horror stories appear – baby chicks slaughtered, cattle withdrawn from market, lumber exported to Japan only to

[5] John Kenneth Galbraith, *Economics and the Public Purpose*, (Houghton, Boston, 1973) p. 196.

[6] See Dale E. Hathaway, "Food Prices and Inflation," *Brookings Papers on Economic Activity*, 1, 1974: pp. 63-116; and William Nordhaus and John Shoven, "Inflation 1973: The Year of Infamy," *Challenge*, May-June 1974, pp. 14-22.

*be reimported at uncontrolled prices and so on. In short, the second
freeze was useless at best, counter-productive at worst.''*[7]

Thus the task of incomes policy in the industrial world is immensely
complicated by the fact that some of most important prices it seeks to
influence are not subject to its control. Milton Friedman is comforted
by the conviction that OPEC's oil cartel will soon break up and that the
"return of the free market" will result in much lower oil prices.[8]
However, others' perception is that, prior to OPEC's display of mus-
cle, oil prices were set low by the oil companies based in the consum-
ing countries – thus by a "consumers' cartel."[9] This cartel endured for
several decades, until the key member – the U.S. – ceased to be a net
exporter of oil, and until various political developments centered in
the Israel-Arab confrontation, enabled OPEC to turn the tables.
     Not being as sure about anything as Friedman is about every-
thing, I do not pretend to know how successful OPEC and other "third
world" producer cartels will be in tipping the terms of trade in their
favour over the long run. However, I share the perception of most
economists that ours is a world of a mixture of competitive and power
relationships, and that the powerful – nations, multinational corporations, unions – enjoy important success in shaping outcomes to their
purposes. History therefore makes a strong case that OPEC's power is
more likely to be accommodated to, contained, or countervailed, than
that it will fail. And certainly OPEC and other producer cartels' attempts to control their markets will all be in the direction of higher
prices and thus inflationary. Already OPEC has attempted to "index"
oil prices to industrial prices, giving an important inducement to
industrial countries not to attempt to restore the old terms of trade by
inflating industrial prices.
     The very fact that world commodity prices are not under the
control of any one nation's price controllers will act as a spur to the
development of more comprehensive national incomes policies. For
repeatedly it has been balance of payments difficulties, rather than
perceived domestic frictions and injustices, which have compelled
nations to enact controls. The oil crisis has given much of the world an
inflationary, depressionary, balance of payments deficit of unprecedented proportions. Sophisticated incomes policies can help deal
with this crisis, so that unavoidable changes in relative prices – in oil,
raw materials, food and increasingly, pollution control equipment –
need not result in cumulative inflation.

The General Aversion to Controls and Friedman's Fables

Before lawyers, economists and legislators will tackle seriously the
difficult task of designing such policies, we must be successful in the
"struggle of escape" from the old ideas, "which ramify, for those of us
brought up as most of us have been, into every corner of our minds."[10]
     For the instinct which causes neoclassical economists to resist
"wage and price controls" is sound, if the object is to conserve
"intellectual capital" rather than to understand unpleasant realities.

---

[7] Nordhaus and Shoven, "Inflation 1973: The Year of Infamy," p. 20.

[8] Milton Friedman, "The Economy and the 1976 Election," *Newsweek,* February
17, 1975, p. 80.

[9] See Victor Perlo, "Behind the U.S. – OPEC Conflict, *"Challenge,* September –
October 1975, pp. 49-54.

[10] *G.T.* viii.

As Joan Robinson puts it,

"Perhaps the idea that the value of money lies in relations between people, not in a solid, objective standard against which individuals can measure themselves, was a greater blow, even than the idea of unemployment policy, to the complex of vague but powerful traditions inherited from the heyday of laissez faire."[11]

Or as Galbraith writes,

"Price and wage controls . . . are psychologically the most difficult of all the measures here proposed for the defender of the established view to accept. Other instruments employed by the planning system – control of individual prices, control of cost, organization of supply at those costs, provision of an internal source of capital, persuasion of the state as regard procurement – can be ignored or minimized by the person who is determined to do so. It takes effort to achieve this absence of perception, but the rewards in intellectual and pecuniary capital conserved are great. The market survives. With wage and price controls the game is up. A market system in which wages and prices are set by the state is a market system no more. Only the blithely obtuse can reconcile 'this Free Enterprise System' with the enforcement of wage and price controls."[12]

The depths of neoclassical aversion to mandatory controls may be seen not only in the "hard core" of monetarist conservatism, but also in the bastard Keynesian mainstream. In 1968 after the abandonment of the almost wholly voluntary U.S. "guideposts" of 1962-66, coupled with the Vietnam War expansion, resulted in accelerating inflation the Johnson administration felt forced to consider compulsory controls as supplements to higher taxes and interest rates. The Council of Economic Advisors rejected mandatory controls with the following stinging comments:

"the most obvious – and least desirable – way of attempting to stabilize prices is to impose mandatory controls on prices and wages. While such controls may be necessary under conditions of an all-out war, it would be folly to consider them as a solution to the inflationary pressures that accompany high employment under any other circumstances. They distort resource allocation; they require reliance either on necessarily clumsy and arbitrary rules or the inevitably imperfect decisions of government officials; they offer countless temptations to evasion or violation; they require a vast administrative apparatus. All of these reasons make them repugnant. Although such controls may be unfortunately popular when they are not in effect, the appeal quickly disappears once people live under them"[13]

Writers for the *Reader's Digest*, their fingers sore from typing endless diatribes against the national debt, will doubtlessly enlist in a thirty years war against the wickedness and folly of wage and price controls. And surely they will draw much of their intellectual ammunition from the fountainhead – Milton Friedman, whose well-known essay,

---

[11] *Economics: An Awkward Corner*, p. 12.

[12] *Economics and the Public Purpose*, p. 312.

[13] Council of Economic Advisors, *Economic Report of the President*, Washington 1968, p. 119.

"What Price Guideposts?"[14] sets forth an uncompromising position against even voluntary controls. Let us examine this Monetarist Manifesto for the quality of its insights into such matters as inflation and depression policy.

I pass briefly over the central argument – that inflation is always and everywhere a monetary phenomenon caused by too much M and cured only by cutting down on M production, since it is familiar to all readers of these pages. What is less familiar, and yet essential to the monetarist argument is his assertion of Say's Law, or perhaps he would prefer, Friedman's Law – for money *ie.* the supply of money is the demand for it.

"Given that people are so stubborn about the amount they hold in the form of money, let us suppose that, for whatever reasons, the amount of money in a community is higher than people want to hold at the level of prices than prevailing. It does not for our purposes matter why, whether because the government has printed money to finance expenditures or because somebody has discovered a new gold mine or because banks have discovered how to create deposits. For whatever reason, people find that although on the average they would like to hold, let us say, the four weeks' income that they hold in the United States, they are actually holding, say five weeks' income. What will happen? Here again it is essential to distinguish between the individual and the community. Each individual separately thinks he can get rid of his money and he is right. He can go out and spend it and thereby reduce his cash balances. But for the community as a whole the belief that cash balances can be reduced is an optical illusion. The only way I can reduce my cash balances in nominal terms is to induce somebody else to increase his. One man's expenditures are another man's receipts. People as a whole cannot spend more than they as a whole receive. In consequence, if everybody in the community tries to reduce the nominal amount of his cash balances on the average nobody will do so. The amount of nominal balances is fixed by the nominal quantity of money in existence and no game of musical chairs can change it.

But people can and will try to reduce their cash balances and the process of trying has important effects. In the process of trying to spend more than they are receiving, people bid up the prices of all sorts of goods and services. Nominal incomes rise and real cash balances are indeed reduced, even though nominal balances, the number of dollars, are not affected. The rise in prices and incomes will bring cash balances from five weeks' income to four weeks' income. People will succeed in achieving their objective but by raising prices and incomes rather than by reducing nominal balances. In the process, prices will have risen by about a fifth. This in a nutshell and somewhat oversimplified is the process whereby changes in the stock of money exert their influence on the price level."[15]

I quote Friedman at such length, repetitions and all, to avoid the charge of unfairness. For he is wrong in his central doctrine that the supply of money is its demand, that "for the community as a whole the belief that cash balances can be reduced is an optical illusion," and it

---

[14] Milton Friedman, "What Price Guideposts?" *Guidelines, Informal Controls, and the Market Place,* George P. Shultz and Robert Z. Aliber eds., (Chicago: U. of Chicago Press, 1966) widely reprinted.

[15] "What Price Guideposts?" p. 29. The same argument reappears almost verbatim in his, "A Theoretical Framework for Monetary Analysis," *Jour. Pol. Econ.,* March-April 1970, pp. 194-5.

is important to see how unqualifiedly, how flatfootedly, he asserts this central error.

If the U.S. Federal Reserve, or the Bank of Canada, were to supply you, or me, or Milton Friedman cash or checks *free,* that is, with no obligation to repay, we would probably increase our expenditures.[16] But this is a most unusual way of getting money into circulation; the usual way is that the money supply expands when someone borrows some of the excess reserves of a bank. The normal world is one in which the borrower feels that money is somewhat "tight", a situation of managed or "rationed money" with a fringe of unsatisfied borrowers at current interest rates so that when the central bank increases commercial bank reserves, the commercial banks find a ready demand for the increased supply of money. It thus appears much of the time that "Friedman's Law" is correct even though it is only an "optical illusion."

If the central bank attempts to increase the money supply at a time when there is a *general* unwillingness of businesses to increase their debts, the bank will be "pushing on a string," to use another homey analogy. For despite Friedman's assertions that the only way one can rid oneself of unwanted cash balances is to spend them, reflection will show that individuals *and the community* can reduce their cash balances and the money supply by reducing their debts to the banks. When expectations concerning the future profitability and safety of borrowing to invest and consume turn pessimistic this is just what they do, and the result is depression. Friedman is committed to the view that if the U.S. Federal Reserve System had more strenuously leaned against contractionary winds after the stock market crash of 1929 the Great Depression would never have happened.[17] While few economists would doubt that Professor Friedman could have done a better job of monetary management than the 1929-30's Fed. – especially if he had tackled the job with the 20-20 hindsight of "the key facts as we now know them," it is highly disputable whether even Friedman at the helm would have been sufficient to prevent serious depression so long as his policy was *pecunia solis.*

Unfortunately there is no way to try the experiment other than by econometric "alternative histories" – and then the result will depend entirely on the specifications of the model. The nearest we can come to sending Friedman back in time to try his hand at righting the economic ship of state is to examine other incidents in the 1930's when the right anticontractionary monetary things were done and observe the results. In view of the fact that I wish to examine Friedman further on his strange misreading of the "lessons of history" it behooves me not to claim too much for these exercises. History never repeats itself exactly; we can run no "controlled experiments," yet it still teaches us something.

---

[16] Though maybe we would be so suspicious of such "irrational" behavior that they could not even "give the stuff away." I understand the experiment of attempting to hand out $10 bills on New York streets had just this result.

[17] Milton Friedman, "The Monetary Theory and Policy of Henry Simons," *Jour. Law and Econ.* 10, October 1967, Reprinted in his *The Optimum Quantity of Money and Other Essays,* See also Chapter Seven of Friedman and Schwartz, *A Monetary History of the United States, 1867-1960.*

Table 8.2.
Indicies of Price (P), Real Output (Q), Money Supply (M₂), Ratio of Money to Goods (r₂) and Velocity (V₂) in the U.S. and Canada in 1929 and 1933.

	U.S.		Canada	
	1929	1933	1929	1933
P	100	77.7	100	81.5
Q	100	69.4	100	70.8
M_2	100	69.3	100	86.8
r_2	100	99.9	100	122.6
V_2	100	77.8	100	65.5

Source: Tables 2 and 4, Chapter 2. appendix

Table 8.2 examines the level of some important indicies in the U.S. and Canada in 1929 and 1933. As the table indicates, real output in Canada fell virtually the same number of index points by 1933 as in the U.S. although the monetary experience of the two countries was quite different. Mismanagement by the Fed., coupled with the uniquely weak U.S. system of tens of thousands of independent banks, and the collapse of demand, resulted in the 30% fall in the money supply (M_2) which Friedman sees as the cause of it all. However, the few, large banks of Canada, with no central bank to fall back upon,[18] did much better at maintaining the money stock, which fell only thirteen index points. Furthermore, there were no bank failures in Canada while the entire U.S. banking system had to be closed down and reopened in the first days of the "New Deal". In Canada, the ratio of money to goods, r_2, rose drastically in the slump, rather than merely remaining constant as in the U.S., but what is the result? If we attribute the differences in the two economies solely to the differing money supplies the answer is given by the table: In 1933 the prices were somewhat higher in Canada, velocity somewhat lower and the depression in real output was just as severe!

If merely maintaining r_2 the same in 1933 as in 1929 was sufficient to cause the Great Depression, what horror might ensue if r_2 were ever allowed to fall? Well, r_2 did fall in the U.S. in 1931, 1933 and 1937 about 8% from the previous year and those were all very bad years. However, as a glance at Chapter Two, appendix Table 4 makes evident, r_2 fell every year from 1947 to 1951 for a total of about 12% and every one of those years except 1949 – when r_2 was virtually maintained – were boom years. Furthermore, as appendix Table 2 of the same chapter makes evident, r_2 in Canada fell in every one of the good years 1927-30, for a total of about 10%, rose from 1930 to 1933 about 27%, fell about 12% during the partial recovery of 1933-37, rose 10% from 1937 to 1939, then fell with the war boom until 1942 before rising strongly to a 1949 peak.

Were I as given as Friedman to sweeping claims based on casual empiricism, I would hail the "dramatic illustration" offered by Table 8.2. as "proof" that "money does not matter" as "one of those beautiful examples that history turns up for us from time to time in which experience is almost in the nature of a controlled experiment, because the difference in the character of the monetary phenomena is so great compared to differences in other relevant respects."[19] However, "the other relevant respects" *are* important. The fact that the depressed U.S. economy was ten times as large as the Canadian

[18] The Bank of Canada came into existence only in 1934.

[19] "What Price Guideposts?" p. 32.

economy, and that Canada – like poor Mexico – is "so far from God and so near the United States," and trades so actively with the U.S., meant that Canada could not avoid deep depression no matter how expansionary her monetary policy had been. This does not at all demonstrate that an isolated economy could not be controlled by monetary policy, but merely that other things besides the money supply "matter."

The second well-known vignette for Friedman to account for is the failure of the U.S. economy to respond from its 1937 slump despite massively expansionary monetary policy. The basic facts are presented in every *Historical Chart Book* issued by the Fed. and are here reproduced as Figure 8.1. The dramatic "skyscrapers" to the left of the figure are powerful refutations of the contention that once the central bank supplies money the rest of us must demand it, so it also refutes the contention that *pecunia solis* can cure depression. The tale is quickly sketched: After the calamities culminating in the 1933 collapse of the U.S. banking system, for which the Fed. was partly to blame, it embarked upon an expansionary monetary policy. Easier money plus deficit finance and other "New Deal " measures and, perhaps, the "natural resiliency" of the "market economy" resulted in a partial recovery of real output and employment by 1936 (Unemployment was 25% in 1933 and "only" 17% in 1936). Thereupon recovery was dealt the "old one-two" by 1) the Federal government proudly "balancing" the 1937 budget by cutting expenditures and upping taxes and 2) the Fed. cutting bank excess reserves (by doubling the reserve ratio requirements) removing the psychological cushion of cash badly shaken commercial bankers had "needed."

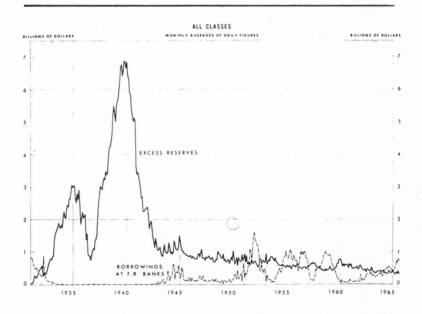

Figure 8.1. Excess Reserves and Borrowings of Member Banks of the U.S. Federal Reserve System 1929-1965, Source *Historical Chart Book,* 1965, Board of Governors of the Federal Reserve System, Washington, p. 6.

For these and other reasons (business fear of such socialistic experiments as the TVA and the Wagner Labour Act) the economy slid back into deeper depression (Unemployment 19% in 1938) despite the massive and unprecedented piling up of excess reserves seen in Figure 8.1, as the Fed. pushed hard on its "string". Although by 1940 excess reserves reached almost $6 billion (versus less than $1 billion in the decades of increasingly "tight" money since) full employment was not restored until the bombs struck Pearl Harbor (unemployment 15% in 1940, 10% in 1941, 4.7% in 1942). Here we see Keynes' "liquidity trap" in a novel and little remarked form – as excess reserves which commercial bankers were either unable or unwilling to convert into active money, thus invalidating "Friedman's Law" and demonstrating that fiscal policy, (massive deficits for war), not monetary policy or "nature" ended the Great Depression. Or does Friedman wish to argue that the fall of France and the bombing of Pearl Harbor were somehow caused "with a lag" by monetary overexpansion in 1938? Farfetched? Not much more farfetched than some "historical" arguments Friedman *has* made, as we shall see presently.

That Friedman is given to extravagant flights of fancy in overemphasizing monetary matters is evident in this same piece we are examining. He holds that even weak price and wage controls such as the U.S. Guideposts will do "untold damage" to the economy because "Suppressed inflation is worse than open inflation" as "suppression prevents the price system from working."[20] To illustrate the wreckage suppressing inflation by wage and price controls can bring about Friedman offers the following historic homily:

A dramatic illustration of the difference between open and suppressed inflation is the contrast between the experience of Germany after World War I and after World War II. This happens to be one of those beautiful examples that history turns up for us from time to time in which experience is almost in the nature of a controlled experiment, because the difference in the character of the monetary phenomena is so great compared to differences in other relevant respects. After World War I, Germany had an open inflation of extremely large magnitude. It is difficult for us to contemplate the kind of inflation Germany experienced at that time because it is so extreme . . . In the German hyperinflation after World War I, there were periods when prices doubled every week and some occasions on which they were doubling every day. Indeed, it got to the point that firms started to pay their employees their wages three times a day – after breakfast, lunch, and dinner, so that they could go out and spend them before they lost their value. That was really a whopping inflation, yet it went on for something like three years.

The inflation did untold harm to Germany. The impoverishment of the middle classes, the arbitrary redistribution of income, and the frantic instability unquestionably helped to lay the groundwork for Hitler's emergence later. Looked at however, from the purely technical point of view of its effect on production, the astounding thing is that until the last six months of the inflation, total output in Germany never declined. Indeed, Germany was one of the few countries in the World that did not experience a great depression in 1920-21, when prices in the gold standard part of the world dropped by 50 per cent. Total output remained up. Why? Because the inflation was open. Prices were allowed to rise freely and hence the price system could still be used to allocate resources. Of course, after a time people

---

[20] "What Price Guideposts?" pp. 31-2.

started to use all sorts of escalation devices to link their contracts to the value of the mark in the foreign exchange market, which was also a free market price, and so on. The price system, however, could work even under those handicaps.

After World War II, Germany was under inflationary pressure as a result of an increase in the quantity of money during the war and the fixation of prices. By our usual standards, the pressure was substantial. If prices had been allowed to rise freely immediately after the war, the price level would probably have quadrupled. That is a large price rise. But it is negligible by comparison with the price rise after World War I which has to be described in terms of factors like 10^{10}. The price rise after World War II, however, was suppressed. Ordinarily, it is extremely difficult to suppress a price rise of that magnitude, to enforce price control when the market price would be four times the controlled price. But there were certain especially favorable circumstances from the point of view of enforcing price control in Germany at that time. Germany was occupied by the armed forces of Britain, France, and the United States, and the occupation forces enforced price control.

The result of suppressing inflation was that output in Germany was cut in half. The price system was not allowed to function. People were forced to revert to barter. Walter Eucken in an article describing this period tells the story of people who worked in a factory making pots and pans. They would work there for two or three days and then they would be given their pay in the form of aluminum saucepans. They would take the saucepans and spend the rest of the week scouring the countryside trying to find some farmer who would be willing to trade a few potatoes or other produce for the saucepans. That is not a very efficient way to organize resources. It was so inefficient that something had to be done and something was done. People developed their own forms of money. Cigarettes came into use as money for small transactions and cognac for large transactions – the most liquid money I have ever come across. But even with these expedients, suppressed inflation cut output in half from the level at the immediate end of the war.

In 1948 as you know, the so called German miracle began. It was not a very complicated thing. It amounted to introducing a monetary reform, eliminating price control, and allowing the price system to function. The extraordinary rise in German output in the few years following this reform was not owing to any miracle of German ingenuity or ability or anything like that. It was the simple, natural result of allowing the most efficient technique people have ever found for organizing resources to work instead of preventing it from working by trying to fix prices here, there and everywhere.[21]

Friedman has much competition, but surely for the above he deserves some sort of prize for the ultimate in fantasy, hyperbole and distortion masquerading as history and economics! Yet in his own comments on this extravaganza Robert Solow lets him off with the mild observation that "there were surely other differences between Germany after the First and Second World War, besides the fact that at one time the inflation was open and at the other time repressed. The degree of physical devastation is one."[22]

---

[21] Ibid. pp 32-4.

[22] Robert M. Solow, "Comments" *Guidelines, Informal Controls and the Market Place*, p. 64.

God save the Mark . . . one hardly knows where to begin! To touch
on only a few obvious and momentous differences in "other relevant
respects," after World War I, German industry was physically intact
and under massive "excess demand" to pay reparations to the vic-
torious Allies. After World War II German industry was physically
flattened and the country divided into four occupation zones (not
three as Friedman has it). The Russians proceeded to strip their zone
of whatever movable capital goods the bombs and shells had missed
to rebuild their own shattered economy, and so did the French in
lesser measure.

For well over a year the American policy vacillated between the
infamous "Morgantheau Plan" to "turn Germany into a cow pasture"
and reconstruction. In such a situation of chaos and disorganization it
is sheer fantasy to conclude that "the result of suppressing inflation
was that output in Germany was cut in half . . . from the level at the
immediate end of the war." Further, what are the boundaries of the
"Germany" for which Friedman's supposed statistics apply? Does he
really believe that on VE Day "Germany" was producing more real
output than on the same day two years later? This is not to deny that
the German economy in 1946 and 1947 was in shambles, but merely to
point out the real reasons: Germany had been devastated, defeated and
dismembered by powers which, at least for a time, agreed that she
should never rise again.

By 1948 all of this had changed. The Americans decided to forgive
the Germans for their crimes against the Russians, the Poles and the
Jews partly because they needed an economicly strong Germany to
help "contain communism." So German industrialists were reclas-
sified from "Nazi war criminals" to "model free enterprisers" and
encouraged, rather than thwarted, in their attempts to rebuild their
factories. Marshall Plan aid poured in, the three western zones became politically and economicly united, leading ultimately to the
rebirth of a sovereign Germany – the Federal Republic – and the West
German "miracle" was underway. These enormous changes in the
"other relevant respects" are too unimportant to rate a sentence from
Friedman: to him the German miracle was caused by "introducing a
monetary reform, eliminating price controls, and allowing the price
system to function," period.

It would be closer to the truth to argue the complete opposite to
Friedman's "price controls devastate the economy" fantasy. In all-out
war, the only time we are really serious about maximizing output and
obtaining the optimum allocation of truly scarce resources, all nations suspend the market mechanism and become for the duration
central planners – the plan necessarily including price and wage
controls. Friedman has claimed, "We are all Keynesians now", but in
total war we are all "communists," or "national socialists." And the
result? Is output cut in half? Clearly the result is a flood of output and
productivity boosting innovations. Thus in the U.S. the real output
level of 1944 was not reachieved until 1951 when the Korean War
again brought full employment and price controls. Controls are a
necessary part of wartime mobilization of the economy, but it would
be as ridiculous to give them the full credit for the near doubling of the
U.S. real output between 1939 and 1944 as it is for Friedman to give
them sole blame for cutting post war Germany's output in half!

Friedman's old wives' tale concerning the destruction of the
Reich through "suppressing inflation" reminds one of an "ultra
Freudian" concerned with the psychic damage from repressing sex.
In the following passage, after rejecting the analogy between "direct
control of wages and prices as a reaction to inflation and the breaking

of a thermometer as a reaction to, say, an over-heated room," as good, but not good enough, Friedman offers the following:

"A much closer analogy is a steam-heating furnace running full blast. Controlling the heat in one room by closing the radiators in that room simply makes the other rooms still more overheated. Closing all radiators lets the pressure build up in the boiler and increases the danger that it will explode."[23]

Picture the scene: A proverbial "man from Mars" arrives at Cologne, Essen, Berlin or Düsseldorf in the spring of 1945 in his flying saucer and surveys the lunar landscape; blown up buildings, smoking ruins, craters as far as the eye can see. Having never heard of World War II, Hitler or the B17, he is at a loss to account for this destruction so he seeks out someone to enlighten him. At length he comes upon Milton Friedman standing in the rubble.

Man from Mars: "What the hell happened to this place? What caused all this destruction?"
M. Friedman: "Ach, vage und prise controls!"
M. from M.: "Wage and price controls?"
M.F.: "Ya, ist terrible. Der pressure builts up and builts up until Kapow!!"

But let us examine Friedman's furnace analogy a bit further, he draws the moral as:

"Closing or opening individual radiators is a good way to adjust the relative amount of heat in different rooms; it is not a good way to correct for overfueling the furnace. Similarly, changes in individual prices are a good way to adjust to changes in the supply or demand of individual products; preventing individual prices from rising is not a good way to correct for a general tendency of prices to rise."[24]

Note the assumption that inflation only occurs at full employment – the furnace going "full blast." This ignores the fact that economies increasingly encounter inflation even while there is excessive unemployment. Suppose further that the whole house isn't too hot, but only one or two rooms. In such a case closing, or partly closing, the radiators in these rooms would re-direct the heat to the other rooms and improve the allocation. In some parts of the economy "administered" prices and wages start to rise even when there is slack in the economy as a whole and in the administered market. The price of steel is an often cited example to which we shall return presently. Controlling these prices – turning down the radiator in these rooms – would direct the expansive money supply – the heat – into increasing the output of the other sectors. Only as all parts of the economy approach the optimum level should the question of tapering off the heat arise.

Friedman is uncompromising in setting forth a money alone theory of inflation with the government the only culprit as it controls the central bank. However, on closer examination his uniquely monetary theory consists merely of breaking into an interconnected argument at a certain point – thus a choice of emphasis – and adjectives. Friedman admits, here and there, that such phenomena as "wage push" and "profits push", inflations have occurred, and one assumes that some day he might concede that "tax push" inflation

---

[23] "What Price Guideposts?" p. 20.

[24] Ibid.

has also occurred. However, he concedes the strength of these factors only if "the cost push produces a monetary expansion that otherwise would not have occurred,"[25] thus ignoring the point highlighted by Keynes, that it is just because of the ever upward tendency of the wage-unit that an ever increasing money supply has proved imperative.[26]

As Joan Robinson has pointed out, the only difference between Karl Marx' and Joseph Schumpeter's analysis of capitalism is in the choice of adjectives. Marx hated the capitalist system and Schumpeter admired it, but both agreed that capitalism was merely a transitory form of economic organization which would give way in time to socialism – a "consummation devoutly to be wished" to Marx, but one which saddened Schumpeter. A somewhat similar observation applies to Keynes and Friedman – Friedman concedes *all* of Keynes', and "Keynesians'" non-monetary causes of inflation, but with dismissive adjectives, as in the following quotation:

"One can go back one or two thousand years and more and find that every time there is inflation, two explanations are offered. One explanation is that the amount of money has increased. The other explanation is that something special has happened: wage-earners have pushed up their wages; profiteers have been active; there has been a blockade of the country and as a result supplies could not come in; and so on and on . . . these two separate explanations are not necessarily contradictory, the non-monetary factors may, on some occasions, be the cause of the monetary expansion. For example, when people argue that attempted investment in excess of desired savings is the cause of inflation, that may be the correct description at the second remove. If the attempted investment is by Government and if Government attempts to finance that investment by printing money, then . . . It is a cause of inflation because it produces an increase in the money stock. Or again . . . the trade unions may in fact push up wage rates sufficiently to create unemployment. If the government is committed to a full-employment policy, it may in response thereto expand the money supply . . .

"One thing is clear from the historical record. The actual sources of monetary expansion have been very different at different times and in different places. Hence, if a theory of inflation is going to deal not with the expansion of the stock of money but with what brought it about, it will be a very pluralistic theory which will have many possible sources of inflation."[27]

In the above, Friedman reduces the money supply growth from the all important "exogenous" "cause" of inflation, to just another one of the effects, albeit an effect which is always observed, and this to avoid "pluralistic" theories of "many possible sources of inflation." However, accidents such as crop failures aside, all the "pluralistic" cost-push theories of inflation boil down to a single cause – a quarrel over income distribution, the attempts of participants in the economic process collectively to receive more income than they have produced real output. The neoclassical economist, monetarist or not, is dedicated to the proposition that if everyone seeks to maximize his own gains the result of this heedless selfishness will be social harmony.

---

[25] p. 21.

[26] *The General Theory* p. 340n.

[27] Milton Friedman, *Dollars and Deficits:* Inflation, Monetary Policy, and the Balance of Payments, © 1968, pp. 29-30. Reprinted by permission of Prentice-Hall, Inc., Englewood Cliffs, New Jersey.

The flaw in the argument was obvious from the beginning, and Adam Smith spent many pages worrying about it. Instead of competing "purely" people will form groups and achieve monopoly power in varying degree, and thus avoid the "discipline of the market." Friedman knows all this, but again dismisses it as of secondary importance.

As for the rest of the argument, the fact that A and B always "go together" does not necessarily make A the cause of B or vice versa, for both A and B may be caused by C. Indeed, by the "general equilibrium" argument everything is caused by everything else. The fact that "substantial changes in prices have always occurred together with substantial changes in the quantity of money" does not prove that "changes in the quantity of money" are the cause of "substantial changes in prices."

If in the following paragraph by Friedman, the word "monetary" were replaced by "wage level" and the words "quantity of money" each time they appear were replaced by "level of wages", the rewritten paragraph would be much more "true" than the original. For as we saw in Chapter Two, "k" is so much more constant than "V" that the EOE price level "law" was contradicted half the time, while the WCM "law" was seldom contradicted.

"Yet, the central fact is that inflation is always and everywhere a monetary *phenomenon. Historically, substantial changes in prices have always occurred together with substantial changes in the* quantity of money *relative to output. I know of no exceptions to this generalization, no occasion in the United States or elsewhere when prices have risen substantially without a substantial rise in the* quantity of money *relative to output or when the* quantity of money *has risen substantially relative to output without a substantial rise in prices . . . I doubt that there is any other empirical generalization in economics for which there is so much organized evidence covering so wide a range of space and time."*[28]

Despite the above concession that money expansion is just an effect of deeper causes – and thus the concession of his entire solely monetary theory of inflation, Friedman treats of these deeper cause with dismissive adjectives.

"Despite its popularity, this cost-push theory of inflation has very limited applicability. Unless the cost-push produces a monetary expansion that would otherwise not have occurred, its effect will be limited to at most a temporary general price rise, accompanied by unemployment, and followed by a tendency toward declining prices elsewhere.

Suppose, for example, a strong (or stronger) cartel were formed in steel, and that it decided to raise prices well above the level that otherwise would have prevailed. The price rise would reduce the amount of steel people want to buy . . . and . . . the price of substitutes would rise . . . But . . . Steel producers would hire fewer workers and other resources. These would seek employment elsewhere, tending to drive down wages and prices in other industries . . .

"The only example I know of in United States history when a cost-push was important even temporarily for any substantial part of the economy was from 1933 to 1937, when the NIRA, AAA, Wagner Labor Act, and associated growth of union strength unquestionably led to increasing market power for both industry and labor and thereby produced upward pressure on a wide range of wages and

---

[28] "What Price Guideposts?" p. 25; Emphasis added.

*prices . . . the cost-push does explain why . . . despite unprecedented
levels of unemployed resources, wholesale prices rose nearly 50 per
cent from 1933 to 1937, and the cost of living rose by 13 per cent.*"[29]

As Winston Churchill once remarked in another context, "different
things strike different people in different ways." Whereas "Everything
makes Milton think of money," as Solow put it, others wish to see
beyond this "veil" to the underlying social and economic realities
which make the money and real magnitudes behave as they do. Other
casts of mind, noting as Friedman does, that government aided market power could raise wholesale prices 50 per cent in the midst of
desperate depression, might suspect that this power had something
to do with the continuation of inflation ever since. If they bought
Friedman's dubious argument that for a continuing cost push "it is
not enough that there exist monopolies of business and labor; it is
necessary that monopoly power increase;"[30] they might look for evidence of such increasing monopoly power in the post World War II
world. Such evidence is not lacking. Thus Willard Mueller[31] has found
that the level of aggregate concentration in American manufacturing
has risen substantially since World War II so that in respect to assets,
"by 1968 the top one hundred companies held a greater share than
that held by the top two hundred in 1947."[32] Lee Preston writes, "The
conclusion that aggregate concentration within the industrial sector
of the economy has increased over the last two or three decades
seems inescapable."[33]

As for increased labour union power one may confine ones' self
to details, such as the payment of unemployment compensation to
strikers as strengthening labour's hand, but that is not the important
change between the 1920s and now. The vital change which has given
the world secular slow inflation since the 1930s has been the commitment of "Bastard Keynesian" Governments to near full employment fiscal and monetary measures without the corresponding
Keynesian revolution in incomes policies. We may, I believe, end
these many pages on Friedman's "right wing" fears that "wage and
price controls" will destroy the economy, with the conclusion that his
fears are without substance. They will cause the economy to behave
differently; "better" if they are well designed and administered,
"worse" if they are poorly done, like most policies. There is ample
room for improvement over the current welter of inconsistent
policies.

There is, however, a "left wing" attack on the Keynes "center"
argument for incomes policy to supplement fiscal and monetary
policies. Thus D.M. Nuti[34] warns all good radical economists to have
nothing to do with the "conservative" and "iniquitous" attempts to

---

[29] "What Price Guideposts?" pp. 21-2.

[30] Ibid p. 21n.

[31] Willard F. Mueller, *Monopoly and Competition* (New York: Random House,
1970).

[32] Ibid, p. 26.

[33] Lee E. Preston, *The Industry and Enterprise Structure of the U.S. Economy*,
(New York: General Learning Press, 1971) p. 8.

[34] D.M. Nuti, "On Incomes Policy", *Science and Society*, 33, 1969 pp. 415-25:
reprinted in *A Critique of Economic Theory*, E.K. Hunt and J.G. Schwartz eds.,
(Baltimore: Penguin, 1972) pp. 431-41.

make capitalism viable with incomes policies and concludes, "Incomes policy can be acceptable only after the replacement of capitalism with a socialist society."[35]

As Joan Robinson puts it:

"Incomes policy is an expedient to cope with a pressing situation. There is no articulate philosophy behind it . . . it is both a rejection and an acceptance of laissez faire. It emphatically rejects laissez faire, since it expresses the acknowledgement that the free play of the market does not establish the equilibrium price level, rather a progressive degeneration in the value of money. At the same time it tacitly accepts the distribution of real income that the market throws up . . . The problem of prices under full employment brings sharply into focus the contradictions of modern capitalism."[36]

"An incomes policy which would check inflation by preventing overall money incomes from rising faster than overall real output would require a general acceptance of some pattern of rewards for various kinds of work. Once traditions have been questioned, there is no acceptable criterion for deciding what it should be. Still less is there any acceptable criterion for deciding the general distribution between work and property . . . Moreover . . . to apply it would require a fundamental change in the traditional powers of both workers and employers which neither side is willing to accept. Perhaps the revival of a doctrine so unconvincing as the quantity theory of money can be explained as a refuge from the uncomfortable thought that the general level of prices has become a political problem."[37]

The lot of the liberal reformer is hard – denounced as he is by the "right" as a communist, and by the "left" as a capitalist apologist. So Keynes found it and so in their own turn have Joan Robinson, Paul Samuelson, J.K. Galbraith; and many others.Their advice is that we "tinker with what is," "Fix it up, make it do, Keynes will make it work like new", rather than regarding what is as perfect, or perfectly intolerable – that we avoid large changes by being willing to make many small changes. It is the wisdom of the peasant maxim, "a stitch in time saves nine", rather than of "give an inch and they'll take a mile." Fortunately or unfortunately no peasant maxim expresses all truth and each of them is true some of the time. Furthermore, the end result of numerous small changes satisfies no one's taste for coherence and logic. For example, the present status of the House of Windsor satisfies no constitutional theorist with a tidy mind. In theory Elizabeth II enjoys all the absolute royal powers and privileges of Elizabeth I, but while all the feudal forms remain the same, England has evolved through a semi-capitalist, semi-democracy into a semi-socialist semi-democracy. For all the incoherence of such a state of affairs it seems far better than change by bloody revolution, or the complete social immobility which has so often led to revolution.

---

[35] Ibid, p. 425.

[36] Joan Robinson, *Economics: An Awkward Corner*, pp. 12-5.

[37] Joan Robinson, *Economic Heresies: Some Old Fashioned Questions in Economic Theory*, (New York: Basic Books, 1971) pp. 93-4.

Towards Better Incomes Policies

Let us draw together some of the implications for incomes policy of our analysis. The recognition that the price level is basically a political rather than a purely "economic" problem points toward political solutions. In a way it is unfortunate that we must look to the government for the solution of inflation, when government has been so much the cause of inflation, but that is the nature of political problems. For Friedman is surely right in laying most of the blame for inflation at the door of the government, but he is overly narrow in focusing solely upon its role in creating too much money. Government "policy push" has also caused inflation by its expanding relatively to the economy as a whole, necessitating an increase in the "social lien" of taxes, by favouring rentier incomes through a high interest rate policy, and by the bad example politicians, whether Presidents, Prime Ministers or Parliamentarians set for the rest of us in the overgenerous raises they have awarded themselves. When President Nixon decided that he had twice as high a marginal product as President Johnson and therefore deserved twice his salary, and Congress concurred and helped themselves to a generous increase also, he made it difficult, to say the least, for union leaders to ask their "rank and file" to exercise "statesmanlike" restraint. Private and corporate businessmen are often extremely generous with themselves and at the same time niggardly with their employees – since there is a direct connection between the level of their salaries and profits and their ability to minimize costs. Not so politicians and bureaucrats. Since the money is not theirs and their own rewards are not from cost minimization or profit maximization, but from empire building, they are apt to be much more generous in granting raises to the underlings and in hiring as many of them as possible. Perhaps Friedman can be induced to employ his considerable polemic powers against these inflationary propensities and give the "Fed" a rest, who being bankers as well as bureaucrats were rather stingy with their money back when I worked for them.

To the extent that the government is merely an extension of "us" and we all believed that more before the U.S. government waged war in Vietnam for ten years against ultimately near unanimous opposition by its citizens – it is true to say with Pogo "We have met the enemy and he is us," regarding inflation as regards so much else.

However, governments – which themselves often behave so badly – by the very nature of their "maintain law and order" function – compel you and me to behave much better than we would otherwise. Furthermore, the pressure on the sovereign to "set a good example", though regrettably not always effective, still is in the long run, a potent force. We may expect, therefore, rather than merely hope, that the increasing recognition by governments that they have themselves been a major cause of inflation, directly and indirectly, will lead to salutory changes in their behaviour as they lecture and compel us to behave better.

If the policy goal is to *reduce* the price level, as Friedman in his more perfectionist moments advocates, the only feasible way to achieve this is to freeze the general level of wages and then check to see that firms in fact lower their prices in accordance with sectoral productivity gains. Some adjustments in relative wages could be allowed to correct the more glaring injusticies resulting from pre-freeze power relationships, so long as the average wage is kept from increasing very much. Thus, given the convention that wages cannot be rolled back, even a wage "freeze" would have to involve a rise in some wages during the transition period. Such a policy of constant wages – "forever" has much to commend it. The nominal rate of interest on savings could fall to zero and still gain the saver a "real" rate of 3%, provided productivity gains continue at about that rate in the future as in the past. Business and government borrowing rates of interest could be set low and "confirmed by the market" once it is realized that a slow deflation is the order of the day ahead. The housing industry could cease from being the economy's whipping boy. Friedman could be given the job of seeing to it that the money supply grew but little faster than the population growth – (subject, of course, to some "emergency over-ride" provision in case the economy takes a downward lurch).

Surely, no one today would advocate that we go beyond the above goal to reduce the wage level or freeze the money supply, as Henry C. Simons once did. In fact, most discussions of incomes policies assume that the goal is a constant price level, a goal which should be approached only gradually from the rapid inflation now besetting us. Thus Abba Lerner advocates a "taper off" rather than a "cold turkey" strategy for ending inflation. Clearly, a sudden end to inflation would cause some personal and corporate bankruptcies as debts contracted at 12% interest rates on the expectation of rapid inflation had to be repaid in dollars of constant purchasing power.

Turning from goals to means, two largely alternative policies are possible. Since the market or "planning" power of business and labour is the mechanism by which the push is effected, the government could either attempt to break up such concentrations of power or prescribe rules or constraints under which the power may be retained but not used to cause inflation. The first approach is "antitrust", the second the "controls" approach to incomes policy. Needless to say, neither approach has had much success to date, but neither is lacking of advocates. Although "trust busting" is often viewed as a conservative programme, since its goal is to make capitalism work by making competition more all pervasive, it is a radical conservative indeed who would seriously advocate dismantling Galbraith's "planning" half of the economy and disbanding labour unions. All too many such proposals may be dismissed as "fun to talk about" but incapable of being implemented. On the other hand, few of the controls proposals seem capable of stopping inflation without either freezing relative prices or involving the government in detailed regulation of allocation; quality control and much more. Here we shall examine an interesting example of each of the two approaches advocated, together with some of the reasons their authors believe they can escape from the weaknesses of such approaches. For the most interesting "trust buster" approach my selection is that of Gardiner Means, long time student of the realities of corporate power and administered prices. The most interesting proposal for controls is the Wallich-Weintraub Tax-Based Incomes Policy (TIP). Both proposals seek to achieve better price level and incomes policy results by enforcement through taxation. Both proposals are designed to deal with the problems of the actual world rather than with a theoretical "pure" world. Thus, I would hold that such proposals as the following are part of the "legitimate Keynesianism" which should replace the bastard variety in a second Keynesian revolution.

Gardiner Means' "New Concept"[38]

Central to Means' concept is the world of the large corporation producing and pricing behind the wall of difficult entry. As many studies
have shown, firms in such markets do not price according to short or
long run profit maximizing calculus – rather they adopt a "target rate
of return on capital" strategy. Means holds that when such firms
adopt a target rate of return but little above the "cost of capital" with
allowance for risk, their prices are in the public interest. Thus, firms
pricing to earn on the average 8 to 10% returns on investment after
taxes (such as Alcoa, International Harvester and U.S. Steel prior to
about 1950) meet with Means' approval. Not so General Motors, Du-
Pont or General Electric which have a "target" of 20% return and in
many years earn considerably more than that.

Moreover, Means argues that the shift of U.S. Steel's management from an 8% target to one closer to GM's target accounts for all
U.S. inflation from 1953 to 1959. When threatened with dismember-
ment by the Theodore Roosevelt administration, the newly formed
U.S. Steel Trust "negotiated" a gentlemen's agreement to behave as a
"good trust" – the definition including, by all accounts, a rate of return
(on admittedly overvalued stock) of but little more than the "normal
return" allowed regulated public utilities. After surviving court tests in
the 1920s, the company's "public utility" approach to pricing was well
established. Since U.S. Steel has from its birth in 1901 been the
largest U.S. steel-making firm (65% of capacity initially and over 30%
today) it quickly became the price leader, so that its moderate target
limited the mark-ups competing firms could charge. (However, many
of its more efficient competitors have earned higher returns than the
giant under its price umbrella, a very different situation than that in
automobiles.)

As Means sees it, U.S. Steel ceased to price in the public interest
in the early 1950s.

*"In 1951, United States Steel adopted a new bonus system which puts
great pressure on management to increase corporate profits. According to the Chairman of the Board, 'The plan was adopted to provide an
incentive for the top-management group of United States Steel Corporation.' Under this plan, key individuals in the management of the
corporation were given 10-year options to buy the common stock of
the corporation at the price which prevailed at the time the options
were given. Since gains from the purchase and subsequent sale of
such stock could be treated as capital gains, the issuance of such
warrants placed the management under tremendous pressure to increase corporate profits so as to increase the market value of its
stock. Such a bonus system was an open invitation to drop the 8
percent target in pricing and use pricing-power to the full extent of
making the maximum profits allowed by the wall of difficult entry.*

*Under this new incentive, steel prices were raised much more
rapidly than steel costs increased. Between 1953 and 1958 steel
prices were raised 34 percent. This was so much more rapid than the
rise in costs that the break-even point, the point at which the corporation would neither make nor lose money, was very much reduced. At
1953 prices, wage rates, and productivity United States Steel could
just break even if it operated at 47 percent of capacity. At 1958 prices,*

---

[38] Gardiner C. Means, "Pricing Power and the Public Interest," *Administered
Prices: A Compendium on Public Policy* (U.S. Government Printing Office:
Washington 1963) pp. 213-44. See also Gardiner Means, John Blair *et al. The
Roots of Inflation*, New York: Burt Franklin, 1975.

wage rates, and productivity the company would make substantial profits at this rate of operation and would just break even if it operated at a rate of around 30 percent of capacity. In 1958, United States Steel produced only two-thirds as many tons of steel as in 1953 but its reported profits after peacetime taxes were higher than in 1953 ... If the 1953 and 1958 figures are adjusted to an average rate of operation, the resulting figures would show more than a doubling of the after-tax profit per ton shipped.''[39]

Figure 8.2 is Means' Chart XVI to illustrate his argument that the inflation of the 1950s spread from U.S. Steel headquarters at 71 Broadway, in lower Manhattan to the U.S. economy as a whole.

Means demonstrates that the rise in steel prices cannot be attributed to a general excess demand inflation, as the proportion of labour force and industrial capacity utilized fell through the period, nor was there excess demand for steel, and he argues that only about one-quarter of the post-1953 price rise was attributable to labour's drive for increased wages while "three-quarters was due to managements' drive for a higher rate of return on capital.''[40]

This pattern has continued in more recent years. As Walter Adams puts it; after World War II "there was an almost unbroken climb in steel prices, in good times and bad, in the face of rising or falling

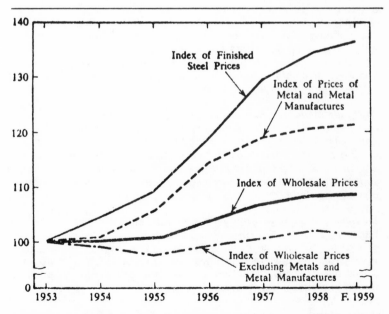

Figure 8.2. Steel and Other Wholesale Price Indexes 1953 – Fiscal 1959 (1953 = 100). Source: *Means*, p. 226.

[39] Means, pp 223-4. "Pricing Power and the Public Interest"

[40] Means, p. 226.

demand, increasing or declining unit costs. Prices rose even when only 50 percent of the industry's capacity was being utilized."[41]

Means' solution grows out of his analysis of the problem: confront the largest firms with the choice between pricing to achieve a low target return, a heavy excess profits tax, or being broken up into smaller enterprises. He summarizes his proposals as follows:

"Given this pricing power problem, the solution I propose is the passage of an act –it might be called the Economic Performance Act – which in broad outline would:

1) *Establish a new legal category for tax purposes, including only those few collective manufacturing enterprises whose pricing power is found to be vested with a substantial public interest.*
2) *Provide especially favorable income tax treatment for performance bonuses received by the management of corporations in this new category.*
3) *Require that, in order to receive the favorable tax treatment, the corporation must adopt pricing policies aimed to produce an average rate of return on capital commensurate with the cost of capital.*
4) *Provide that a corporation falling in the new category should have three options (1) to remove itself from the category by a breakup into smaller enterprises no one of which has substantial pricing power, (2) to stay in the new category but be subject to a heavy excess profits tax, or (3) to adopt the new pricing policy and a performance bonus plan."*[42]

Means' "performance bonus" proposal reflects his argument that a) profits are not the sole relevant test of management performance in the planning sector and b) a system of bonuses for reducing costs, improving products or operations are needed to keep management efficient.

Means' plan, if enacted, would permit some rollback on prices in the planning sector and thus a "one shot" reduction or reversal of inflation and in the profits share. He argues further that once his Economic Performance Act were in operation "the danger of administrative inflation would be largely taken care of so far as management initiative is concerned," but concedes that:

"Administrative inflation could still come from the side of labor if wage rates were pushed up faster than the average increase in national productivity. But . . . If the big price leaders no longer used pricing power to make excessive corporate profits but used this power in the public interest, there would no longer be a potential source for financing excessive wage increases or the justification for demanding them."[43]

Means is perhaps overoptimistic in this last statement, as a GM which had been earning 20% on invested capital which after the E.P.A. law settled for 10% would be able to pay higher wages and reraise its prices. Clearly, however, the moral case for labour restraint would be a real one and any reduction in consumer prices would put wage indexing clauses into reverse.

---

[41] Walter Adams, "Competition, Monopoly, and Planning," *American Society, Inc.* M. Zeitlin ed., (Chicago: Markham 1970) pp. 241-50. See also Jerry E. Pohlman, *Economics of Wage and Price Controls*, (Columbus: Grid 1972) pp. 100-2.

[42] Means, p. 232.

[43] Means, p. 239.

The Wallich-Weintraub TIP plan aims directly at inducing corporations to slow the pace of wage gains.

The Wallich-Weintraub TIP Proposal[44]

The Wallich-Weintraub Tax based Incomes Policy proposal likewise grows out of its authors' analysis of the roots of inflation. Wallich and Weintraub (WW henceforth) see corporations as all too ready to acquiesce to inflationary wage demands as they expect to mark-up and pass on these costs in higher prices, confident that governments committed to full employment will increase the money supply accordingly. The proposed solution:

". . . is to levy a surcharge on the corporate profits tax for firms granting wage increases in excess of some guideposts figure. If the wage guidepost were 5.5 per cent, and a wage increase of 7 per cent were granted, the corporate profits tax for the firm would rise above the present 48 per cent by some multiple of the 1.5 per cent excess . . . The added tax burden may be expected to stiffen the company's back in wage negotiations. The result would be a lower rate of wage increase, and a slowing of the rate of inflation."[45]

Among the advantages claimed for TIP are administrative simplicity. All corporations and non-corporate businesses of any important size already supply rather full information on their wage costs, number of employees, revenues and profits to the government when paying the corporate profits tax and when turning over the amounts withheld from paychecks for incomes and social insurance taxes. Therefore, it is a fairly simple matter to calculate from year to year whether employee compensation has increased by more than the wage norm figure and to levy the appropriate "fine". Thus WW seek to avoid the specter of the "army" of wage and price controllers conjured up by Friedman. As Weintraub puts it,

"What is proposed has an analogy in traffic fines for speeding. These have as their object not revenue, nor really incarceration of speeders, but eliminating dangerous driving . . . firms could puncture the wage norm, just as speeders can violate the posted limits – but at a penalty."[46]

A subsidiary advantage claimed is that both wages and executive salaries would be included in calculating the rate of increase of wages. Thus unions could still bargain for above average pay boosts through inroads on salary increases.

Further, for administrative convenience, WW would not apply TIP to all business, only those whose profits are above a certain size – say $1 million a year.

---

[44] Henry Wallich, *Newsweek,* September 5, 1966, December 14, 1970; Sidney Weintraub, "An Incomes Policy to Stop Inflation", *Lloyd's Bank Review,* January 1970; H. Wallich and S. Weintraub, "A Tax-Based Incomes Policy", *Journal of Economic Issues,* June 1971, pp. 1-19, (reprinted in S. Weintraub, *Keynes and the Monetarists,* (New Brunswick: Rutgers University Press, 1973) pp. 103-24).

[45] Wallich and Weintraub, "A Tax-Based Incomes Policy", p. 2.

[46] Sidney Weintraub, "Remedying the Inflation Bias in the Incomes Mechanism", *Common Sense Economics,* University of Waterloo, Vol. 3, No. 2, 1975.

Figure 8.3 is adopted from WW to illustrate the "back stiffening" properties of TIP. In wage negotiations the two parties start off far apart and eventually come together and settle.

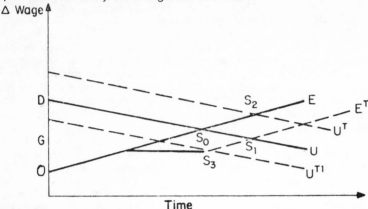

Figure 8.3.

O   = Original employer offer
E   = Employer settlement curve
E^T = Employer settlement curve after imposition of a tax on firm
D   = Original union demand
U   = Union settlement curve
$U^{'T}$ = Union settlement curve after imposition of tax
G   = Guidepost level
U^{T1} = Settlement if labour reduces its demands in light of imposition of tax on firm
S_0, S_1,
S_2, S_3 = Alternative points of settlement, allowing for the alternative taxes.

Source: *Wallich and Weintraub*, p. 7.

In the figure, D represents the wage increase initially demanded by the union, while O represents the initial, considerably lower, offer of the employing firm, and G represents the guidepost figure. Left to themselves the union and firm would haggle, threaten, bluff and perhaps strike their way to an eventual bargain where the two settlement curves U and E intersect at S_0, here somewhat above G. The enactment of TIP with a given schedule of penalty rates of taxation for settlements above G causes a lateral displacement of the employer's settlement curve at the guidepost level, resulting in the kinked settlement curve E^T. The employer is willing to undergo the cost of additional weeks of haggling and perhaps a shut-down rather than pay more than G to avoid the payment of TIP. After some weeks, however, the strike losses would exceed the potential TIP payment and the firm would offer more than G to settle the strike. If the enactment of TIP shifts the employer settlement curve to E^T and does not shift the union settlement curve, the final settlement comes at S_1, thus at a lower wage increase than that granted in S_0. Note, however, that under these circumstances strikes would be of longer duration than without TIP with consequent losses to employees, employers, and the economy as a whole.

It is likely, however, that the enactment of TIP would induce unions to lower their settlement curve as to $U^{T'}$, in recognition of the fact that firms are less willing and able to pay above guidepost amounts if they have also to TIP the government. Here, the result is settlement at the G level with little or no increase in the average duration of strikes.

Since the object of TIP is not to collect more taxes from corporations, but to induce them to be less generous in raising wages, why
not tax excessive wage gains directly? WW argue, and our analysis in
the above chapters support the point, that increased wage taxes
would lead to an upward movement in union settlement curves, here
to U^T as they seek to "get higher wages to pay the higher taxes". The
result, given the initial E settlement curve, is a still higher wage
settlement at S_2 after a prolonged strike.

It may be objected, however, that corporate taxes can be shifted
forward in higher prices, as we saw in previous chapters, so why
would not firms *raise* their prices to pay government its TIP? WW
argue that such conduct, while possible, is unlikely because a) profits
per unit of sales vary greatly among firms and "a tax that affects cost
per unit very differently among firms evidently is harder to shift than a
tax that affects all firms equally."[47]

b) *"It is sometimes argued that the degree of shifting of the corporate
income tax depends upon the structure of an industry. Highly
concentrated industries might find shifting easier than highly
competitive industries. If this effect were pronounced, however, it
would tend to make concentrated industries more profitable than
competitive industries, that is the rate of return on capital would be
higher in the former. There is no strong evidence that this is
generally the case."*[48]

c) Even if some shifting does occur the effect upon the rate of inflation
will be small as long as the revenue from the surcharge was small.

*"An average surcharge of 5 percentage points on the corporate in-
come tax would amount to less than $2 billion at present. Spread over
a GNP of $1 trillion, the effect on prices would be minimal."*[49]

---

[47] Wallich and Weintraub, p. 4.

[48] Ibid. The above quote is hard to accept since "everyone knows" that the rate of
return is generally higher in the concentrated then in the non-concentrated
industries. Monopoly and oligopoly theory would lead us to expect the rate of
profit to be an increasing function of the degree of concentration in an
industry, and most empirical studies support theory here. Important studies
include: Joe S. Bain, "Relation of Profit Rate to Industry Concentration:
American Manufacturing 1936-1940", *Quarterly Journal of Economics,* 65,
August 1951; Victor Fuchs, "Integration, Concentration, and Profits in Manufacturing Industries", *Quarterly Journal of Economics,* 75, May 1961; Leonard
W. Weirs, "Average Concentration Ratios and Industrial Performance,"
Journal of Industrial Economics, 11, No. 3. However, George J. Stigler, in his
major study *Capital and Rates of Return in Manufacturing Industries* (National
Bureau of Economic Research, Princeton University Press, 1963) concludes
that concentrated industries do not have rates of return which are always
significantly higher than those in non-concentrated industries. Three recent
studies reconfirming the hypothesis of a positive relationship between concentration and the rate of profit in Canada are, Donald G. McFetridge, "Market
Structure and Price-Cost Margins: An Analysis of the Canadian Manufacturing
Sector", and J.C.H. Jones, L. Landadio, and M. Percy, "Market Structure and
Profitability in Canadian Manufacturing Industry: Some Cross-Section Results", both in *Canadian Journal of Economics,* August 1973, and Harry Bloch,
"Prices, Costs, and Profits in Canadian Manufacturing: the Influence of Tariffs
and Concentration", November 1974.

[49] Wallich and Weintraub, p. 5.

WW elsewhere advocate that the revenues collected by TIP be used to cut the corporate profits tax, or in other ways used to reward firms which hold the wage line, so the above inflationary effect could be offset. For further analysis concerning this important point see Peter Isard,[50] who finds zero and full shifting to be polar cases. See also the study of Kotowitz and Portes.[51]

d) *"Most students agree that more shifting will occur in the long run than in the short. Unless a firm expects to be paying TIP tax continuously, it can hardly plan on long-run shifting. Its expectations of being able to shift in the short-run will be relevant."*[52]

Since, as I believe has been demonstrated above, tax shifting is part of the business "game", it might be well to go beyond the WW proposal somewhat as follows: enact that any corporation which has become a "habitual offender" against TIP – say by paying a significant TIP tax in 3 of the past 5 years – shall have its prices frozen for a year, with yet stronger penalities possible if it continues to offend. This carries Weintraub's speeding ticket analogy a step further, to license suspension for the perpetually dangerous driver, and threat of jail if he drives without a license. Again, the purpose of Incomes Policy is not to jail business men or union leaders, but to induce them to "slow down".

WW have given considerable thought to the problems of loopholes in defining the wage index, problems which need not detain us here, though they will loom large when such plans are enacted.

Weintraub has recently suggested a variant mode of attack on the problem on which Means focuses – excessive profit margins in the strongest firms.

"To encourage general price cuts, all firms who trim profit margins would qualify for tax relief. If the normal profit mark-up is 30 per cent, by topping it out at 25 per cent a lower corporate income tax rate would enable firms to recoup some or all of the profit sacrificed through lower prices."[53]

Without some such mechanism to induce restraint on profits, TIP restraint on wages might swell margins of the firms enjoying the greatest productivity gains, rather than being reflected in lower prices – as has happened several times already with U.S. "guideposts" and "Phase II" alike.

Weintraub further proposes that the personal income tax be amended to entitle those whose pre-tax income rose less than the guidepost percentage to a rebate, and those gaining more to a surcharge. WW concede that TIP will not work in the world of "collapsing corporations" such as abound in construction and that "direct" controls are necessary here.

---

[50] Peter Isard, "Using the Tax System to Curb Inflationary Collective Bargains", *Journal of Political Economy*, May/June, 1973.

[51] Y. Kotowitz and R. Portes, "The TIP Tax and Wage Increases", *Journal of Public Finance*, 1974.

[52] Wallich and Weintraub, p. 5.

[53] S. Weintraub, "Remedying the Inflation Bias".

Concluding Comments

Stagflation has discredited the "conventional wisdom" of the "bastard Keynesian" mainstream and its right wing "monetarism" and cleared the decks for a second "Keynesian" or "Ultra Keynesian" revolution in economic theory and policy.[54] Coherent, conscious and permanent incomes policies are an essential part of this second revolution, as modern fiscal and monetary policies were of the first. This is necessary for survival in the face of intolerable inflation. On moral grounds we should probably aim at nothing less than a new "social contract" increasingly to share the benefits of progress, or mitigate the effects of resource exhaustion, more justly between the haves and have nots, not only domestically, but internationally.

It may be that the British, who provided leadership out of the Great Depression, will lead also in the second revolution, not because they are brighter than others, but because England's present situation is so intolerable. At the present writing it is not clear whether Harold Wilson's new incomes policy proposals will survive the parliamentary and TUC congress at Blackpool tests, or whether the proposed limit to raises will be adhered to so long as the programme is "voluntary".* But if voluntarism fails it seems the objective facts should compel the government to make compliance mandatory, and at least this time there is no illusion that controls can be temporary. For what matters is not so much the particular provisions of the programme, which will undoubtedly need revision over time, but the maintenance of the commitment to the permanent rational planning of income growth within the limits imposed by the growth of society's real income. This is an extraordinarily difficult task for governments based on consent of the governed to undertake. Their task is made the more difficult because most economists have refused to face up to the necessity of articulating and weighing incomes policy proposals for the real world and instead have contented themselves with elaborating ever more fine-spun theories about a world which never existed. As Joan Robinson puts it, "The soothing doctrines of the bastard Keynesians have been a very poor preparation for the actual problems of modern capitalism."[55]

---

[54] See John Knapp's excellent, "Economics or Political Economy?" *Lloyd's Bank Review,* January 1973, pp. 19-43. See also Alfred S. Eichner and J.A. Kregel, "An Essay on Post-Keynesian Theory: A New Paradigm in Economics," *Journal of Economic Literature,* XIII, December 1975, pp. 1293-314.

[55] Joan Robinson, *Economic Heresies,* p. 95.

* Ah, the delays of publication! Since the above was written, Harold Wilson has resigned and James Callaghan has become Prime Minister. The U.K. rate of inflation has been cut in half and will be halved again if the TUC will, as seems likely, accept the tax cuts conditional on restraining wage hikes to 5% contained in Denis Healey's new budget. Three years of tight money failed miserably to stop the British inflation, but now the monetarists are claiming credit for the recent improvement! (See David Laidler, "Lord Kahn on Monetarism," *Lloyds Bank Review,* April 1976, pp. 47-8. As Laidler states, " . . . in 1973 monetary policy became extremely restrictive and has remained restrictive ever since . . . Monetarists attribute the current high level of unemployment and the recent rapid fall-off in the inflation rate to the fact that monetary variables are much more important than fiscal variables.") Monetarists seem unable to learn that to what extent M changes Q rather than P depends on what happens to w, t, and i, and these nonmonetary policies can much change. Ah, the delay in paradigm change!

At present writing the Canadian federal government's new *Attack on Inflation* system of price and wage restraints on the largest firms, coupled with a promise to restrain the increase of federal spending is a much needed step in the right direction. For Canadian inflation is considerably more rapid than U.S. inflation and the cause is clearly the more rapid pace of Canadian wage hikes. The long-sought "goal" of the CLC of wage "parity" of their members with their U.S. counterparts has been achieved and exceeded in many cases, but at the cost of a fall of the level at which $C "floats", a loss of international competitiveness, a housing slump, and runaway land speculation. A recent assessment, and tepid support, for the new programme is given by Frank J. Reid.[56]

The British and Canadian governments have suffered comparatively little erosion of traditional respect – of their ability to get their citizens to follow if they show strong leadership. Not so the United States government. The present crisis in the capitalist world is compounded by revelations of the degree to which the U.S. federal government has corrupted itself in the pursuit of its world-wide "anti communist" crusade. It is painful to prescribe an increased role for a government which contains a merged CIA and MAFIA (or MACIA). The threat of a lurch to outright fascism hung over the entire Watergate affair, and there is much to fear in this direction still. It is chilling to recall that it was the German social democrats who worked out the anti-depression policies which Hitler corrupted to war preparations. Moreover, it was particularly the Americans who bastardized Keynesian fiscal and monetary policies, into "military Keynesianism" – the maintenance of near full employment by armaments spending and "bush-fire" wars.

Thus the economic aspects of our present crisis are part of a larger crisis of government and civilization. The collapse of bastard Keynesianism and its replacement by the legitimate variety, while a gain, is by no means sufficient to end this time of troubles. Like Lear's Britain, the capitalist world has far worse sorrows than those involving Gloucester's bastard son Edmund and legitimate Edgar.

Messenger: Edmund is dead, my lord.

Albany: That's but a trifle here.
You lords and noble friends, know our intent.
What comfort to this great decay may come,
Shall be applied . . .
[To Kent and Edgar] Friends of my soul, you twain,
Rule in this realm, and the gored state sustain.

Kent: I have a journey, sir, shortly shall I go.
My master calls me; I must not say no.

Edgar: The weight of this sad time we must obey,
Speak what we feel, not what we ought to say.
The oldest hath borne most; we that are young,
Shall never see so much, nor live so long.

Exeunt with a dead march.[57]

---

[56] Frank J. Reid, "Canadian Wage and Price Controls," *Canadian Public Policy,* II Winter, 1976, pp. 103-13.

[57] William Shakespeare, *King Lear,* V, iii.

Acknowledgements

Permission to reproduce previously published articles as chapters 3 and 6 was generously granted.

"Effects of Tax and Interest Hikes as Strengthening the Case for Incomes Policies – or a Part of the Elephant," *Canadian Journal of Economics,* May 1971.

"Harrod's Dichotomy and the Price Level," *Economic and Business Bulletin,* Spring – Summer 1972.

I am indebted to the following journals and publishers for permission to quote from others' published works.

American Economic Review
The Brookings Institution
Econometrica
Harcourt, Brace, Javonovich, Inc.
Houghton Mifflin Company
Richard D. Irwin Inc.
Journal of Economic Issues
Journal of Economic Literature
Journal of Political Economy
Macmillan and Company, Ltd.
McGraw-Hill Book Company, Inc.
Newsweek Inc.
Oxford University Press
Prentice Hall Inc.
St. Martin's Press
University of Chicago Press, G.P. Shultz and R.Z. Aliber, eds., *Guidelines, Informal Controls, and the Market Place,* © 1966 by the University of Chicago. All rights reserved.

Index